BACKDOOR to EUGENICS

BLACKJACK & EUGENICS

BACKDOOR to EUGENICS

Second Edition

 TROY DUSTER

ROUTLEDGE
New York and London

Published in 2003 by
Routledge
29 West 35th Street
New York, NY 10001
www.routledge-ny.com

Published in Great Britain by
Routledge
11 New Fetter Lane
London EC4P 4EE
www.routledge.co.uk

Library of Congress Cataloging-in-Publication Data

Duster, Troy.
    Backdoor to eugenics / Troy Duster.— 2nd ed.
        p.   cm.
Includes bibliographical references and index.
    ISBN 0-415-94805-3 (Hardcover : alk. paper)—ISBN 0-415-94674-3
(Paperback : alk. paper)
  1. Eugenics. 2. Human chromosome abnormalities—Diagnosis—Social aspects.
3. Genetic disorders—Social aspects. 4. Eugenics—United States. I. Title.
    RB155.D87 2003
        363.9'2—dc21

                                                                    2003010961

Contents

Foreword: Advocating a "Genethics"

Conservatism has always been linked to forms of thought that tend to reduce the social to the natural—the historical to the biological. But something new is happening in this era of cultural reaction: Recent progress in molecular biology and the discovery of the genetic basis of certain illnesses are beginning to revive the old eugenics (which had been discredited by association with the Nazis) and above all the old mythologies, which, clothed in the biological sciences, were sometimes used to legitimize social differences. If it is true that some genetic deficiencies are unevenly distributed among ethnic groups, why couldn't it be so for many other traits? And why shouldn't we ask genetics for the explanation for differences in intelligence, criminality, and mental illness? We know that at the end of the 1960s, a Berkeley psychologist reopened the old debate about the genetics of intelligence, arguing in the *Harvard Educational Review* that blacks performed more poorly than whites on IQ tests because of their genetic makeup. This was a reaction to prevalent views about the social determination of behavior, and it was quickly picked up by neoconservatives at *Commentary* and elsewhere. Today the new genetics brings a "halo of legitimacy" to racist and reactionary stereotypes: Purely genetic arguments are invoked with increasing frequency to account for behaviors which, like intelligence and the propensity to violence, are the results of complex combinations of factors.

Troy Duster, a sociology professor at Berkeley, well known for his works on morality and law (especially *The Legislation of Morality: Law, Drugs and Moral Judgment*), here draws the connections between the resurgence of essentialist thinking and the rise of the new biotechnologies—technologies that have demonstrated the greater frequency of certain genetic deficiencies among "risk populations," which correspond rather precisely to ethnic groups. He cautions us against the risks of stigmatization, discrimination, and marginalization inherent in screening policies, and in the increasingly sophisticated tests they bring to bear, in a society where power

vii

is unevenly distributed. Will the systematic use of such tests by insurance companies, employers, courts, schools, and even public health professionals create a caste of "biological pariahs," defined by their biological or neurological status as unfit for education, employment, or insurance? State bureaucracies (such as the National Center for Human Genome Research) are sociologically disposed to perpetuate themselves and increase their reach, notably by extending the range of available tests and by making some screening obligatory. Isn't there a risk, in this process, of slipping from mass screening to the screening of target populations, and from voluntary to mandatory testing? And shouldn't we fear that the uses of genetics will be determined more by economic and social power relations than by scientific or purely medical needs (as the differential treatment of groups such as blacks and Jews suggests, who differ in terms of genetic risks but more importantly in their social positions)?

The worst outcome, without question, would be if routine bureaucratic practices of genetic intervention slowly imposed the eugenic worldview and a form of scientifically and bureaucratically accredited racism. It is clear that the indisputable therapeutic virtues of many forms of genetic screening risk granting a renewed legitimacy to old attempts to ground the social structure on eugenics—whether a eugenics of criminal tendencies or of intelligence. How can we deny the link between the forceful return of conservative thinking and the favorable climate offered by progress in genetics, when we observe that "a review of the *Reader's Guide to Periodical Literature* from 1976 to 1982 revealed a 231 percent increase in articles that attempted to explain the genetic basis for crime, mental illness, intelligence, and alcoholism during this brief six-year period. Even more remarkably, between 1983 and 1988, articles that attributed a genetic basis to crime appeared *more than four times* as frequently as they had during the previous decade" (see p. 93, chapter six). There is no need to evoke the Orwellian myth of a controlled society based on genetics to understand the danger of a state-controlled genetic database. (This is no longer a utopian fiction: In California, every pregnant woman receives a genetic examination, and all anomalies are recorded in a central database at the Centers for Disease Control in Atlanta.) It is this kind of covert eugenics, perhaps more dangerous because it is more refined, that Troy Duster reveals here. In doing so, he brings together the talents of the sociologist with those of the most lucid and courageous geneticists, in the service of what one of them, David Suzuki, has called a "genethics" based on the refusal to establish simple and direct causality between the genetic properties and the behaviors of individuals.

—Pierre Bourdieu
Translated from the French by Emmanuelle Saada

Preface to the Second Edition

When the first edition of this book was published at the beginning of the 1990s, it was literally "the dawn of the Human Genome Project." It is perhaps fitting then, that the re-release occurs just as the Genome Project leadership announced "the sunset"—completion of a full human genetic map and sequence (in the spring of 2003). In the ensuing years, we have learned much about the prospects, promises, and limits of human molecular biology. For one, the diagnostic power has greatly exceeded the capacity to intervene therapeutically. We have learned a lot more about who is likely to have a genetically-based illness than how to treat that illness. Cystic fibrosis is a good example. When the first gene mutation for this disorder was discovered in the early 1990s, a ray of hope as penetrating as it was unrealistic spread quickly through the cystic fibrosis community. In a study that I was conducting at the time,[1] several families in which there had been a pre-natal diagnosis of cystic fibrosis decided to carry pregnancies to full term, because of what they thought was the high prospect that a cure was "right around the corner." These promises have not been fulfilled—and we have learned that it is very difficult to cure a genetic disorder. Gene therapy has proved to be the highest hurdle, and the successes have been rare. Thus, we have mainly opted for ameliorative interventions, settling for pharmaceuticals or special treatments for symptomatic relief to lessen the effect of the disease. Accordingly, this one set of eugenic concerns has been muted.

Yet there have been instructive "eugenic success stories." The island of Cypress has become the new model for cooperative consenting eugenics, joining the Tay–Sachs screening history chronicled in the first edition of *Backdoor to Eugenics*. Well into the 1980s, Cypress was afflicted with a relatively high rate of *thalassemia major*, a condition caused by a genetic mutation resulting in a debilitating and sometimes fatal blood disorder. Signing on to a widely distributed genetic screening program, the great majority of Cypriots not only agreed to be screened, they also came to generally accept a genetic counselor's advice to not have children (either to not

CYPRUS?

marry—if a couple tested positive as carriers of the gene—or to not carry to full term an affected fetus). The outcome over the last decade has been a dramatic reduction of children born with the disorder.

On the other side of the ledger is "positive" eugenics, and this last period did witness the increasing use of sperm banks and *in vitro* fertilization, with many prospective parents articulating explicit eugenic agendas. In the last decade, over 17,000 babies have been born from these procedures, and in many cases the parents openly "ordered up" what they thought would be preferred genes of race, height, intelligence, or musical ability. Yet this is a "mere drop in the bucket" of all human births, and there has not been a substantial eugenic concern generated by this development. The public imagination has been captured instead by debates about the potential for human cloning and the use of embryonic stem cells—with abortion politics as the very loud subtext.

It is once again the subterranean eugenic aspects of the revolution in molecular biology—now flying just under the radar of public consciousness—that I foresee as generating the most profound outcomes. Chief among these are developments in forensic science and the related developments in the new line of forthcoming research (waiting patiently in the wings) on national DNA databanks.

As the national DNA forensic databank grows, there will be increasing pressure for every person in the United States to contribute their DNA. Meanwhile, a new term has entered the lexicon, "ethnic estimation" by use of the DNA—in practice a proxy for the old idea of race. In a new chapter (eight) and the Epilogue, these concerns are addressed in some detail, and serve to complement the earlier analysis of why the backdoor to eugenics will always be a far more attractive entry point for dealing with age-old fears about human decline, illness, crime, and violence.

1. The U.S. Department of Energy (DE-FG03-92ER61393) "Molecular Genetics Meets the High-Risk Family."

Preface to the First Edition

At mid-century, social scientists believed that they had won the battle with hereditarians over who could better explain the great human concerns of our era. Evidence for this belief was substantial. Social theories predominated in the scholarly journals reviewing research on "the causes" of war, poverty, and privileged class position, of the political status of racial and ethnic groups, of crime, health, drug use, and even (increasingly) of mental illness. Moreover, in both public debates among lay persons and in the mass media, the victory was overwhelming. By 1955, few would take the stage to argue for the overarching importance of the genetic inheritance of social position or social condition.

Yet in the last few decades, gradually, almost imperceptibly, our thinking about human social life has shifted to accept a greater role for genetics. This thinking has, in turn, begun to influence matters such as private and personal decisions about prenatal diagnosis, the use of blood banks and the creation of sperm banks, and the genetic screening of workers at the workplace— in short, a whole range of public health policy issues. The last decade has seen a geometric increase in publications pronouncing the genetic basis of such disparate phenomena as shyness, rape, mental illness, alcoholism, crime, even social and economic position.[1] How did we get here, without a road map, a blueprint, or even a trumpet to sound the new day? A review of our history provides some insights, and there are several excellent works on this topic (Haller, 1963; Ludmerer, 1972; Kevles, 1985). In this book I will argue that the social concerns of an age, not the scientific status of the new knowledge-structure of genetics, offer the most compelling answer to this question.[2]

At the turn of the century, real and consequential developments in plant and animal genetics helped fuel an interest in the new science of human genetics. In America the work of geneticists and eugenicists was frequently blurred. Indeed, one of the leading biological scientists of the day was also the head of the two major organizations that funded eugenic research.[3] But some geneticists spoke out and warned about the inappropriate application of the (then) new genetics to human affairs. Those on the fringe of genetics and biology commonly preached the gospel of eugenics, magically converting spurious correlations into causation, and subsequently into social policy. In 1924, the United States passed a law that would effectively shut its borders to those "tired masses" who had come by the hundreds of thousands annually for the previous half-century. The ideological foundation of that policy, which was to form and seal the ethnic and racial composition of the United States, was the new eugenics.

A parallel play is being re-enacted in the late twentieth century, but on a subtler stage set. It is subtler for two reasons. First, the old eugenics movement was not based upon any demonstrable successful intervention by medicine or science into human genetic affairs. The current technology is both eminently successful in its predictive power, and potent in extending its impact to such concerns as the prenatal detection of human birth defects, and the applications of growth hormones from gene-splicing techniques with recombinant DNA. Technical complexities of vanguard research in molecular biology and the promises of success incline us to go limp before such scientific know-how. We give up to "science and expertise" a deep human concern that has little to do with either science or expertise, namely, what kind of knowledge we should pursue in determining what kind of children should be born.

Second, and equally important, the new genetics technology is more immediate in its promise: the mitigation of problems (birth defects, mental illness, nutritional deficiency) not the creation or sustenance of discredited claims of racial superiority or purity.[4] Indeed, one of the significant ironies is that today's technology tells us that socially identifiable groups such as Jews, blacks, Greeks, Italians, and women of a certain age can now be cost-effectively screened for genetic disorders.[5] I believe that this development indirectly has helped to both legitimate and reinvigorate the old nature-nurture debate over the issues of race, ethnicity, gender, and mental capacity.

In the "community" of those screened, louder voices will be heard in the next decade about who screens whom for what purpose. While warnings of impending genocide may be dismissed as unwarranted, I would join other voices in drawing attention to a more insidious general and growing acceptance of the notion that "defective" babies can be prevented. Even the most naive and Pollyannish social analysis must concede that the idea of defective babies has to do with care and feeding, dependency, aesthetics, and the variably constructed meaning of life itself. Such constructions are the basis of social order, and order and control are subtly interlocked.

A racially and culturally homogeneous nation might come to some working agreement about what makes for unwanted babies. In a heterogeneous society, the public forum for this debate needs to be vigorous and informed, not just by modest levels of technical knowledge about genetic or microbiological developments, but about the role of power and social location in determining and applying that knowledge.

There are few prescriptions here, and no injunctions to shape public policy in a particular direction on matters of genetic counseling, screening, or therapies. No genetic counselors could read chapters 6 and 7 of this book and come away feeling more informed about what they do, or that they could do their jobs better, etc. No director of a state public health department could read chapter 4 and come away feeling better prepared to administer the health bureaucracy or resolve the contradiction which I address and emphasize.

Why, then, did I write this book? Because of my belief, based on observation, that an enormous abyss in the public discourse surrounds the new genetics technologies, and that a danger inheres in this situation. Currently, the public debate seems cast in terms of experts (geneticists, medical specialists, researchers, etc.) on the one hand, and on the other, critics who have been portrayed as nannies, naysayers, and know-nothings, Luddites who would put their heads in the sand or try to stop the machinery of progress.[6] I would like to see another level of discussion, in which a far better informed citizenry engaged one another in a spirited debate about matters of privacy and disclosure, therapies or screens, nutrition or genes. Out of this an informed public policy could be generated and shaped. If the debate as currently configured persists, if it is simply left to the experts versus the Luddites, the experts are going to win hands down.[7]

In technologically advanced societies, the ordinary citizen with a cautious query about where we are headed with the new technology is like a "primitive or savage" armed with mere humanistic word-spears, confronting the advancing armies of technological/scientific healthbearers and their moral advantage. The latter, after all, can lessen human suffering. The former are more easily cast as either ostriches or alarmists who are little short of hysterical or fanatical in their attempts to stand in the way of progress.

It is not so difficult to get applause for the technology that permits us to determine whether a fetus has a fatal birth defect such as Tay-Sachs disease, but the warm blanket of consensus begins to fall away when it comes to deciding upon an appropriate "policy" for controlling levels and kinds of hemoglobinopathies (abnormalities of red blood cells, pigment structure and/or function) and levels and kinds of mental retardation.

Where the line is drawn becomes the central issue. And while the major ingredients of such a decision are likely to be political, social, and economic, they will be masked by the technical complexities of "science."

Japan, India, the United Kingdom, and every European nation will join the United States within the next decade, either in deliberately confronting the social policy issues inherent in a pursuit of the new technology, or in back-sliding into unexamined practices with a "eugenic" outcome. To put it metaphorically, when eugenics reincarnates this time, it will not come through the front door, as with Hitler's *Lebensborn* project. Instead, it will come by the back door of screens, treatments, and therapies. Some will be admirably health-giving, and that will be the wedge. But sooner or later, each will face the question of when to shut the back door to eugenics.

The route by which we are moving towards a new kind of genetics is indirect, subtle, and nonlinear. It is impossible to establish this point by looking only at genetic screening programs, at the profession of genetic counseling, at a state public health department, or at the history of genetic screening legislation.[8] While I will spend some time looking in each of these directions, this is not a study of genetic screening or counseling, nor of the Massachusetts or California health bureaucracies. Studies of these areas have already been done, based on some excellent and even superb work by a number of other scholars and researchers.[9] Moreover, while an early chapter addresses the issue, I am not trying to use these pages to singularly establish that science has a social basis, that genetic explanations of intelligence are greatly exaggerated, or that racism can creep into decisions about screening for inherited disorders.

The case for each of these has been made by others, and I refer the reader to those other sources. I try to produce a mosaic of these many concerns, providing a different kind of picture that can come into better focus only when one places together a number of disparate developments that otherwise seem isolated. This different look at converging technologies, interests, and disease-prevention policies takes on an increasingly eugenic character.

Acknowledgments

In a work that has spanned so many years and covered such a wide territory, it is impossible to acknowledge all the persons with whom I had rewarding conversations, or who reviewed and commented on various segments and drafts at different stages. The following paragraphs gratefully acknowledge just some of those colleagues and friends.

An early research group at the Institute for the Study of Social Change at the University of California, Berkeley were vital in helping to shape the initial ideas for this book, and included Diane Beeson, Elaine Draper, Judith Ellis, Michael Flowers and Terry Lunsford. I have a special indebtedness to Diane Beeson, who was the first person to bring to my attention the enormous sociological implications of the new genetic technologies. Bert Thomas and George Cunningham were gracious in giving their valuable time and providing access to information at the California State Department of Health.

A second and more recent study group reviewed portions of an earlier version of this manuscript, and gave me valuable advice about where to delete and where to develop. This group included Bob Blauner, Elliot Currie, David Matza, David Minkus, Lillian Rubin, David Wellman, and Norma Wikler.

Then at various junctures, I received cogent, critical and constructive commentary from Ken Bock, Aaron Cicourel, Russ Ellis, Hardy Frye, Joan Fujimura, Howard Becker, Thelton Henderson, Judith Auerbach, Ron Roizen, Robert Yamashita, Jerome Karabel, Karen Garrett, David Chandler, Ernest Landauer, Kenneth Polk, Sally Simpson, Martin Sanchez-Jankowski and Anselm Strauss.

While they are hardly responsible for any lapses in my portrayal of genetic issues, the manuscript was much improved in this area from critical readings from Gordon Edlin, Marc Lappé Bert Lubin, and Leon Wofsy. Irene Fereti was pivotal to my successful field trip to Orchomenos, Greece, both strategically and intellectually. Other colleagues from Europe and the United Kingdom who greatly assisted me in discussions about the advantages and limits of cross-cultural comparisons include Pierre Bourdieu, Barbara Lal, Yoka Haafkens, and Sabine Lang.

Annette Flowers provided excellent bibliographical assistance, and the congenial and supportive environment of the Institute for the Study of Social Change is directly attributable to Janice Tanigawa. My editor at Routledge, Maureen MacGrogan, has always exhibited unflinching support. Finally, Deborah Woo helped provide some strong focus on the key themes at a very critical juncture in the completion of the manuscript.

The research was supported by a Senior Research Fellowship from the Ford Foundation and grants from the National Institute of Child Health and Human Development and the Committee on Research for the Berkeley campus. I would also like to thank the publishers of the *San Francisco Chronicle* for their permission to quote from an article on sickle-cell screening regulations published July 8, 1976.

BACKDOOR to EUGENICS

1

Inherited Genetic Disorders and Inherited Social Orders

In the fifteenth-century Spain of Torquemada, people routinely raised the question about the biological differences between believers and heretics, between Christians and Jews, posited the natural superiority of one group over the other, and invoked the known procedures for coming to terms with the available knowledge. Just before and during the Inquisition, the most important biological argument for the persecution of the Jews centered around the concept *limpiezza de sangre* or purity of the blood (Lea, 1906). Limpiezza decrees were used to prohibit intermarriage and, quite significantly, required that a candidate for a particular ecclesiastical or secular post prove his Christian ancestry (Coulton, 1938).[1]

Efforts to attribute human traits or behaviors to the influence of biological inheritance are seemingly limitless: they have focused on such widely diverging matters as eye color, blood type, poverty, fingerprints, heretical beliefs, aggression, intelligence, unemployment, birth disorders, mental illness, skin color, rape, ethnic purity, and musical ability, with varying degrees of success. The first question that comes to mind is: What is the level of truth of each claim of hereditary basis? While blood types and skin color can now be shown to be hereditary, the conventional wisdom in the contemporary West is that heretical beliefs and unemployment are not biologically inherited. While there is currently wide agreement as to the biological basis of many birth defects, there is no consensus in the scientific world about whether the "genetic account" is appropriate for many traits, behaviors, and disorders. Contemporary science is fairly well equipped to assess any particular truth claim.

There is an equally important question, however, which receives comparatively little attention: Why, in any given society, do studies of heritability focus upon trait A versus B or behavior C versus D? Once the credibility of the truth claim is bracketed, it is possible to see how a sociology of knowledge provides some answers, however tentative, that are directly related to consequences that ensue with the formation of organizational developments and institutional machineries.

Heritability as the Recurring "Sirens' Call"

Despite alternating periods of attraction and wariness, the relationship between genetics and society has been passionate for a full century; beginning with an early absorbing mutual interest (1900–1935), surviving an abrupt disenchantment and apparent divorce (1940–1965), and now on through a resurgent warming trend (1970–1990). The "prism of heritability"[2] is very seductive. Even when the genetic explanation for some arena of human life has been discredited or fallen from favor, the appeal of such accounts somehow remains just beneath the surface.

There is no easy or simple explanation for this. One must look at more than the discoveries and refutations in a field of inquiry to explain the spread of ideas. It is by now almost a truism that science both shapes and is shaped by social, economic, and political conditions (Harding, 1986; Knorr-Cetina and Mulkay, 1983; Keller, 1982, 1984; Zuckerman, 1977; Knorr-Cetina, 1981; Merton, 1973). The science of genetics and the society in which it is located are in a special kind of tension. Even after lying dormant for a time, in a period of rapid transformation, the appeal of a biological destiny can be irresistible (Pickens, 1968). The shifting status of the explanatory power of race is an example. At certain points, race is invoked to explain social status, as with slavery in nineteenth-century America. A combination of Nazi atrocities and social science research converged in the mid-twentieth century to undermine the explanatory power of race (in its biological status) as either a popular[3] or a scientific accounting for human behavior.

Then, just at the point in the intellectual history of the West when "race" was getting to be treated in both scientific and enlightened lay quarters as something no more than skin-deep, just when the social sciences thought they had won the battle with hereditarians over the fundamentally *arbitrary* importance of race[4] in society, a new development came along to shake this assumption at its core: the growth of a body of research showing that *genetic disorders were distributed differently through different racial and ethnic groups*. Jews, African Americans, Asians, North Europeans, etc., are at different risks for genetic disorders. This was no longer a matter of social science theorizing about the significance or insignificance of race for social position. Now there was empirical evidence that one group was more likely to have a genetic disorder than another. Even though socially enforced patterns of mating had produced this development, the new technology would give race and ethnic categorization a potential for a different and independent reality.

This new impetus created a body of research and the related genetic screening programs that would emerge as cost-effective only if greatest-risk populations[5] were identified. This radically altered the discourse about race and rearranged the landscape between the social and natural sciences on this topic. The importance of race and ethnicity in cultural history has re-fueled the old logic to give rise to a new question: *If genetic disorders are differentially distributed by race and ethnicity, why aren't other human traits and characteristics?*

Popular accounts in the mass media of the new technology in molecular biology and genetics emphasize such matters as frozen embryos, test-tube babies, baboon heart implants in humans, and the prospective cures for cancer and diabetes with recombined DNA. Moreover, scholarly journals and literary monthlies publish lengthy and frequent debates by scientists, ethicists, theologians, and politicians on the real and imagined prospects and deeper meanings of these developments.[6] We are a long way from the kind of genetic manipulation that would permit a dash of blond hair or Olympic gymnastic potential here, a gene splice for some genius there, or a snippit of strand X to intercept schizophrenia and heart disease. Nevertheless, the considerable attention given to highly selective developments affecting only the tiniest fraction of the population has diverted our attention away from real and significant developments that already engulf us.[7] I would point to two major issues.

First, genetic screening programs, already in place throughout most of the United States, can be distinguished from all previous health screening in the degree to which "risk-populations" to be identified have frequently been linked to ethnicity and race. In sharp contrast to mass health screening for contagious diseases, these programs cannot be made as appealing to all groups in behalf of the common good. Yet, mandatory newborn screening is already underway for a sizeable proportion of the population, and prenatal diagnosis of several hundred genetic disorders is now possible.

Second, state and national registries for information received from newborn genetic screening programs are already in place, collecting data in the chromosome and genetic trait status of millions of infants. These data are collected for health and medical reasons, and often deal with whole populations, not just those at greatest risk. Such information, recorded and stored in archives for both immediate and long-range retrieval, may prove useful to health professionals who dedicate much of their time and lives as counselors and treatment specialists trying to improve the condition of those with birth disorders. But these registries, now in their beginning stages, are part of the *machinery in place* (organizational, institutional, legal, and physical) which will slowly, subtly, sometimes almost imperceptibly, help shift the refraction of human traits, characteristics, behaviors, disorders, and defects through a "genetic prism."[8]

In the midst of these developments, the United States is undergoing its second great economic and political transformation. At the turn of the century, the country changed from an agrarian to an urban industrial society. The urban areas of the emerging industrial sectors of the Northeast and Midwest were mainly white, with ethnic diversity largely imported from Europe.[9] During this first great transformation, genetic explanations played an important role in providing an "understanding" of rapid changes and a measure of legitimacy to public policies to "correct" the problem (Kamin, 1974; Ludmerer, 1972; Haller, 1963; Kevles, 1985; Pickens, 1968).[10] The last decades of the century are the locus of the second great economic transformation. The shift to a service economy has brought about dramatic social dislocations, much of it centering around racial and ethnic differentiation.[11] It is impossible to document a shift in the *zeitgeist*, but there is a sense in which a new "genetic understanding" of the conditions we live in is penetrating the popular discourse.[12] As we shall soon see, of the various strands to the field of genetics, it is molecular genetics which has been mainly responsible for the new technological developments. The older strands of population genetics and the search for Mendelian laws of inheritance have always had amateur as well as professional and scientific research spinning off to impute the genetics of many different phenomena regarded as social problems.

Currently, only a very small part of the population is using the new technologies of prenatal detection, which, along with postnatal interventions and the promises of human gene therapies, now have the potential for reducing human suffering.[13] At the same time, a genetic screen is a genetic screen. Although not generally available, prenatal diagnosis is possible before the end of the first third of a pregnancy.[14] Screening for a defective fetus where there is near universal consensus about the seriousness of the defect is one thing. When there is high variability in the clinical expression of a genetic disorder,[15] a host of new issues surfaces. When there is disagreement about the very nature of whether a "defect" is a defect or an arbitrary social assessment of aesthetics and or potential dependency, the issue then shifts away from the advisability of medical intervention strategies for health purposes to the question of who should decide.

As noted above, however, the more immediate concern that already affects the lives of millions of people is the development of the earliest stages of genetic screening and its overlap with existing social groups. Table 1.1 summarizes some of the research of the last several decades documenting the ethnic distribution of genetic disorders.[16]

These tables on the ethnic distribution of disorder[18] are consequential. This knowledge, even as imprecisely constituted, can and does become the foundation upon which the social organization of real genetic screen-

Table 1.1 *Selected High Incidence of Genetic Disorders*

Condition	Estimated Incidence*
Cleft lip/palate	1 in 675 individuals
Club foot	1 in 350 individuals
Cystic fibrosis	1 in 2,500 Caucasians
Diabetes	1 in 80 individuals
Down syndrome	1 in 1,050 individuals
Hemophilia	1 in 10,000 males
Huntington's disease	1 in 2,500 individuals
Duchenne muscular dystrophy	1 in 7,000 males
Phenylketonuria (PKU)	1 in 12,000 Caucasians
Rh incompatibility	1–2 in 100 individuals
Sickle-cell anemia	1 in 625 African-Americans
Tay-Sachs disease	1 in 3,000 Ashkenazi Jews
Beta-thalassemia (Cooley's anemia)	1 in 2,500 Mediterranean people

*The above figures vary according to ethnic background. For example, Rh incompatibility is much lower among those with Asian ancestry. Phenylketonuria is rare in those of Black or Ashkenazi Jewish ancestry (most Jewish people in the United States are of Ashkenazi descent).

Table 1.2 *Ethnicities/Groups Primarily Affected by Disorders (USA)*

Condition	Ethnicities Primarily Affected
Duchenne muscular dystrophy	Northeastern British
Adult lactase deficiency	African-Americans, Chinese
Cleft lip/palate	North American Indians/Japanese
Cystic fibrosis	Northern Europeans
Familial Mediterranean fever	Armenians
Phenylketonuria (PKU)	Caucasians (especially Irish)
Sickle-cell anemia	African-Americans
Alpha-thalassemia	Chinese, Southeast Asians
Beta-thalassemia	Mediterraneans
Spina bifida/anencephaly	Caucasians (especially Welsh and Irish)
Tay-Sachs disease	Ashkenazi Jews (origins in central and eastern Europe)

From L. Burhansstipanov, S. Giarratano, K. Koser, and J. Mongoven, *Prevention of Genetic and Birth Disorders* (Sacramento: California State Department of Education, 1987), 6–7.

ing programs develop, and also provides the guideposts to gene therapy research. Gene screening programs feed data back into a growing scientific data base, and buttress select arguments of the scientific structure because there are data on that topic. The order and manner in which those discoveries are made, who makes them, and the sense that is made of it all should be at the core of research on the social organization of knowledge. In this chapter, I will try to show that certain genetic and biological explanations of heritability can be traced directly to prevailing social concerns.

Genetics: Multifaceted, but
Converging Questions around "Target" Populations

The field of genetics is broad and encompasses different types of research and analysis, including population genetics, Mendelian genetics, and molecular genetics. *Population geneticists* tend to work primarily with large population statistics. The original goal of the field was to unlock the key to Darwinian evolution by applying statistical methods.[19] Were there patterns that showed up in a population by chance or by pattern, and how much of that could be attributed to genes? This strategy and the new discipline that emerged around it[20] gained their strongest foothold in Britain and on the European continent. Perhaps one reason is that the relative ethnic homogeneity of the populations there meant that a concerted search for differences in intelligence would focus upon class differences. One of the central tasks of any social order is to convince its members that the current system of social stratification is legitimate. Gould (1981) demonstrates how scientists in the nineteenth century purposefully and determinedly aimed to show how the higher classes ascended by natural biological superiority.

The word *population* has a specific and technical meaning for the geneticist. At the broadest level, it is any interbreeding aggregate—thus, a *species*. But species have subpopulations that interbreed only among themselves. In humans, customs, laws, traditions, geography, ethnicity, klan, etc., work as barriers to interbreeding for the whole human race. Anthropologists and sociologists chronicle hundreds of differing forms of laws of endogamy and exogamy, incest taboos and arranged marriages. States have created and enforced inheritance entitlements based upon professed beliefs and professed heresies. All this variation in human interbreeding has produced both observable patterns and variations in the species. In evolutionary theory, the idea of the survival of the fittest generated the intellectual and political interests of population geneticists, many of whom were trying to find an evolutionary tree *within* homo sapiens. Here we come to the intellectual birth of population genetics, and the basic relationship to the matter of what is being looked for:

A preliminary step in analyzing the genetics of a population, then, is to measure allele frequency. . . . Theoretically, it is very simple to measure allele frequencies: *one simply looks at a population* [italics mine], assumes that each person is just one cell (perhaps the zygote from which he developed), and counts how many alleles of each kind there are for any particular locus. (Suzuki and Griffith, 1976:405)

Theoretically simple, and practically possible for blood groups, where one can count and measure *allele*[21] frequencies. But population geneticists, beginning with Pearson,[22] were looking for signs of something called "human intelligence," for which there is no known allele. They were looking for something that would help explain the social evolution of select subpopulations to the top of the social and economic order.[23] The target population of the early population geneticists, then, coincided with smaller, socially configured subpopulations with a social marking.

A very different wing of genetics was fathered by the Augustinian monk Gregor Mendel in the 1860s. Rather than statistical analysis of traits and characteristics in a large population, Mendel and his followers searched for evidence of the appearance of traits in offspring that followed "laws of inheritance" (e.g., Mendel's account of transmission through dominant and recessive genes). After laying dormant for many decades, *Mendelian genetics* was rediscovered in the early part of the twentieth century.

By studying garden peas, without ever seeing a cell, Mendel was able to deduce that certain genes were dominant, others recessive. In crossing purple- and white-flowering plants, the first generation all turned out purple; then

> he planted 929 peas . . . some grew up to be white-flowered. The white character had reappeared. He then did something that, more than anything else, marks the birth of genetics: he *counted* how many there were of each kind . . . the key to the future of genetics. There were 705 purple plants, and 224 white ones. He observed that this was close to a 3:1 ratio (Suzuki and Griffiths, 1976:8).

The significance of the notion of dominant and recessive genes was profound. It meant that a single gene could account for some trait. Those who followed the Mendelian tradition could search through families for evidence of these Mendelian genes. While many genes do not follow such Mendelian principles, it is important at the early juncture to understand Mendel's orientation to the research problem in order to see the direction Mendelian genetics would take in the search for human genetic principles.

Mendelian genetics gained most of its followers in the United States. I noted above that population genetics was more popular in England, and suggested that relative ethnic homogeneity may have played an important role in the search for class differences in, for example, intelligence. The United States was a country of immigrants from a wide variety of nations, mainly European. Notions of "race" and "ethnicity" frequently converged in the nineteenth century, and people spoke freely of the Nordic race or the Slavic race. Until World War I, there was considerable hostility and even open fighting between the population geneticists, mainly English, and the Mendelians, mainly American.[24] Nonetheless, some of these researchers and their followers in the eugenics movement often agreed on what they considered to be wrong at the bottom of the social order.

During the first decade of the century, the American side discovered that Mendel's laws could apply to humans as well as to plants and animals. With the exception of blood types in the ABO system, almost all the traits that conformed to these laws were pathological conditions. Ludmerer (1972:46) suggests that this helps explain why most eugenicists, from the very beginning, were interested mainly in negative rather than positive eugenics.[25]

Population genetics had its own strong tendency to impute a genetic account to a variety of human "traits." After getting school teachers to rank students for such traits as vivacity, introspection, popularity, and handwriting, Pearson found correlations between siblings for these traits to range between .43 and .63. These correlations were about the same as those between siblings for physical traits, which he assumed were hereditary, and so "Pearson concluded that personality and intelligence too were predestined in the germ plasm before birth" (Haller, 1963:13).

On the American side, the Mendelians also found their way to study intelligence as hereditary, but of course thought that it would obey Mendelian laws. H.H. Goddard, a psychologist who was the director of a training school for the feeble-minded, tried to use Mendelian rules to trace the lineage of the feeble-minded at his school (Gould, 1981:162). In this he partook of the spirit of the times, for others had already tried to trace wanderlust through the families of naval captains.

A further convergence between the two traditions would come in the work of statistician and eugenicist Ronald Fisher, who in 1930, showed that Mendel's laws could be used with quantitative genetics to account for the observed similarity between relatives for traits such as height, weight, and, of course, IQ scores (Schiff and Lewontin, 1986:10). In *The Genetical Theory of Natural Selection*, Fisher proposed a theory of evolution and sounded the familiar alarm that, since the lower classes were outbreeding the upper classes, the human species was in danger of deterioration.

While population and Mendelian genetics date back a full century, the field of *molecular genetics* has only emerged as an important approach to join the issue of human genetics in the second half of this century. Developments of the last few decades have produced a converging of the fields of chemistry and biology (biochemistry) in the laboratory study of genes and chromosomes. Cytogeneticists study the cell life and chromosomes as a larger frame for gene studies. Thus, the term *geneticist* covers a range as wide as a molecular-level laboratory scientist who studies the chemistry of DNA all the way to a study of Mormon or Amish family trees, where Mendelian inheritance is the core interest. Now, since many things "run in a family," including wealth, crime, and occupational choice, and since many things "run in large population aggregates," it is of great interest to the social analyst to ascertain and note which of the many human attributes, characteristics, traits, or behaviors that "run in families" get conceptualized as prime candidates for understanding genetic basis, and investigated with a program of research.

The Search for the Genetics of Intelligence: When and Why?

In this century, the empirical research on the genetics/IQ controversy and the attendant policy injunctions have had a remarkably varied history. However, one consistent pattern emerges: the more privileged strata have at each juncture raised the "genetic" question about those at the lower end of the socioeconomic ladder. Depending upon the social and political climate, the relationship of this research and the controversies and claims about it have directly influenced significant social policy shifts in the nation. The genetics/IQ debate has been laced with ideological and political controversy for many decades, including charges of cultural and class bias in the test, reification of the test as intelligence itself, and outright cheating and fraud (Kamin, 1974; Schiff and Lewontin, 1986).

For example, it has long been known that Jews do better in school than gentiles, and they also do better on IQ tests (Terman and Oden, 1947; Belth, 1958; Vincent, 1966; Synnott, 1979; Karabel, 1984). However, during the first part of the twentieth century, Jews did so poorly on IQ tests that scientists testified as to their "genetic inferiority" before the U.S. Congress (Kamin, 1974:16–26). In fact, using this as a rationale, Congress passed restrictive legislation in the 1920s that drastically reduced the immigration of Jews, other eastern Europeans, and Italians from a flood to a mere trickle (Lieberson, 1980:7–12). Armed with two sets of "data" at two different historical periods, scientists have pursued the question of whether Jews are genetically inferior to gentiles, but ignored their potential genetic superiority. Indeed, if Arthur Jensen used the very same methodology that he employed to argue that blacks are genetically inferior to whites, research completed in the last half of the twentieth century would have forced him to conclude that gentiles are genetically inferior to Jews (Jensen, 1969, 1972; Chase, 1977:468–509).

As noted, Jews currently do better than gentiles on IQ tests. They also get better grades and excel on college entrance examinations and on standardized tests for graduate and professional study. This pattern is not limited to the United States. A study in Scotland, for example, compared the measured intelligence of more than one thousand Jewish and non-Jewish schoolchildren born between 1949 and 1954. The data were collected from seventy-eight schools, and the children were between the ages of ten and sixteen when the study was done (Vincent, 1966). The overall mean IQ score for the Jewish children was 117.8; for the non-Jewish children, it was 100.00. The difference in means is statistically significant at a level remarkably comparable to mean differences between blacks and whites in America that Jensen (1969) reported. The author of the Scottish report chose to interpret the results as explainable by *cultural*, not genetic, factors (Vincent, 1966: 103–107).

Despite the evidence that both internally and cross-culturally, Jews have higher IQ scores than gentiles, no body of research has been developed to pursue the question of the possible biological genetic base of this superiority. Much of the explanation can be found in C. S. Lewis's wry formulation that "man's power over nature is really the power of some men over others with nature as their instrument." If Lewis is correct, then "power over others with nature as . . . instrument" may have a bit more to do with the social and political course of knowledge development than intrinsic intellectual interest in biological or genetic imperatives. More precisely, if Lewis is correct, we should be able to find a pattern whereby a group with more power but lower IQ and lower entrance test scores finds a way to get its members into training to become brain surgeons and heart surgeons and judges and lawyers. For many decades before "affirmative action" was in the lexicon, law schools and medical schools and Ivy League schools, including Harvard, Yale, and Princeton, blocked Jewish students from entry, despite the Jewish students' superior grades and, later, superior IQ and entrance test scores (Synnott, 1979; Karabel, 1984). Indeed, the move to introduce standardized testing was explicitly designed in part to reduce the number of Jews admitted to universities and colleges (Wechsler, 1977; Karabel, 1984). This move was a reaction to the fact that Jews had done so well with high school grades, and were competitively superior to gentiles. However, the history of Jews on IQ tests in the early part of the century was poor, and it was believed that introducing a standardized test would lower if not erase this grade point advantage.

Yet at one point a search actually was made in this country for a biological explanation of the IQ performance of Jews. It is crucial to the argument that I am making here to appreciate the social context of this attempt. The emergence, use, and ascendance of the IQ test accompanied the last great wave of European immigration. Historians and sociologists have long noted the importance of this epoch for the development of contemporary thought and social political life. The last reforms and regulations of the Progressive Era, the immigration laws of the 1920s, and two powerful movements (labor and temperance) were all substantially influenced by this immigration. The story of this period is also instructive in illuminating the social basis of claims about the genetic condition of members of ethnic and racial groupings.

At the turn of the century, hundreds of thousands of Europeans were immigrating to the United States annually. During the three decades from 1885 to World War I, more than fifteen million Europeans came to the American shore as permanent emigrés (Sibley, 1953:382). Prior to 1885, European immigration had been primarily from England, Scandinavia, and Germany. However, in the thirty-year period prior to World War I, the "new immigrants" were predominantly Italian, Russian, Polish, Slavic, and Jewish (the last cutting across several national boundaries). Those who had already arrived (English, Scandinavians, and German-Americans) saw real threat in the new immigrants (Kamin, 1974; Gusfield, 1969; Haller, 1963; Ludmerer, 1972). Across many spheres of American life, the self-proclaimed "full-blooded" north and west European-Americans pooled their resources and moved to collectively block further "alien" immigration. Ultimately they succeeded. Congressional action in 1924 slammed the door almost completely shut on those from the southern, central, and eastern parts of Europe.

For example, yearly immigration from the Baltic states and Russia was 250,000 in both 1913 and 1914, but dropped to 21,000 in 1923, then to 1,000 per year for the next fifty years (Lieberson, 1980:9). Similarly, Italian immigration dropped from 222,000 in 1921 to 56,000 in 1924, fell even further in the next decade, and never again approached even the 1924 level.

In congressional testimony to justify the new legislation to stop the flow of this "lower form of human life," the "scientific" IQ test became a powerful justification. Jews (and Russians and Italians) had been revealed by the Binet test as genetically inferior and more prone, biologically, to "feeble-mindedness."

> The mental testers pressed upon the Congress scientific IQ data to demonstrate that the "New Immigration" from southeastern Europe was genetically

inferior. That contribution permanently transformed American society. (Kamin, 1974:12)

The United States passed immigration laws in the 1920s that were unashamedly committed to racial and ethnic quotas, and nearly a half-century elapsed before they were substantially repealed. The first restrictive legislation in 1921 set quotas at 3 percent for immigrants from any nation already represented in the United States population. In the next two years, Congress was besieged by testimony from eugenicists, who argued from IQ test data collected by the Army during universal conscription in World War I. Just closing the borders of the nation was not enough. The eugenicists wanted to impose harsher quotas on the nations of southern and eastern Europe because the test scores were used to show that Italians, Slavs, Jews, and Poles came from inferior racial stock (Gould, 1981:232). They won the fight, and a new, more restrictive law was passed in 1924, resetting the quotas at 2 percent from each nation recorded in the 1890 census. Since north Europeans and the British had predominated in 1890, this effectively shut off the flood of immigration from south, south-central, and eastern Europe. When Calvin Coolidge signed the Immigration and Restriction Act of 1924, he said that "America must be kept American."

The development of intelligence testing and the attribution of genetic inferiority paralleled this explosive immigration growth. In 1905, the Frenchman Alfred Binet developed and administered the first "intelligence" test. His purpose, along with that of his countryman and colleague Théodore Simon, was to help schoolteachers more effectively reach students who had difficulty with standard methods of teaching (Schiff and Lewontin, 1986:8). Binet believed that all children could learn if taught with methods adapted to their condition, and he explicitly rejected the notion of innate stupidity. The origins of the IQ test were therefore well-intentioned, but the uses were hardly benign.

Seven years later, in 1912, the United States Public Health Service invited psychologist Henry Goddard to Ellis Island (the immigrant receiving station at New York harbor) to administer a translated and adapted version of the Binet test and screen the new immigrants (Kamin, 1974:16). Goddard claims he was scrupulously concerned with fairness and applicability of his findings, as is revealed in the following passages of a report that he published in 1917 summarizing his results:

Confining our study to the Jewish group for the present, we find in addition to these above tests, 75 per cent passed questions ... They are therefore valid tests. (Goddard, 1917:247)

The Binet-Simon Scales gives a person a chance to make a rating of XII. But the usual scale is shown by these data to be not valid for this group of immigrants, because certain questions are not passed by 75 per cent of them. Nevertheless after omitting these non-valid questions, there is still enough left of the scale to give the examinee the chance to make a rating of X. More than 40 per cent of the Jewish immigrants fail to do even this. According to this criterion more than 40 per cent (for all groups it is 39.1 per cent) would be considered feeble-minded according to the usual definition. It must be admitted that this gives the immigrant the benefit of every doubt. (Goddard, 1917:249)

More than 40 percent of the Jewish immigrants tested showed up "feeble-minded" from this research. In the context of a period in which the public arena was saturated with social evolutionary theories adapted from Darwin's bioevolutionary theory, the quick attribution was that this inferiority was genetic.[26]

The IQ test was institutionalized in 1917, when the United States began testing Army conscripts. Robert Yerkes, professor of psychology at Harvard, had been longing for an opportunity to prove that psychology could be as rigorous and scientific as physics. He, like most of his contemporaries, "equated rigor and science with numbers and quantification" (Gould, 1981:193). He was embarrassed by poorly trained amateurs who were using the newly arrived mental tests without systematic controlled methods of inquiry (Chase, 1977:242). He successfully lobbied the government to permit the mental testing of 1.75 million Army recruits during World War I.

The tests corroborated the worst fears of the eugenicists. The most recent immigrants from southern and eastern Europe scored lower on the IQ tests than the older immigrant groups from northern Europe. Although skeptics pointed out that Italians and Poles who had been in the country longer scored much higher than the more recently arrived, this criticism never undermined the importance of the genetic explanation (Gould, 1981:221). On average, African Americans scored lower than European Americans. Northern blacks scored higher than southern whites. Undaunted, the staunch defenders of the genetic interpretation speculated that the more intelligent blacks had moved north, and that, coincidentally, they also probably had a higher proportion of "white blood."[27] Even though this was a period of legally mandated segregation of schools, with most blacks (who lived in the South) consigned to inferior schools, no mention was made of these rather important environmental factors influencing the scores.

Probably the most use made of the tests inside the Army was the screening of men for officer training. The Army IQ tests had their greatest impact on civilian life. Educational institutions lined up to use the IQ test, not as Binet had intended as a device for individualized assessments of how instruction might be improved, but to assign students to categories of smart, normal, moron, etc.[28] The use of mass testing had firmly established *the machinery* for screening far beyond the reaches of the military.

In 1923, Yerkes' disciple, C. C. Bingham, a professor of psychology at Yale, published *A Study of American Intelligence*. In this work, he noted how the Army tests, like the Goddard tests at Ellis Island, revealed that recently immigrated Jews had low intelligence. Thus, we see how the question of the genetic basis of Jewish intelligence only surfaces for scientific investigation under select historical, economic, and political circumstances.[29]

The Shifting Focus of the Genetics of Intelligence

Between 1925 and 1950, attention shifted away from the lower IQ scores of the presumably "feeble-minded" Jews to the lower IQ scores of blacks. In 1920, most blacks still lived in the rural South. New York City had the largest black settlement in the North. But the total number of blacks in the city was 150,000; in contrast there were nearly a million Jews, 800,000 Italians, 750,000 Germans, 220,000 Russians, and even the Poles, 160,000 strong, outnumbered the blacks (Lieberson, 1980:60).

In 1920, only a few years before massive new European immigration was to end, 85 percent of all blacks lived in the South. Three-fourths were still in the South when the United States entered World War II. This figure decreased in succeeding decades, thanks to the massive changes during and after the war, but in 1970 a bare majority of blacks were still living in the South. (Lieberson, 1980:9)

By 1950, the demographic picture had changed dramatically, and several northern cities had begun to bulge with black ghettoes. There were even then the harbingers of red-lining, and with government approval, the refusal to provide federal housing loans to blacks (Abrams, 1966), the subsequent development of residential segregation, and the emergence and coalescence of slums (Chase, 1977). This was also the period in which the already-arrived working-class whites in these cities began to increase their expression of concern about black strike-breakers, and competition from black low-wage workers (Schuman et al., 1985). For those who have grown accustomed to the 1980s phenomenon of black youth unemployment being three to four times that of whites, it will come as a surprise to learn that in 1954, unemployment rates for black and white youth in the urban North were about the same. Indeed, white youth unemployment actually slightly exceeded that of blacks in the 16–19 age group (Kasarda, 1983). But blacks soon replaced whites in the formerly white neighborhoods and urban school systems, and deindustrialization soon shifted employment sites away from these black communities (Bluestone and Harrison, 1982; Squires, 1982; Freeman and Holzer, 1986).

The social and behavioral scientists of the period were busily explaining all of this by reference to social, economic, and political forces, rather than biological ones (Dollard, 1957; Clark, 1965; Osofsky, 1967). They were correct. Within a decade, America would experience some of its most powerful movements for social change. The nation would remake its laws in response to the social protests and the demands for social justice. But all the turmoil and strife, the ghetto rebellions and racial confrontations, all the rapid dislocations of American institutions, had the collective potential of jostling, if not fully awakening, the dormant genetic accounts of some of these new patterns, new social arrangements, and old stereotypes.

Still, the *zeitgeist* of the 1960s was such that few would take the *public* stage (or publish in scholarly journals)[30] and argue the "genetics" of intelligence, crime, or athletic or job performance. There were minor skirmishes about such matters as an extra male chromosome, and debates about whether research on the early identification of potential criminals should be funded (Reilly, 1977). But this was the era of President Lyndon Johnson's *Great Society,* the *War on Poverty,* and *Head Start*—in short, of programs that emphasized social intervention. In this setting, two developments occurred. The first was the prominent and controversial publication of an article asserting the genetic inferiority of blacks. Using primarily arguments and techniques of population genetics, the article was published in the *Harvard Educational Review* in 1969 by an educational psychologist in Berkeley, Arthur Jensen.[31] The article received immediate attention from *Newsweek, Time,* and other major print media, and even got international coverage.[32]

The second development was a quiet, unobtrusive, barely noticed phenomenon emerging out of the new technologies in molecular biology and biochemistry. In 1961, Robert Guthrie reported that he had uncovered a method of detecting high levels of phenylalanine in the human bloodstream (Stine, 1977:457). It would lead to genetic screening. At the time, scientists believed that high levels of phenylalanine were likely to be explained by the presence of phenylketonuria (PKU), an "inborn error of metabolism" which, if untreated in the newborn, could lead to mental retardation.[33] By using Guthrie's new test, a physician could take a newborn who tested positive and initiate treatment by monitoring a low phenylalanine diet, thereby "treating" PKU. Advocates of the new testing procedure argued persuasively to members of state legislators that gene screening for PKU would be cost-effective. While a screening program might cost $33,000 per infant with the disorder, the state would save the $365,000 it would otherwise cost to take over as a ward of a single victim of mental retardation (Reilly, 1977:19). Thus was born the biochemical basis of mass gene screening in the United States. Massachusetts passed the first state law mandating such screening in 1962, and within five years, 3.5 million newborn were being screened annually across the nation.[34]

The two sets of events, were, of course, unrelated. Jensen had rekindled an old flame using population genetics, with a nod to Mendelian principles. He asked how much IQ scores could be boosted by means of social and educational programs aimed at improving the lower achievement scores of blacks. Since his answer was that the problem was primarily a genetic one, the implication was that these social interventions were doomed to failure. The newly perceived social threat, and the fear of a drain on the public revenues, help explain the level of heat in the debate and the ensuing public controversy, the direction of the new targets of the hunt for low IQs, and, later, attempts to account for high crime rates and their biological or genetic base. The 1960s, while ushering in a new era of social activism concerning race and racial equality, also renewed an old debate (Jensen and the IQ levels of those at the bottom of the social order) and saw a completely new incarnation of the relationship between genetics and the social order.

Summary

The story of the search for genetic explanations of intelligence in the early part of the century reveals that the empirical focus was not at the molecular level, but was based instead upon statistical manipulations of large aggregates of data (population genetics methodologies), or, alternatively, upon studies contrasting the trait, behavior, or condition of blood relatives with adopted children, and so on (i.e., Mendelian methodology applied to humans). The first two strategies have been used for over a century, and scientists and laity alike can argue back and forth about how convincing the data are, why "intelligence" was chosen as a subject, why it is measured with an IQ test, and why we make a Mendelian or population study of crime, or indeed, of any phenomenon.

The strategy for addressing the "genetics" of any phenomenon in a large aggregated population is to infer from observed frequencies the statistical probability of occurrence by inheritance pattern, chance, etc. The proponents of the IQ, race, and intelligence research were inferring in part from the statistical methods and background assumptions the salience of a mean difference of fifteen points between blacks and whites on IQ tests, built upon further inference about the genetics of the phenomenon from twin or adoption studies. Although the two fields started off in an adversarial relationship, population genetics, as noted, later intersected with Mendelian genetics. Still, the attempt to see if a phenomenon "runs in families" is predominantly a Mendelian strategy. This would be a prime methodology for trying to locate "the genetics of a phenomenon" by looking at the genealogies of older, stable communities with good record keeping. This included the Amish and the Mormons, among others, and the questions taken on would include crime, intelligence, alcoholism, schizophrenia, and retardation.

In the midst of these ongoing tussles came molecular biology, using developments in biochemistry. Spectacular successes have accompanied these developments,[35] providing both health and medical gains. Equally significant, these successes were undoubtedly fused and confused in the body politic and the general public. The laity, in absorbing accounts of new "discoveries," are not likely to sift and sort the genetic traditions from the molecular to the population to the Mendelian logical inference. Indeed, sometimes the researchers themselves merged seemingly disparate concerns. In 1981, the *Journal of Medical Genetics* published an article entitled "Genes for Super-Intelligence?" The authors concluded the article in the following manner:

> It is possible that future investigations will further confirm the association between various inherited disorders and superior intelligence, and that, as the biochemistry of the disorders becomes better understood, there may be direct demonstrations of intellectual enhancement by the products of the genes involved. (Sofaer and Emery, 1981:412)

In any event, the developments in molecular biology inevitably gave new legitimacy to many of the formulations of genetic accounts that had been lying fallow for decades.

It was not just the population geneticist technique of getting at the "genetics of a phenomenon" that received a new halo. This would also affect the search for and attribution of Mendelian principles that might throw some "genetic light" on such matters as crime, alcoholism, and mental illness. It is clear that an analysis of "which questions" is important to pursue for genetical studies of kinship lines. That is, we can profitably ask what factors direct a body of research in a given society at a given historical moment to study the heritability of crime or heresy or intelligence "as it runs in families." It is equally (if somewhat more subtly) important to raise the matter of "which questions" when reviewing how and why population statisticians search for select matters of heritability for a large social aggregate. Finally, when it comes to the search for chromosomes and genes of an inherited disorder at the molecular level, the perspective on "which questions" is more difficult to sustain, but no less significant for increasing our understanding of the architecture of knowledge structures. The search for single dominant genes for *wanderlust* at the turn of the century, or for shyness and inhibition during the 1980s, may seem unlikely enterprises to some, but that should not lead one to underestimate the importance of single major genes. More Mendelian traits are known for humans than for any other organism (McKusick, 1983; Ludmerer, 1972:59). Thus, it is the search for these traits that should demand the closer attention of social analysis.

At the beginning of this chapter, I mentioned briefly that something new has happened in the field of molecular genetics as applied to humans. In later chapters, I will argue that the new genetics has provided a new halo of legitimacy around long-standing issues and concerns, and has refueled old notions about the "genetics" of a wide host of issues in social life.

The "old" genetic intersection with race, ethnicity, and social class concerned the "lower intelligence" of those at the bottom of the social order. The new genetic intersection with race concerns a far more neutral, scientific, even health-beneficial issue—screening for genetic disorders. How the new prism refracts and thereby selects problems for inquiry, research, screening, and treatment is a matter for the sociology of knowledge.[36] It is far more subtle, however, because health, science, and medicine are the banners of the new molecular genetic technology.[37] Before turning to the advances, accomplishments, promises, and problems of the new technologies as they apply to genetic screening of a population, we will first turn to some concerns with the sociology of knowledge.

2

The Prism of Heritability and
The Sociology of Knowledge:
What Questions? Whose Questions?

The sociology of knowledge is, in its broadest conception, an approach to the social conditions of thought. It is not equipped to assess the validity of the truth claim, nor to evaluate the pragmatic fit of a worldview. As a field of inquiry, its roots are traceable to Karl Mannheim (1936) and Max Scheler (1926). Mannheim often referred to the "existential conditions of thought," and variably referred to the "sociology of cognition." While neither Scheler nor Mannheim provided a systematic or single method of getting at the subject, it is possible to distill from their works, and from the works of those who followed them, some key principles. Foremost among them is the perspective that (a) individuals are located in groups, (b) groups have an interested position towards the existing order of things, and (c) the organization of human thought (in individuals) can often be better understood by discerning the relationship between *(a)* and *(b)*.

> People . . . living in groups do not merely coexist physically as discrete individuals. They do not confront the objects of the world from the abstract levels of a contemplating mind as such, nor do they do so exclusively as solitary beings. On the contrary, they act with and against one another in diversely organized groups, and while doing so they think with and against one another. These persons, bound together into groups, strive in accordance with the character and position of the groups to which they belong to change the surrounding world of nature and society or attempt to maintain it in a given condition. It is the direction of this will to change or to maintain, of this collective activity, which produces the guiding thread for the emergence of their problems, their concepts, and their forms of thought. (Mannheim, 1936:3)

To illustrate the bearing of this perspective upon a "genetic prism," a social analysis in the tradition of the sociology of knowledge investigated the social backgrounds of the adversaries of the genetics and IQ controversy. The finding: those scientists who pursued research claiming that high IQ was genetic and was located in the privileged strata were more likely to have come from upper-middle-class backgrounds; in contrast, those pursuing the adversarial environment argument were more likely to have come from humble social origins (Sherwood and Nataupsky, 1968).[1]

While it is probably rare that social factors so crudely explain the behavior of scientists engaged in research that is socially controversial, this study does suggest that a systematic investigation of the interplay of social factors would add to our understanding of the nature and direction of human work, of which science is a subset.

The inevitable question, however, can understandably come down to: "I don't care who started it, nor why the question was asked. Just tell me whether or not there is any truth to the claim that IQ is related to race." It is important to state at the outset, and it is worth repeating, that the sociology of knowledge does not address the truth claim. In that sense, it can be infuriating if the credibility of the formulation is the main question to be addressed. Sometimes the drive to uncover the legitimacy of the "truth claim" is so strong that even those employing the sociology of knowledge will unobtrusively, perhaps even inadvertently, slip into a posture to address the degree of truth. But that is a different kind of investigation, to be left to the procedural rules for getting at the degree of truth in the claim. Of course, at any given moment, members of a society firmly believe that their procedures are adequate to the task.

Framing the Issues and the Sociology of Knowledge

How differing interests shape the questions that in turn are the building blocks of knowledge structures is at the core of a resurgent "sociology of knowledge" (Knorr-Cetina and Mulkay, 1983:2).[2] In a sacred society, it makes common sense for the members to concern themselves with the relationship between heresy and deep evil, heresy and intelligence and wealth, and blasphemy and moral turpitude. The fifteenth and sixteenth-century Spanish tied their concern for purity of the blood (*limpiezza de sangre* decrees) to belief versus heresy. When twentieth-century Americans have expressed concern for purity of the blood, it has usually been tied to the question of race.[3] The biological question of blood purity is inevitably connected to the particular substantive concerns of the society. Thus, in a culture where race and sex are firmly rooted categories of differentiation and sustained stratification, we should expect both common sense and probing inquiry into the intelligence differences between the races and into the biological destiny of females (Corea, 1985). Thus, Arthur Jensen was taken quite seriously when he posited a relationship between race and IQ. He would be taken far less seriously in the National Academy of Sciences if he did, or if he advocated studies of the relationship between IQ and head shape, IQ and height, IQ and arm length, or IQ and hair color.[1] But we have seen from the last chapter that it is largely a matter of the social framework of the times. Gould (1981) has rendered both a vivid history and a superb analysis of how the measurement of heads captured the imagination of nineteenth-century scientists. We are not so distant from that past. The question of the relationship between IQ and physiognomy, skin color, and hair texture was treated as worthy of serious investigation by members of the National Academy of Sciences in the 1970s precisely because skin color is such a salient feature of American life, and has been so for four hundred years.[5]

The study of knowledge formation is at once one of the most fundamental and complex issues in human history. At specific points in time, select social questions emerge for critical, detailed, close inspection and the laying on of the tightest strictures of the prevailing epistemology of a culture. In the present period, this path is identified as science, but every culture and every epoch has its equivalent claim to faith in procedures of investigation that resolve matters in areas deemed knowable and worth knowing.

Whatever may be our historical hindsight of the Salem witch-hunt trials, nearly three hundred years later, Boyer and Nissenbaum (1974) have shown that the judges were scrupulous and meticulous in admitting into evidence what was considered for those times only the most carefully screened information inferentially relevant to the findings and "knowing" of who the witches were.[6] But we need not go back so far in history. In late nineteenth-century Italy, celebrated scholars raised questions about the biological differences between law-abiding citizens and criminals, posited the natural superiority of one over the other, and invoked the known procedures of investigation to sustain the distinction and argument (Gault, 1932). There is continuity to the biological study of crime even today, as there is between IQ and race, and the genetics of mental health issues. In later chapters, we will return to the long legacy.

The Sociology of Science (Knowledge) and the Game of Go

From Latour and Woolgar (1979) we have the notion that science is in practice much like the Chinese game of Go, in which the number of possibilities is infinite as the game opens, but where each move restricts the remaining options. In theory, science differs in that one can always retrace one's steps and head off in a new direction. But in practice the social organization of a particular Go strategy is so embedded in routine assumptions and so costly in career-risk terms that practitioners are in perpetual danger of reifying a particular line of inquiry or pathway to knowledge. Laboratories are set up moving in one direction, and whether "it works" is only one ingredient for its continual operation, as cancer research analysts know very well (Hilgartner, 1986; Fujimura, 1988; McIntyre, 1980).[7]

The success or failure of a paradigm or an arraying of a set of facts is not necessarily the major component of its longevity in science. But as Gould (1981:21–23) points out, it does not follow that one must then fall victim to the polemical trap of concluding that the organization of knowledge structures is entirely or even primarily political. Rather, it is the interplay of science and external forces, much as it is the interplay of genes and environment, that will best account for the outcomes we observe in behavior.

As an example, in cancer research, if the apparatus of research institutions is set up to look primarily for the molecular genetics of cancer, nutritional studies which might illuminate how different diets affect cancer rates are less likely to get funded by the peer review process.[8] Even so, distilled by that process, excellent path-breaking research with treatment possibilities may well be conducted in the molecular genetics of cancer, and so to reduce the distillation process to "politics" is as absurd as to deny the role of extrinsic forces. The Nobel Prize is more likely to lie in the higher technology adventure of the latter, not the arena of prosaic controlled experimental studies of nutritional intervention. In the zero-sum of scientific energy and resources, other approaches (prisms) get less attention, less status, and ultimately a weakened capacity to do empirical battle with the dominant paradigm.

There is a parallel for high-technology medicine, apparent when we contrast prenatal or postnatal intervention in the health problems of low-birth-weight infants. If the issue is entirely a concern with the "health dimension,"[9] then the burden should be to provide strong evidence that the resources and money that go into this kind of work are likely to be more health-beneficial. An abundance of empirical research[10] has established the efficacy of primary maternal health care during the first two trimesters of pregnancy, but the lower glamor and social status of this kind of work in the health profession has made for weaker advocates who are often pushed to the sidelines to watch the march towards expensive high-technology postnatal intervention.

At the beginning of this section, I used the metaphor of the game of Go to suggest how the earliest stages of a research program structures whole fields of scientific work, that in turn shape and delimit the way in which many research projects develop for decades. Even when scientific work on some topics has long been demolished as fraudulent, the prism can be a difficult one to discard. For example, the earliest work on twin studies and IQ has long been discredited, with demonstration of unconscionable cheating and fraud in the earliest reports of "research findings" (Kamin, 1974; Schiff and Lewontin, 1986). Cyril Burt, for decades perhaps the leading figure in the world arguing from his published materials for the innate mental differences between the classes, fabricated data to claim that identical twins reared apart were strikingly similar in IQ. He was knighted for his work in England, and in the post–World War II era, his research was used as a primary justification to implement a class-based tracking system in the British schools (Schiff and Lewontin, 1986:11). Even though now thoroughly discredited, this research continued to be the foundation of twin studies for a quarter century. Jensen's article leaned upon Burt's "findings," and later Jensen (1974), disavowed this work.[11]

It is less well appreciated, but now well documented, that the history behind the body of research now claiming a genetic basis for schizophrenia has origins that are as suspicious as the Burt fabrications. The father of the genetic theory of psychiatry, Ernst Rudin, was a eugenicist who advocated the sterilization of schizophrenics in Hitler's Germany (Lewontin et al., 1984:206). His student was Franz Kallman, a scientist as influential in using twin study data to claim the genetics of schizophrenia as Burt was in claiming the genetics of IQ. In 1984, Richard Lewontin, Steven Rose, and Leon Kamin published a dissection of Kallman's work, in which they demonstrate the unlikely nature of the extremely high correlations for schizophrenia that Kallman claimed to have found between identical twins (Lewontin et al., 1984:206–214). Kallman found the rate of similarity to be 86 percent, a figure so high that no researchers since have been able to duplicate, or even come close to it. Lewontin et al. point out that while Kallman's data recently have been dropped from a body of acceptable evidence, just as Jensen stood on the shoulders of Burt in his 1969 article, so citations to Kallman persisted in the literature for many years, as if the research were respectable. In the tradition of the sociology of knowledge, the major point here is that even when there is fraud, bodies of scientific work on the genetics of a phenomenon in such a hotly contested arena take on lives of their own, and often can produce and have direct social policy spinoffs.

Just as there are spinoffs to other research within science, there are also spinoffs to social and public policy that make use of that science. As I indicated at the outset, this is a two-way street. Scientists produce work that dismantles outmoded thinking about race, as in research on race/IQ and on the genetics of enzymes and proteins, and science has also produced work that ushered in unjust and unwarranted mandatory sterilization. Both occurred in this century. It is only in hindsight that we understand the problematic character of social policy based upon a series of (what was determined later to be) uncertainties. We need to better appreciate that, at a given historical moment, we always believe that the current technology, being up-to-the-minute, is "correct." What follows are two contrasting examples of the spinning off of the original Go game into the organizational apparatus of the state, in this case, the military. In one case, a research program was generated; in the other, "only" a policy initiative.

The Search for Genetic Explanations of Inexplicable Experiences at High Altitudes

In the eleven-month period between March 1968 and February 1969, four isolated instances of death occurred among approximately four thousand blacks going through basic combat training for the U.S. Army (Jones et al., 1970). The training camp where the deaths occurred was at an altitude of 4,060 feet. All four men had originated from low-altitude areas, were apparently healthy, were between the ages of nineteen and twenty-one, and had no family history of anemia.

One collapsed after a 40-yard crawl and a 300-meter run. The second complained of feeling faint after a 20-yard crawl during his first day of training, lost consciousness, and was dead upon arrival at the medical clinic. The third collapsed and died after a mile run. The final case was even stranger. On his very first day, this recruit simply ran once around the barracks, expressed concern about numbness in the legs, and lost consciousness. Although he regained consciousness for a time, he died within eight hours (Jones et al., 1970:323).

In the research report that revealed these incidents, we are not told if any whites died during this eleven-month period. An autopsy revealed that all four blacks had experienced severe sickling of the red blood cells. As Kevles (1985:278) and others have pointed out, the sickling could have been a consequence of death, not the cause.[12] Ordinarily, to be a carrier of a recessive gene has no notable effect upon experience, behavior, or appearance. One can be a carrier of the recessive gene for blue eyes, but have brown or black eyes, for example. However, to be a carrier of the sickle-cell gene, depending upon place and circumstance, can be either an advantage or a problem. It is a particular advantage in areas where there is malaria. Studies from Africa and the Mediterranean basin indicate that people with sickle-cell trait are less susceptible to lethal malaria than those without the trait (Stine, 1977:405; Edelstein, 1986:46–48). While there is some controversy over degree of risk, sickle-cell carriers are thought to be at slightly greater risk than the rest of the population for certain kidney and spleen problems. Nonetheless, it is very uncommon for blacks who have sickle-cell trait to experience any discomfort or problems associated with the trait.

When the report of the four blacks who died in basic training was first published in the *New England Journal of Medicine* in 1970, it reverberated in profound and revealing ways. The responses within the medical profession ranged from a call for pre-induction genetic screening for recruits (Stone, 1970) to exemption from the draft (Mosher, 1970), to skepticism about the interpretability of the results (McCurdy, 1970). The National Academy of Sciences–National Research Council set up a committee to investigate (Powledge, 1974). While the committee concluded that data on the topic of the pathologies associated with carrier status were inadequate, they recommended that all recruits for basic training, regardless of race, be screened for both the trait and the disease (NAS/NRC,[13] 1973). The committee also recommended that limits be placed on the activities of those who are carriers, including exclusion from copiloting an airplane.

Undoubtedly, the committee was well intentioned. However, the essential controls and comparisons were absent, and if one is merely observing frequencies, there is great danger of spurious relations and false conclusions. Indeed, at about the same time as the report about the four deaths and the reaction was setting in, a study of black professional football players revealed that 7 percent have sickle-cell trait (Murphy, 1973). Players in the National Football League are exemplars of the healthy, powerful, agile American male, exercising continuously in the most adverse circumstances, from moderately high altitudes to snowstorms and below-zero weather. The occurrence of sickle-cell trait in the National Football League is higher than in the general population, although not significantly different from what one would expect in the African American population (Powledge, 1974). If one were doing a simple linear interpretation of these frequencies without controls informed by theoretical sampling, as in the case of the four black Army recruits, the straight linear conclusion would be that having sickle-cell trait means one's chances for superlative athletic accomplishment increases. Despite what is undoubtedly "strenuous physical exertion," no blacks in the National Football League with sickle-cell trait have collapsed and died after such physical exertion at Mile High Stadium in Denver, week after week, over many decades, often in front of a national television audience.

To return to the matter of the deaths of the four black recruits at the military training camp, the committee of the National Academy of Sciences was correct in saying that the data were inadequate. What was needed was a series of rigorous studies, in which controls and comparisons were employed for those who are carriers and those who are not, both within and between groups, at various altitudes. Instead, armed with this National Academy of Sciences recommendation, for the next six years the Air Force Academy carried out a policy of excluding blacks with sickle-cell trait. Here is the text stating the position by a ranking official in the Department of Defense ("Hb AS" refers to carrier status):

1. Candidates with Hb AS will continue to be disqualified for attendance at the Air Force Academy. Applicants to the Air Force with Hb AS are fully acceptable for Air Force commissioning by other routes, such as Air Force ROTC programs. These other routes, particularly the Air Force ROTC, provide the great majority of commissioned officers in the Air Force.

2. The military departments will continue to disqualify applicants with Hb AS for aviation and flight crew training. It is my opinion that the rigors of aviation duties in combat operations are potentially so severe that it is medically imprudent and militarily unwise to have military members with Hb AS in flying status.

3. The Department of Navy has been testing all Navy and Marine recruits for Hb AS for over two years. The Navy is testing virtually all officers coming on active duty; a few officers receiving direct commissions such as medical personnel, lawyers, chaplains may not be tested at the time of their entry because of difficulty of administratively securing samples from them. The Air Force is in the process of implementing an Hb AS screening program for enlisted and officer members similar to the Navy program. The Army is at this time only testing those members who apply for airborne, ranger or flight crew training. (Bowman, 1977:129)

The best (and only) reported scientific research up to this point in time was to be found in two studies. One was an autopsy study "in which there was no difference among normals and sickle-cell trait carriers coming to autopsy, which suggests no difference in mortality. The second was a prevalence study in California of sickle cell trait at various ages. . . . No differences in sickle cell trait frequency were found" (Hilton et al., 1973:163). Despite this state of knowledge in the world of scientific medicine, almost all of the major airlines grounded or fired their employees with sickle-cell trait in the early and mid-1970s (Bowman, 1977:129).

In 1979, Stephen Pullens, a black, was forced to resign from the Air Force Academy when blood tests revealed that he was a carrier of the recessive gene for sickle-cell. The story is replete with irony. Pullens was a former state champion high hurdler and four-sport star athlete whose best times were at high altitudes.[14] He was also a mountain climber and testified that he never experienced problems at high altitudes. Nonetheless, the Air Force Academy had instituted a policy of summary disqualification of blacks with sickle-cell trait, so Pullens was dismissed. Undaunted, he filed a lawsuit, and within two months of this new development, the Air Force Academy ended this policy.

This story of an appropriated genetic explanation, unsubstantiated by a developed body of research, is in sharp contrast with another instance involving the American military and inexplicable events at high altitudes.

In the first few years of jet travel, pilots often reported "strange rushes of feeling" while flying for long periods. There was a pattern to their experiences, in that these feelings usually came over them after they had been flying alone, in straight, level flight, for three-quarters of an hour or more (Solomon et al., 1961). Sometimes these sensations, or "hallucinations," would prove quite dangerous, even fatal. For example, the pilot would be flying level, read the instrument panel correctly, but "feel" that the plane was turning. The pilot would then "correct for" the turn, and the plane would head into a tailspin. In one such report, the pilot returned to the base for a medical check-up, only to learn that medics could determine nothing physically wrong with him. Moreover, a thorough check of the airplane showed no leakage of gases and correct operating air compression. Further investigation ruled out other potential mechanical explanations.

These kinds of strange experiences happened just often enough that medical doctors who examined the pilots began to suspect that what happens to certain people in this circumstance might be worth investigating. A study was done on jet aviators in the United States Navy and Marine Corps (Clark and Graybiel, 1957).

Of the 137 pilots interviewed, 48 reported that they had experienced sensations of "spatial disorientation" in which the self is in an eerie detachment from objects, a sense of physical separation. The explanation would come later, but Bennett (1961) described the problem quite vividly. He observed that jet pilots flying alone at 35,000 feet, with the plane straight and level, have very little to do. There is no appreciable change in the instrument panel, the pilot is strapped into his seat, he can see neither the wings behind him nor the nose of the plane sloping away in front:

> The background noise of the engines and of the oxygen system is monotonous and unvarying. Outside, there is an unchanging vista. At 45,000 feet the horizon is over 200 miles away, and the eye cannot detect any movement over the earth's surface, supposing that it is visible and not obscured by haze or cloud. The aviator is suspended in his transparent canopy in the sky. (Bennett, 1961:171)

Since one-third of the pilots in the Clark and Graybiel study admitted to the experience of spatial disorientation while flying, it was clearly a widespread problem. The task was to explain this spatial disorientation and occasional hallucination. The first strategy of detective work was to examine the physical condition of the plane, then to examine the physical condition of the pilot, and finally the psychological condition of the pilot.

When the first two provided no leads, there was increased speculation about the explanatory role of sensory deprivation in monotonous environments. A series of studies on this topic was launched, perhaps the most famous being a three-and-a-half-year study at McGill University.

In the tradition of the times (1951–1954), male college students were the subjects of this experiment. They were paid to lie on a comfortable bed in a room barren of any other objects of furniture for twenty-four hours a day, for as long as they could take it (Heron, 1961:8–9). They wore cotton gloves that limited their ability to touch, except when eating (by the bedside) or going to the toilet (in an adjacent room). They were not told the time, and the room was nearly soundproof. Most of the subjects refused to continue after only forty-eight to sixty hours. Of the twenty-nine experimental subjects, twenty-four reported hallucinations of some sort.[15]

Culling material from this experiment and a number of other studies of sensory deprivation, some scientists began to theorize about the necessity for cerebral stimulation and activity, and where such activity is not stimulated from sources outside the brain, then the brain will activate its own—that is, hallucinate. Indeed, later studies, of rapid-eye-movement (REM) sleep would corroborate these early theories of the necessity of regenerative stimulation of the brain. The point of the story, for our purposes, however, is not that monotonous environments produce hallucinations, but that a whole line of inquiry and knowledge development ensued along a particular line in relation to some practical problems the military perceived relevant to these early experiences in jet aviation.

The response of the military and the subsequent structuring of knowledge development was quite dramatically different with the discovery of an apparent problem for carriers of the recessive gene for sickle-cell anemia. Once again, it is not a comparison of truth claims that is the major issue here. With respect to the Air Force response to the sickle-cell carrier cases, if there had been a body of commissioned research, there would have been an answer to the question of whether and why sickling can and does occur with more carriers, why, etc. It would be important to know if this occurs, since there is a strong interest in screening pilots who might have such health problems. In the case of sickle-cell, the screen was set up only to block, not to provide the grounds for further empirical investigation. In the case of the otherwise inexplicable hallucinations at high altitudes, the monotonous-environment research turned up some fascinating results. A whole body of work emerges from the latter set of questions and problems, whereas a potentially equally important and consequential set of questions and problems was ignored in the former.

Scientific Knowledge and Its Application:
The Case of Sterilization

In chapter 1, we noted that the old eugenics movement was near the peak of its power in the 1920s, playing an important role in the justification of exclusionary immigration laws. The movement was not at the fringe of society. It was at the very center, counted among its number federal judges, university presidents, literary figures, eminent scientists, expanded to include a wide band of the political spectrum, and spanned two continents. Even President Theodore Roosevelt enjoined the "better social classes" to produce more or be threatened by "race suicide" (Ludmerer, 1972:67). Roosevelt also railed against the "yellow peril" of too many Asians, although there was only a trickle of immigrants from that part of the world, Asians having been subjected to specific and pointed exclusionary laws several decades earlier. In addition to centrists and conservatives, other eugenicists were George Bernard Shaw, a Fabian Socialist; Sidney Webb, a Socialist; and literary giant H. G. Wells (Haller, 1963:18). In the United States, members of key institutions were movement sympathizers, including David Starr Jordan, president of Stanford University, and Oliver Wendell Holmes, a member of the Supreme Court. Both men espoused eugenic views about the bad human genetic stock at the bottom of society. For detailed accounts of how highly placed, outstandingly intelligent people in the United States and England advocated eugenics programs in the early part of this century, see Ludmerer (1972), Haller (1969), and Kevles (1985). Buoyed by the legal success that resulted in the immigration gates closing to the "lower forms," eugenicists turned their attention to attacking the problem of the polluted gene pool inside the borders. Successful lobbying resulted in the passage of several state sterilization laws aimed at the mentally deficient.

In 1927, the Supreme Court ruled in a famous decision that permitted eugenic sterilizations. The Court reviewed a 1925 Virginia State Supreme Court ruling that had upheld a sterilization law. The appellant was a woman named Carrie Buck who, like her mother before her, was committed to the Virginia State Colony for Epileptics and the Feebleminded. Carrie's newborn daughter had also been "tested" and found to be feebleminded. This convinced the officials of the institution that the linkage was genetic. The Supreme Court upheld this decision in its 1927 ruling *Buck v. Bell*, in which Oliver Wendell Holmes, concluding for an overwhelming majority, stated in a phrase that was to ring ominously down through the next half century that "three generations of imbeciles is enough." In fact, Carrie Buck's daughter had been tested at the age of one month; later, when the child developed to a stage where testing was more reliable, she proved "to be above average in intelligence" (Reilly, 1977:125).[16]

With this Supreme Court ruling as a backdrop, the next decade saw twenty states pass sterilization laws, through which more than twenty thousand Americans were sterilized. By the end of World War II, the number had more than doubled, and by 1956 the total had reached fifty-eight thousand (Reilly, 1977:126). The eugenics advocates were in retreat during this period, partly because of the way the Nazis had become associated with eugenics, partly because their single-gene theory of criminality, alcoholism, epilepsy, sexual degeneracy, and retardation was being refuted by accumulating empirical evidence. However, these facts did not begin to undermine the rate of sterilizations until the 1960s, some thirty years after the first strong evidence was reported that no single-gene theory could explain these "antisocial" behaviors. Moreover, most states have not bothered to repeal their sterilization laws even in the 1980s, despite the decline in reported sterilizations in the last fifteen years. The currency of these sterilization laws, the precedent of the 1927 Supreme Court decision in *Buck v. Bell*, and the continued concern for crime and "criminal types" in America, combine to make the connection between genetics, crime, and the law an ongoing political issue.

Just fifteen years after the Supreme Court upheld the right of the state to sterilize in cases of "imbecility," it was again faced with the constitutionality of a sterilization law. The defendant, named Skinner, was an armed robber, chicken thief, and most importantly, a three-time criminal offender. In the State of Oklahoma, the law permitted sterilization of a person convicted of three felonies on three separate occasions. The important thing about *Skinner v. Oklahoma* (1942), however, is that while the Supreme Court eventually declared this sterilization law unconstitutional, the basis for the ruling was that the law violated the equal protection clause, not that sterilization for inheritable antisocial behavior was itself objectionable. Skinner's social background placed him near the bottom of the social order. Because the Oklahoma statute mandating sterilization excluded certain white-collar crimes such as embezzlement, the Supreme Court ruled that Skinner had been denied equal protection, violating his constitutional rights under the Fourteenth Amendment. The argument was framed, in other words, in terms of a class discrimination in the application of the laws (Reilly, 1977:127). By not overturning *Buck v. Bell*, the Supreme Court left compulsory sterilization as an option, and genetic sterilizations continued. Indeed, one of the concurring justices asserted the potential and likely association of criminality and genetic inheritance. The unmistakable implication of this ruling is that if a general association can be demonstrated between criminal behavior and genetic makeup, and if it did not so blatantly exempt one class of criminal offender, then sterilization by the state is permissible.

Given that the Supreme Court has upheld the right of the state to sterilize when there is evidence of genetically inherited antisocial behavior, genetic research has profound potential implications. Indeed, contemporary research on XYY chromosome males makes the Holmes doctrine "three generations of imbeciles is enough" an ominous and potential, if not imminent danger. This is particularly salient since the U.S. prison populations are becoming more racially and ethnically segregated with every succeeding decade.[17]

There are many ways to interpret this situation. The prevailing economic interpretation explains crime rates in terms of access to jobs and unemployment (Quinney, 1979; Freeman and Holzer, 1986; Currie, 1985). A cultural interpretation, tries to show differing cultural adjustments between police and those apprehended for crimes. A political interpretation sees criminal activity as political rebellion, or prerevolutionary (Hobsbawm, 1965). A conflict interpretation sees this as an interest conflict over scarce resources (Chambliss and Seidman, 1971). And over all these years of the last century, there is a genetic interpretation, which tries to account for criminality in terms of the genetic makeup (Mednick, 1984, 1985; Rowe:1986).

The XYY controversy is directly relevant to the issue of crime and color, for it is demonstrably the thin edge of the wedge for the linkage of criminality and chromosomes. There are those who maintain that our prison population contains a higher proportion of XYY males than could be expected by chance (Jacobs et al., 1965). Careful critiques of these studies (Dershowitz, 1976; Suzuki and Knudston, 1989:141–159) reveal that early conclusions about especially notable aggression among XYY males was based upon specious reasoning and seriously flawed methodology.[19] However, we cannot underestimate the force of "genetic knowledge" once it penetrates the social world of routine understandings of deviant behavior. When the Supreme Court ruled as it did in 1927, there was no knowledge about the genetics of mental retardation. The DNA code was not broken until a quarter of a century later. The new technology permits the detection of several forms of mental retardation, Down syndrome (by amniocentesis, prenatal) and phenylketonuria (by a blood test with newborn screening) being well-known examples. Both are screened for. Specialists know that chromosome abnormalities and "inheritance" can be quite different matters. Yet, the lack of this knowledge did not inhibit the Supreme Court from an inferential determination and ruling on inheritability in 1927. The Court can be much more certain now, with established mapping of select genes linked to genetic disorders.

However, there are also important empirical studies that show that, just as in the case of Carrie Buck's daughter, much that goes under the category of mental retardation is actually to be explained by social and cultural differences (Mercer, 1973; Mehan et al., 1986).

Two sides to a conflict are already in formation. Prospective parents may have a number of reasons for wanting to have the child, ranging from personal preference to strong religious or cultural beliefs. The state, as we have just noted, can overrule such "personal" preferences. The state and the individual will not always agree about whether the fetus should come to full term, or even when a "disorder" in the fetus is a disorder. Since the state has an interest in reducing costs by limiting the numbers of infants who end up as its wards, there is a potentially serious interest conflict. There are precedents on the abortion issue. At various junctures, federal funding for only certain kinds of abortions has been permissible, codified in law and regulations. For all the popular media attention to twenty-first-century images of genetic engineering, the social and political uses and consequences of this emerging technology should capture our attention at least as much as its genetic uses and health and medical consequences.

Sex Determination: Individual Autonomy vs. Cultural/Social Interests

The new technology in genetics will bring new controversies and exacerbate some old ones. The tension and conflict between the rights of individuals and the interests and control of some collectivity is as old as society itself. With prenatal determination of the sex of the fetus and the attendant matter of sex selection, there is a new arena for this old conflict. When the question is posed in the following way, the issue is clear: the right of individuals to choose the genetic destiny of their offspring is counterposed against the interests of the collectivity (the state, the ethnic group, the kinship lineage) in maintaining a balance of the sex ratio (Etzioni, 1973:119–122). A very small fraction of the earth's population is already experiencing this tension, but the numbers will expand and the controversy will intensify in the next decade with the diffusion of technology. Some commentators have minimized this as an issue.[20] Williamson (1983), while acknowledging the limited research in this area, suggests that concerns about distorting the sex ratio, or projections of untoward social costs and effects, are probably exaggerated, at least for technologically developed countries. For developing countries, she acknowledges that the picture is muddier. In any event, the main point for our purposes is that different nations will respond differently to the uses of the new technologies, and that sex selection is an example of this national, cultural, or ethnic difference. India's experience of the sex selection controversy may well be a harbinger of things to come.

The Sex Selection Controversy in India

The sex ratio of India has undergone a significant but patterned variation since records have been kept. At the turn of the century, there were 97 females born in the country for every 100 males, a relatively normal sex ratio. However, by 1970 that figure had fallen to 93 females per 100 male births, and remained constant at that level through the mid 1980s (Rao, 1986:202). This last ratio figure had nothing to do with amniocentesis, which was only introduced in 1974. Rather, the likely explanation is infanticide (*India Today*, 1982:94). Since Indian society produces a setting in which preference for a male child is so great as to incline a substantial fraction of the population to engage in infanticide to get rid of females at birth, consider how much greater the potential for reducing female births when prenatal detection is widely available. Rao (1986) reports a study of Bombay in which, of 8,000 abortions, 7,997 were female fetuses.

Following is an excerpt from a general letter sent out by Bhandari Hospital in early 1982:

> Most prospective clients in quest of a male child, as the social set-up of India demands, keep on giving birth to a number of female children, which in a way not only enhances the increasing population, but leads to a chain reaction of many social, economic, and mental stresses on these families. . . . Antenatal sex determination has come to our rescue and can help in keeping some check over the population as well as give relief to the couples requiring male children. (*India Today*, 1982:94).

In 1971, India passed the Medical Termination of Pregnancy Act, which stipulates that a women can be given an abortion only if there is a life-threatening situation, or grave injury to her physical or mental health. Amniocentesis began in India in 1974, at the Human Cytogenetics Unit in New Delhi. There were early reports that the test was being used less for the detection of birth defects than for sex determination. The Indian medical establishment, the Indian Council of Medical Research, requested that this practice be discontinued. While the New Delhi clinic complied with the request for the most part, private clinics sprang up in several cities to fill the very determined requests for prenatal knowledge of the fetuses' sex. Within two years, more than a dozen such places were in operation all over India.

So many Indian physicians have ignored the 1971 law prohibiting abortion for sex preference that the government began a new round of hearings in the late 1980s to consider legislation to restrict the use of the new technologies for sex determination of the fetus.[21] In 1988, the State of Maharastra introduced legislation to ban the use of prenatal diagnosis for sex determination, after a report estimated that approximately 78,000 fetuses were aborted in India between 1978 and 1982 (Rao, 1988).

India is hardly alone in its official concern, certainly not in developing nations, nor even in the West. During the same period, the physicians in the United Kingdom made the decision to withhold the sex of the fetus from their reports of laboratory analysis unless there was some direct clinical relevance (e.g., sex-linked genetic disorder) for the fetus (Hultjen and Needham, 1987:190). But under the same banner of health (sex selection for X-linked inherited disorders), the Japanese have recently been experimenting with a technique that has been used to select for females (Swinbanks, 1986:720).

As events move us closer to general mass-use technologies for sex determination in time for first trimester abortion, every nation will experience some version of what is happening for the few who can afford it now in India. However, rather than confronting the issue of the role of the collectivity[22] versus the role of the individual in determining the legitimacy of a bit of genetic decoded information for the termination of pregnancy, we are likely to witness protracted litigation on constitutional concerns that will delay or avoid a direct confrontation with the substantive problem.

One-dimensional solutions are tempting when the real issues demand attention to the cultural complexities of individual rights versus social interests. This is true at both a national level, and later, more complexly, at the level of subnational ethnic population variability in many parts of the world. In India, social and cultural forces best explain why there is such a premium on having a male child that a part of the population practices infanticide on its females at birth. In Scotland, an array of social forces such as relative racial, cultural, and ethnic homogeneity go far to explain why a national registry of genetic defects is conceptualized entirely as a medical or health problem. In Japan, the medical profession routinely refuses to disclose anything other than what the doctors have decided is a "medical" piece of information, and for a variety of social and cultural reasons, the Japanese population acquiesces in that decision. Meanwhile, in the United States, ethnic and racial heterogeneity and a completely different (litigious, individualistic) tradition have produced the "right to know" for individuals. In coming to believe that "individuals" should make decisions about genetic destiny, we can be blinded and then broadsided by the social frame of those decisions.

So it is that every nation, culture, and society has its own version of how to handle or what to do with sex determination, and how to handle the information (or squelch it, bury it, leave it only in the hands of the physicians, etc.). Consequently, there will be systematic social patterning in the world on this matter of how to handle information garnered from prenatal diagnosis. Moreover, every "minority" culture within a nation will vary systematically on this matter. Thus, what appears to be only "the behavior of individuals," will in the next decade emerge as a *de facto* ethnically patterned variation in such matters as sex determination. Moreover, this "behavior of individuals" will manifest itself among social aggregates living within defined geographical boundaries, and the application of "personal choice" will have little predictive utility when compared to simple designations of the larger unit of analysis (Robinson, 1950). Armed with an ideology of "individual choice," select Western nations will either have to confront the social control of this new technology by explicit devices (state), or watch social control be taken over inadvertently by the routine practices of social groups. Sex determination and sex selection are only one aspect of this matter, other issues are only as far behind as the respective imperatives of the prevailing culture or society.

Summary

The prism of heritability is, at first, a social matter. Why, when, and how a given society's members employ that prism on any one of an infinite variety of possible human traits is a matter for an approach that attempts to illuminate the prior question of knowledge production (including the choice and formulation of questions), and later reception and application of that knowledge. But such an approach cannot settle or even address the truth claim of those who assert the "genetics of x, y, or z." What the sociology of knowledge can do, however, is point more clearly to how members at any given historical moment, convinced that they have it right, erect machinery of two varieties. The first is the machinery of proof, research programs that by their very nature include or preclude particular lines inquiry. The second is a machinery of public policy, where rules, regulations, laws, and bureaucratic forces can congeal to produce their own internal logic and their own tendency for self-perpetuation.

There is a tendency to confuse heredity with inevitability and destiny, and to adopt a fatalistic stance. As early as 1927, some far-sighted observers lamented the fact that the medical profession placed so little emphasis upon genetics because of the mistaken view that no intervention or therapies are possible, once something has been determined as "inherited" (Ludmerer, 1972:67). However, the technical meaning of heritability is an accounting for how much variability in the appearance of a trait within a population can be explained by genetic differences among individuals. Flexibility, adaptability, even treatability are totally different matters. For example, a particular visual impairment might be 100 percent inherited, but it might be 100 percent *correctable* to normal vision with glasses or contact lenses (Gould, 1985:326). It is vital to keep this distinction in mind when engaged in a debate about an appropriate response to something that is regarded as "inherited." That may be only a small part of the matter, and not the central part.

Genetic research and the screening for genetic disorders have the potential for doing great amounts of good, and great amounts of harm. The way in which human societies deliberately move into this arena will be shaped as much by social forces as by concerns for the general public health. The next section makes an effort to address that issue, and to make more explicit what is now only implicit and generally unavailable for public scrutiny.

3

The Genetic Screening of "Target" Populations

Approximately one in every 16 babies born in the United States has some birth defect. Translated into yearly rates, that means approximately 250,000 children born annually will be so victimized (Apgar and Beck, 1974:4; Flynt et al., 1987:1).[1] In 1985, birth defects accounted for nearly 9,000 infant deaths, or about one-quarter of the total. However, only about one-third of these quarter-million birth defects are attributable to known specific factors[2] (OTA, 1985).

Considerable fatalism has traditionally accompanied major birth defects, and still does, despite the inroads that have been made in the diagnosis of genetic disorder. While we still do not know the source of the bulk of these birth defects, we do know that approximately one-quarter are attributable to a combination of single-gene defects and chromosomal abnormalities. By the mid-1980s, with the aid of new technologies, prospective parents[3] could discover whether the fetus was likely to be born with any of 380[4] genetic disorders (Weaver, 1988:253). This has placed much greater choice and control simultaneously at the disposal of individuals, interest groups, and governments. If at one end of this continuum there is the lone and isolated prospective mother making a personal decision, then at the other is state-controlled mass genetic screening. Even in its earliest stages, gene screening has produced a series of new concerns about the nature of state monitoring and information control and the relative vulnerability of differing groups because of the uneven social and political power of those being screened.

As was noted in chapter 1, several important gene disorders tend to overlap racial or ethnic groups. Since these racial and ethnic groups, in turn, are stratified, genetic screening programs are now forced to confront socially sensitive issues. Public health screening was not always so politically problematic. In the first part of the twentieth century, the United States screened the public for communicable diseases, primarily syphilis, tuberculosis, and malaria (Wilson and Jungner, 1968; Powledge, 1974:26). Since the general population was at risk, consensus and compliance were not so difficult to achieve. *Mass screening was transparently in the general public interest.*[5] This ceases to be the case when screening is aimed at a specific population with its "own" health problem, and when the cost effectiveness of such screening is assessed by those not in the screened population. This form of genetic screening, therefore, requires a whole different level of political and cultural sensitivity.

Laws that mandate screening of designated groups are in a very delicate area whenever they specify such "target" populations. Identifying populations-at-risk by statute raises the specter of practices condemned sharply by the Nuremberg trials of German war criminals after World War II: namely, *the specification of ethnic and racial groups in legislation by the state.* Coming in the wake of the genocidal annihilation of Jews and gypsies, the Nuremberg trials served to dramatize the moral consensus of the war's victors against the designation and possible scapegoating of a single ethnic or racial group by state power. The United States is in a relatively unique position among nation-states with regard to its monitoring and evaluation of the health, economic, educational, and general welfare conditions of its ethnically and racially diverse population. This is partly a function of the fact that the U.S. has had a long head start in dealing with ethnic and racial diversity as a public policy matter. In 1981, the Center for Disease Control began collecting data on the race and ethnicity of malformed infants born in the United States. The organizational rubric reads like a series of tree limbs: the Birth Defects Monitoring Program of the Birth Defects and Genetic Diseases Branch of the Division of Birth Defects and Developmental Disabilities, of the Center for Environmental Health and Injury Control . . . of the Center for Disease Control. The Birth Defects Monitoring Program monitors 161 diagnoses, collecting data from approximately 1,500 hospitals in the United States. In the period 1981–1986, the Birth Defects Monitoring Program catalogued 4,617,613 births (Chavez et al., 1988:18).

Most nation-states still do not keep vital statistical records with ethnic and racial designations, and therefore health statistics on ethnic and racial minorities are often impossible to obtain. Currently in France, if one asks for the infant mortality rate of recent immigrant Arabs from North Africa, or of Caribbean blacks, no one in the government knows, because they do not keep statistics that way. In Italy, if one asks about unemployment and morbidity rates for differing recent immigrant groups, no one in the government knows, because they do not keep statistics that way. Brazil keeps no records monitoring the health and welfare "by color," even though the 1980 Brazilian census resumed a color classification system. But as medical science and molecular genetics converge, important differences for genetic disorder risks will inevitably show up in differing populations. Greeks, Sicilians, and Arabs are at greater risk for sickle hemoglobin than north Europeans (Stamatoyanno-poulos, 1974; Hollerbach, 1979; Bowman, 1977); north Europeans are at greater risk for cystic fibrosis and phenylketonuria than south Europeans, and so forth.

As Europe as a whole moves rapidly towards becoming a political-economic regional community in the 1990s, national boundaries relevant to public policy regarding "health of citizens" may become blurred through the pooling of resources towards dealing with common problems. Under the aegis of health screening programs that can be justified on grounds that they are cost-effective, a screening for inherited disorders would force some new thinking about abandoning a long postwar tradition enshrined at Nuremberg. It is likely that European nations, under the banner of health, will move towards keeping records where race and ethnicity are (as in the U.S. Center for Disease Control national registry) relevant categories.[6]

Newborn Screening Legislation as the Early Wedge

Legal mandates to screen populations for inherited disorders began when Massachusetts passed the first such law in 1963 for phenylketonuria (Reilly, 1977:39–61). Because phenylketonuria (PKU) screening is post-natal or *newborn screening*, it is the least controversial form of genetic screening: it is done (1) for medical intervention and treatment, not for termination of a pregnancy or dissuasion of mating, and (2) on a mass level for *all* newborn, not for a specific high-risk group.[8] Phenylketonuria legislation was the "foot in the door." In only four years, forty-three states passed phenylketonuria[9] screening laws. Within the next few years most states had "add-on" legislation which included provisions for *prenatal* and even *carrier* screening, two forms of screening that are far more politically controversial. For example, in 1971 the Massachusetts state legislature[10] passed a law requiring blood tests for both sickle-cell trait and sickle-cell disease as a prerequisite to school attendance.[11] This had direct implications for carrier screening, and on this matter blacks have had an ambivalent position. While many blacks had complained about the neglect of sickle cell, the new attention that was being given in this era was often not of the desirable kind, because of minimal health implications, capricious targeting of youthful carriers, and the associated stigmatization without treatment or counseling (Powledge, 1974; Bowman, 1977).

It is difficult for the law to take into account the variability of the economic, social, and political positions of the ethnic and racial groups screened. Yet, as soon the programs are set up for administration, the relative economic and political position of the groups comes to the fore.

Later in the chapter we will see how objections were raised against California state regulations mandating sickle-cell screening of all blacks admitted to hospitals for whatever reason. In order to understand the rationale behind these programs, and sometimes the irrationality of attempts to set up a screen, we must spend a few pages reviewing the basic classification system for genetic disorders. Without this understanding, later references to kinds of genetic screening will make no sense.

Classification of Inherited Disorders

In the late nineteenth century, it was discovered that when a special dye is added to the cell of a living organism during certain stages of that cell's development, tiny thread-like structures in the cell absorb that coloring and thus become easier to see. The Greek word for color is *chroma;* the Greek for body is *soma.* Thus, the origin of the name for chromosomes, parts of each cell which contain extraordinarily complex sets of instructions for how the organism will develop, ranging from vision and lung tissue to body shape and hair color. The most important part of a chromosome is its deoxyribonucleic acid (DNA), a long, ladder-like structure which has specific sections that give out a particular code for a precise bit of genetic information. Each such specific section is called a gene. No one knows how many genes a human cell contains, but some estimates are as high as twenty thousand for each individual chromosome.

It is therefore a very complex problem to locate or "map" a particular gene for a particular instruction. In fact, single-gene causation in many areas of human development is contrary to overwhelming evidence. While the issue of single-gene determination is important on the matter of genetic disorders, there are a group of so-called genetic disorders that are multifactorial. That is, they are caused by an unknown combination of factors, of which the genes comprise only one component. They are the fourth major group in the classification scheme of inherited disorders, and an understanding of this category is critical to my later argument about the problematics of screening and the appropriation of genetic explanations. Inherited disorders are broadly categorized under the following headings:

1. Autosomal dominant
2. Autosomal recessive
3. X-linked
4. Multifactorial[12]

Each human carries forty-six chromosomes. Forty-four of these are paired into twenty-two sets that are called "autosomes." Each parent contributes one-half of this set of twenty-two pairs. The two remaining chromosomes are the sex chromosomes, called "X" and "Y" chromosomes. Each parent provides a single sex chromosome to the fetus. With each parent providing twenty-two autosomes and one sex chromosome, the child usually has the full complement of forty-six. Typically, males have one each X and Y, females typically have two X chromosomes. If the combination is X and X, the child will be female. If the child is X and Y, it will be a male. Every now and again, an extra Y sex chromosome appears, making the male child XYY, and some researchers have suggested that XYY males are more prone to retardation and/or aggressive behavior. Indeed, some studies have been under way for years to ascertain whether XYY males commit more crimes than XY males (Dershowitz, 1976).[13]

Autosomal dominant disorders are those in which a single gene from one parent is sufficient to produce the inherited disease or disorder in the offspring. Although there are nearly fifteen hundred known autosomal dominant disorders, their statistical appearance is rare. The two best-known are achondroplasia (dwarfism) and Huntington's disease. The latter appears only after full adult development and causes neurological degeneration. When someone with an autosomal dominant gene for the disorder mates with someone who does not have the gene, the chance for each live birth to be affected by the disorder is 50 percent. Only one of the paired chromosomes that splits off will carry the gene to the child.

Autosomal recessive disorders, of which more than a thousand are known, appear in the offspring only when both parents contribute a gene that, when paired, causes the disorder. All humans are thought to carry at least four to six autosomal recessive genes, which, though harmless to the carrier, would be lethal or seriously deleterious to the health of the offspring if paired at conception with a mate who also was a carrier.

The significance emerges from that fact that, when groups intermarry for centuries, there is a pooling of these recessive genes. Thus, social groupings, such as ethnic or racial, with a strong endogamous tradition are at higher risk for pairing recessive genes and passing on a disorder.

The best-known of these clustered autosomal recessive disorders are Tay-Sachs disease, beta-thalassemia, sickle-cell anemia, and cystic fibrosis. For Tay-Sachs, concentrated primarily among Ashkenazi Jews of northern and eastern European ancestry, about 1 in 30 is a carrier, and approximately one in every 3,000 newborn will have the disorder. Approximately 1 in every 12 African Americans is a carrier for sickle-cell and 1 in every 625 African American newborn will have the disorder.[14] Irish and north Europeans are at greater risk for phenylketonuria. In the

United States, 1 in 60 whites is a carrier, and about 1 in every 12,000 newborn is affected.

When both members of a mating couple are carriers of the autosomal recessive gene, the chance for each live birth to be affected by the disorder is 25 percent. However, being a carrier (also known as having the trait), or passing on the gene so that one's offspring is also a carrier, typically poses no more of a health threat than carrying a recessive gene for a different eye color. That is, carrier status typically poses no health threat at all. The health rationale behind carrier screening is to inform prospective parents about their chances of having a child with a genetic disorder.

The two most widespread genetic screening programs for carriers between 1965 and 1985 have been for Jews (Tay-Sachs) and for blacks (sickle-cell). There has been prenatal screening for both disorders, and by 1988, newborn screening for sickle cell had become common. It is the autosomal *recessive* disorders, located in risk populations that coincide with ethnicity and race, that will be of special interest as we move later to a discussion of genetic screening for populations that are at greatest risk for a disorder.

X-linked conditions, as the name indicates, are those that are attached to the X (female) chromosome. It may be surprising, at first glance, to learn that X-linked conditions appear almost exclusively in males. Recall that females are XX and males XY. The second X for the female serves to negate the first X-linked gene for a disorder. However, the Y chromosome has no capacity to counteract the deleterious X-linked chromosome, and so it is that males are at risk for X-linked disorders. There are some two hundred X-linked disorders, of which hemophilia is the most common. Disorders that are X-linked provide grounds for the prenatal determination of sex. Under this cover, some prospective parents have made sex selection of the fetus (Hultjen, 1988).

Finally, *multifactorial disorders,* which are a combination of genetic and environmental factors with unknown permutations, relative weights, and interactionism, constitute the largest number of "inherited" disorders. When disorders are said to be both genetic and environmental, there is an unknown interaction between them, and yet they still get the label of "inherited disorders" (McKusick, 1988).

> The precise contribution of the different genes to any one multifactorial disorder is as yet poorly understood. Conditions like diabetes, neural-tube defects, congenital heart malformations and hypertension all appear to be multifactorial in origin. . . . Only rarely is a neural-tube defect like anencephaly (the failure of completion of the brain) or spina bifida (an opening at a place along the spinal column) found in both individuals of a pair of genetically identical twins. Results like these suggest the effects of powerful non-genetic influences, probably of environmental origin. (Lappé, 1979:26)

In sum, although a number of genetic disorders can be classified in terms of autosomal dominant and recessive, and X-linked, there is a large residual of multifactorial disorders where heredity and environment interact in ways that can not now be explained. At a subsequent point in this chapter, and in chapter 6, the importance of the category "multifactorial" will be re-examined in relation to the issue of an encroaching "prism of heritability" described in the beginning sections of the first chapter. In the next section, we briefly examine the two principal screening programs for single genes as they affect the two major targeted populations, Jews and African Americans. The variable histories will tell us much about what we might expect to surface as issues in future screening programs.

Tay-Sachs Screening

In 1881 a British physician named Tay noted a rapid-onset degenerative disease pattern that affects the central nervous system of infants in the first six to eighteen months of life. Several years later, an independent description was made by an American neurologist, Sachs, who noted familial patterns in the transmission of the disorder. The infant with Tay-Sachs disease has a normal appearance in the first half-year, but the degenerative process is rapid, with an inexorable decline toward death by age four. There is no cure, and parents can only watch helplessly. Estimated costs of medical care in the last year alone average about ninety thousand dollars. Prior to the carrier screening program initiated in the 1970s, incidence of Tay-Sachs among Ashkenazi Jews in the United States was 18 per 100,000 live births (Goodman and Goodman, 1982:21). In 1970, 22 of the 30 infants born with Tay-Sachs were Jewish. The incidence is about a hundred times more frequent among Ashkenazi Jews as in the general population.

> Examining the data and records of tuberculosis among American Jews of Eastern European origin, Myrianthopoulos found that TB was three times more prevalent among immigrants from the southern regions of Eastern Europe, where TSD was rarest, than among immigrants from more northern regions, where TSD was most common. (Goodman and Goodman, 1982:21)

From these data one theory that has been proposed is that being a carrier of the Tay-Sachs gene provides some greater protection or resistance to tuberculosis. If both members of a couple are carriers, however, the chances are one in four that the fetus will have the disease. Because of the inevitability of early mortality, Tay-Sachs is the limiting case of an inherited disorder for which genetic screening can obtain widespread support. One analyst concluded:

> Thus, in Tay-Sachs carrier screening, an easily identifiable population is offered the chance to greatly lower the incidence of an irrevocably fatal disease and help assure the birth of unaffected children. It becomes very difficult to find telling arguments against screening in this situation. Any other course appears inhumane. (Powledge, 1974:34–35)

A community carrier screening program[15] was initiated in the greater Washington, D.C./Baltimore area in the early 1970s. The program had the support of the leading rabbis, and brochures from supportive physicians blanketed the Jewish community. Mass mailings and television and radio spot announcements were also used, all in support of a community-ratified voluntary screening program. Before the program, 98 percent of the 240,000 Jews in the area had never heard of Tay-Sachs. Within a year, not only were 95 percent aware of the disorder, but thousands volunteered for screening (Stine, 1977:465). In the first year of the program, 7,000 adults, approximately 10 percent of the total eligible population,[16] were screened (NAS, 1975:169). One of the key architects of this program, Michael Kaback, perhaps the world's leading specialist on the topic, had this to say about the issue of voluntary versus mandatory screening:

> An alternative approach, mandatory (or legislated) screening, although easier to implement perhaps, was regarded as unwarranted, unnecessary and ethically unacceptable. (Kaback et al., 1974:148)

Estimated cost of the program was sixty-four thousand dollars to provide equipment, supplies, and personnel. All those screened were asked to contribute five dollars, and most did so. Couples at risk received counseling, and reports indicate that it was direct, careful, and sensitive (Stine, 1977:465). The success of the initial Baltimore/Washington project was such that scores of Jewish communities around the United States followed suit, and were later joined by Jewish communities in five other countries. By the early 1980s, over 310,000 Jews around the world[17] had been screened *voluntarily*, with identification of 268 couples where both were carriers. In contrast to the generally positive response quoted above, the Goodmans (1982) have offered a dissenting view on the advisability of Tay-Sachs carrier screening. They argue that couples at greatest risk are those with a history in the family, who would come in anyway for clinical genetic counseling. Thus, they were critical of what they characterize as an "over-selling of anxiety" among the Jewish population, and stigmatization of carriers without a balanced assessment of benefits. However one comes down on the balancing scales, the major fact remains that a decade of Tay-Sachs carrier screening was carried out in the United States (and in five other countries) with the general full support of the Jewish community.

Sickle-Cell Screening

The history of Tay-Sachs carrier screening is in sharp contrast to screening for sickle-cell anemia among American blacks, a potpourri of programs that, taken collectively, can only be described as a public policy disaster, and as for carrier screening, on balance a health and medical failure. In chapter 1 we have already had a glimpse at mandatory and punitive treatment of carriers. While Tay-Sachs carrier screening was typically voluntary and had the enthusiastic support of the Jewish community, sickle-cell carrier screening was frequently compulsory, written into law in more than a dozen states (Powledge, 1974). In the mid-1970s, six states[18] and the District of Columbia required by law that children be tested "for the presence of a sickle cell gene before they can enter school" (Stine, 1977:508). Why any six- or seven-year-old should be screened for a trait, and either be told directly, or have his or her parent so informed, makes no sense in terms of health or medicine. *Despite the fact that Tay-Sachs is a much more fatal disorder, it was sickle-cell carrier screening that became mandatory.*

In the United States, approximately one in twelve blacks are carriers. Because of this, sickle cell is popularly thought to be a "black person's disease," and this image penetrates the consciousness of those who are even partially informed about these matters.[19] In fact, sickle hemoglobin is found in a small Greek population at about double the rate among American blacks (Stamatoyannopoulos, 1974; Kenen and Schmidt, 1978; Hollerbach, 1979), and it is not uncommon among Arabs, Sicilians, and other groups in the Mediterranean region.

A person who has sickle-cell anemia (homozygous, with two defective genes, one from each carrier parent) has red blood cells that are impaired in the capacity to carry oxygen. Moreover, in trying to rapidly carry blood to a certain part of the organism, these red blood cells tend to sickle or change shape, blocking the small blood vessels. This can produce a "crisis" at that particular juncture, and depending upon how vital the organ, joint, or muscular tissue is, can cause mild to severe pain, or even death (Stine, 1977:121). There is high variability in persons with sickle-cell anemia. Some have moderate and mild crises and live for many years. A child with sickle cell has a better than 50 percent chance of living well into middle age, and some survive into their 60s. Despite this, there is a tendency for even some of the most informed people to "collapse the category" and not deal with this complexity. Here is a quote from one of the more humane of the most visible scientists of our time, two-time Nobel Prize–winner Linus Pauling:

> I have suggested that there should be tattooed on the forehead of every young person a symbol showing possession of the sickle-cell gene or whatever other similar gene, such as the gene for phenylketonuria, that has been found to possess in a single dose. If this were done, two young people carrying the same seriously defective gene in single dose would recognize this situation at first sight, and would refrain from falling in love with one another. It is my opinion that legislation along this line, compulsory testing for defective genes before marriage, and some form of semi-public display of this possession, should be adopted. (Pauling, 1968)

As for Pauling's credentials as a scientist with specific knowledge of sickle cell, it should be recalled that it was Pauling and his colleagues who first detected the mutant form of hemoglobin associated with sickling cells in 1949 (Edelstein, 1986:46) and gave it the name "hemoglobin S." The quotation above from Pauling is another reminder of the dangerous problematics of the halo of generalized expertise and solid thinking for those who make important scientific discoveries with respect to their views about social policies and the social implications of their work.

The Comparative Politics of Genetic Screening

In California, Tay-Sachs screening has gone on without much in the way of vocal negative public reaction. The bureaucratic structure for administering Tay-Sachs screening is quite different than that for sickle-cell anemia, although the language of the laws that generate and under-pin such programs gives no indication of this organization. In southern California, Tay-Sachs screening was for several years funded through a principal investigator, a private physician, and highly esteemed research specialist, who then in turn made funding allocations to various agencies and organizations that wished to participate in Tay-Sachs screening. The situation was quite different for sickle-cell anemia. Screening programs for this disorder required approval by a central coordinated agency of state government. The agency sent out "requests for proposals" and then assessed whether the various applicants met the criteria to warrant funding.

This difference can be explained by a number of factors, but a social scientist looking at the problem cannot help but isolate as a central factor the relative structural location of Jews and blacks, their relative educational and economic positions, and the comparative level of trust and confidence one might therefore expect these programs to generate.

Sickle-cell screening programs developed during the same period of the black power movement in the mid- and late 1960s. The Black Panthers collected for sickle cell on the street corners of major cities and, with others in the movement, used political rhetoric to reshape the consciousness of much of the population to the historical neglect of this disorder.[20] When community and neighborhood groups emerged to direct and staff such programs, they often did so with the rhetoric of "control over our own lives." This meant that black groups from the black community should be in charge of these programs.

The hostility and suspicion with which blacks treated white medical professionals who suddenly showed up in the black community to conduct genetic screening between 1969 and 1972 was predictably fierce and effective. But a very uneasy relationship was to develop out of these programs precisely because blacks are at the base of the economic order. The very groups that surfaced to work on any well-funded black community-based programs were those groups who had been warriors in Lyndon Johnson's War on Poverty. When this social strategy gave way to the Nixon-Moynihan policy of benign neglect, they were suddenly out in the cold. Many of these *emeriti* "poverty warriors" would discover a natural affinity with community-based sickle-cell programs. While they were not the majority, in urban centers they were often the most visible political force.

There was a parallel between community-based sickle-cell screening programs and many of the methadone maintenance clinics across the country. The latter were frequently based in the black community, with federal and state funding essential to the continued livelihood of the staff. As the sociologists of organizations and bureaucracy have long noted, the interests of the staff in the perpetuation of the bureaucracy will almost perforce supersede the original intent of a program. Methadone maintenance became an essential element on the continuation of funding, and so it became the interests of the staff to find more people to serve as warm bodies in the body count in the war on heroin. There was a similar development with sickle-cell programs. While many volunteers were drawn mainly if not exclusively to the health and medical issues, a sizeable proportion had come out of community-based programs from which they had forged a political relationship to funding agencies, and had developed a political analysis of the process. Moreover, for the set of reasons just noted, they also had an economic interest at quite a different level from the many community participants in the Tay-Sachs programs.

With this political and economic reality at the base of many urban community-based sickle-cell programs, it is not difficult to imagine how an entrenched, physician-oriented and -controlled state department of public health would view such groups. State monitoring requirements were routinely built into the programs. Nonetheless, intense adversarial social and political pressures of the moment could and sometimes did mute the public health interests of such monitoring. Responding to community pressure groups to have a community-based genetic screening program for blacks in 1971, the Chicago Board of Education approved a People's Health Coalition to perform screening and to counsel the blacks who were screened. Health workers from the community, many of them from the then "politically correct" Black Panther party,

> had screened several thousand school children for sickle hemoglobin by using the Sickledex R test, a solubility test for sickle hemoglobin, which only detects the presence or absence of sickle hemoglobin. It does not delineate between sickle cell trait and sickle cell disease. The health worker stated that the Black Panthers discovered that 10 per cent of black children have sickle cell disease . . . that whites knew of this high disease frequency in blacks but had done nothing about it; therefore this was another means of genocide. (Bowman, 1977:124)

In fact, of those 10 percent referred to in the passage above, more than 90 percent were only *carriers* of the gene, and would live as healthy a life as anyone else.[21] The Panthers' exaggerated fears were in the larger context of the politically tense, indeed hostile, relationship between the screeners, the screened, and the state apparatus.[22] This was also the period in which the Tuskegee syphilis experiments on blacks were still going on, an embarrassing and shameful episode in American public health history, which would break in to news stories during the same era.[23]

The social-economic stratification of ethnic and racial groups reproduces itself in the kind of "community-based" programs that attend the medical problems of the respective groups. For blacks, the staffing of these programs was much closer to a basic fundamental issue of economic livelihood, and mired in political suspicion. For Jews, the health issue became paramount precisely because the political controls were seen to be sufficiently in the hands of the Jewish community. It would be impossible to explain the respective fates of gene screening programs for Tay-Sachs and sickle cell by focusing only on the programs. At the very least, a review of gross data on the income, educational, and occupational situations of the two groups accounts for much of the differences in program development.[24] They manifest themselves again at the administrative and organizational levels in the way in which genetic screening programs were funded, administered, and responded to by the respective communities.

California was an early state to pass laws requiring newborn screening. In 1965, the state legislature passed legislation requiring screening at birth for phenylketonuria. Very shortly thereafter, the Bureau of Maternal and Child Health received a federal grant to establish a special unit dealing with hereditary defects. In five short years, the California legislature enacted a requirement of blood-typing of all pregnant women. One of the most important reasons for screening for inherited disorders is medical intervention. With some problems there is a solution, as in the birth of an RH+ mother (the administration of immunoglobulin can prevent this disorder). But in 1971, the California legislature directed its Department of Public Health to develop a policy for control of sickle-cell anemia. Since there is no cure for sickle cell, the specter of "control" agitated and angered many black medical practitioners in California, who reacted vigorously when the legislature passed a law permitting the Public Health Department to require testing of blacks "whenever appropriate." Following is a segment of a newspaper story that gave the public an account of what transpired:

Sickle Cell Test Rules Scrapped

Controversial State Health Department regulations aimed at screening all black hospital patients in California for sickle cell anemia were scrapped yesterday.

A six-month moratorium on enforcing the regulations was ordered by Dr. Jerome Lackner, the state's director of public health, and at the same time Lackner named a prominent black physician to head a committee that will rewrite the rules.

The committee will have all the time it needs to draft new regulations, Lackner said—even more than six months, if necessary—and will be given staff assistance by the Health Department.

Dr. Lonnie Bristow, a San Pablo physician who is president of the California Society of Internal Medicine, was named to head the committee. Bristow has long been an outspoken leader in the effort by black doctors to encourage widespread testing for sickle cell anemia without imposing mandatory tests that ethnic minorities feel are offensive invasions of privacy.

Bristow and several of his colleagues held a press conference here yesterday to discuss their concerns about sickle cell testing and to announce Lackner's message to them that he was holding up enforcement of the mass screening rules.

The regulations were first drafted in 1973, after a new California law declared it state policy to "detect, as early as possible, sickle cell anemia, a heritable disorder which leads to physical defects."

But the first regulations were rejected by the State Board of Health, an expert advisory agency abolished by the Reagan administration.

The Health Department itself published the regulations two years ago, but delayed enforcing them. Then a department official, without consulting Lackner, notified all the state's hospitals last month to begin obeying them now. This unexpected decision caught black physicians by surprise.

The rules require physicians in hospitals to "determine the sickle cell status" of all black patients by giving them an approved blood test. Patients are permitted to refuse to take the test after the nature of both sickle cell anemia and the test have been explained to them. But the results of the test, or a patient's refusal to take it, are to be entered in the patient's chart. And sickle cell test statistics are to be forwarded regularly to the health department.

Sickle cell anemia is a hereditary disease most prevalent among blacks. Where both parents carry the genetic trait for sickle cell blood, each of their children has a one-in-four chance of developing the disease itself. Carrying the "trait" alone rarely leads to any illness at all.

When the disease does strike, however, it is marked by severe painful and crippling recurrent crises; most victims die before they are 40, and many die long before that.

At yesterday's press conference Bristow noted many difficulties with mass sickle cell tests: It's not always possible to determine "who is black or how black is black," he said.

There is never a guarantee that hospital records will remain confidential, he added, and as a result insurance companies, which can easily learn the sickle cell status of patients, are apt to increase premiums on racial grounds alone.

Nor do most hospital staffs include either doctors or other health workers skilled or sensitive enough to counsel black patients on sickle cell problems, Bristow said. (David Perlman, *San Francisco Chronicle*, 8 July 1976)

We can see from this news story that, from the summer of 1976, the attempt at organizational implementation of state genetic screening laws and regulations for sickle-cell anemia ran into serious difficulties, complications, and, ultimately, reversals.

For those who would doubt the role of political mobilization around the salience of race when it comes to genetic screening, I would simply point out that by the mid-1980s newborn screening for sickle-cell anemia was mandatory in Wyoming, where less than 1 percent of the population is black, but voluntary in the District of Columbia, where over half the population is black (Townes, 1986:1192). But things are not quite so simple as this. In Virginia, newborn screening is mandatory for all screened disorders *except* sickle cell which is voluntary. However, while newborn screening for sickle cell is mandatory in seven states (Colorado, Georgia, Louisiana, New Mexico, New York, Texas, and, of course, Wyoming) and voluntary in three jurisdictions (Maryland, District of Columbia, and North Carolina), most states have no newborn screening programs.

Three Screens and Their Degree of Political Controversy

Apart from patently political motives, genetic disorders—as diseases—affect different groups in the population differently. As noted earlier, one of the most salient issues in screening for genetic disorders is the capacity for medical intervention. Insofar as genetic diseases are chronic, it is difficult to evaluate the success of massive interventions (Wilson and Jungner, 1968:78-133). There is no treatment for the underlying cause. In such instances as hemophilia and thalassemia, patients must be given repeated transfusions and cared for in ways which make them continually dependent on others. To screen for a disorder that cannot be cured can tap a reservoir of latent, recurring fears about the motives of those who would *prevent* genetic disorder rather than *treat* it. *Prenatal* screening, therefore, is far more controversial than *neonatal* or *newborn screening*, which takes place just after the infant is born.[25]

Neonatal screening is the least controversial of the three genetic screens. The infant has already been born, and the arguments for the neonatal screen are always in terms of possible successful medical intervention for the treatment of the disorder. Even when the disorder is chronic and incurable, as in the case of sickle-cell anemia, the physician can more accurately diagnose the problem, and provide some treatment for symptoms and temporary relief. Moreover, the parents have an account when the child complains of pain, and can act with this knowledge. The advantages of early and accurate diagnosis in the kind of neonatal screening are generally accepted.[26]

Much of the screening for sickle-cell anemia had shifted to neonatal detection by the late 1980s. Black infants are given a blood test in the first weeks after birth. If the test is positive, then parents and physicians know more about how to intervene if and when the child begins to complain of pain that is otherwise "inexplicable."

The social and political controversy level heightens with the second kind of genetic screen, *prenatal diagnosis*. This kind of screen heavily implies that if one finds what one is looking for, then termination of the pregnancy is high on the list of potential intervention strategies. However, there is considerable variation both between and within "birth disorders." It is obviously a serious mistake to lump these genetic disorders together and treat them generically. But even within disorders, the variation can be considerable. We have noted that a child with sickle-cell anemia may live a full life with minor symptoms, or another child with sickle-cell anemia may experience excruciatingly painful crises with some frequency, or perhaps die at an early age. A child with Down syndrome might be only moderately retarded, or even if substantially retarded, might live a life that is rewarding, both for the self and for others in the family.

As will be seen in chapter 4, the new technologies will move large, impersonal forces almost inexorably to "screen" against such "outcomes" in "cost-ineffective" terms. This touches directly upon the social and cultural aspects that frame and give meaning to a genetic screen or a genetic disorder. Lappé (1972) has argued forcefully and effectively that the "genetic burden" to the society is the wrong formulation, and that instead, the major burden is upon the family. He believes that the society should provide maternal and postnatal care, even if and when that means support of the congenitally handicapped. However, the thrust of prenatal screening for an inherited disorder gravitates towards the termination of a pregnancy. Since that joins the debate even within a single society, it is easy to see how different societies will behave quite differently when it comes to this matter of whom to screen, why, and for what purposes. Just as some cultures not only tolerate but support the "village idiot," perhaps even as *idiot savant,* others deride and denigrate, ridicule, and incarcerate the "idiots" in their fold. A current illustration of the high vulnerability is the way in which different societies relate to the sex selection option presented by prenatal diagnosis technology, discussed in chapter 2.

Prevention of a birth that is only potentially a debilitating genetic disorder is more likely to generate controversy and conflict within a society or family. It is qualitatively different than newborn screening, where there can be a straightforward argument for intervention where treatment is indicated. There is likely to be systematic social conflict depending upon such distinctions as class position, ethnic, racial, and cultural history, sex, customs, and tradition. Professional women in their early thirties who have delayed pregnancy in order to pursue a career have it in their interest to consume the new technology as liberating. Men from backgrounds and traditions that have minimal contact with newborn nurturance and child care are less predictable. But these are only a few early and illustrative considerations. As the technology shifts and is made available to women of all ages, there are predictable shifts in the political and social consciousness, and in the level of controversy over its variable uses. The next chapter demonstrates that the new technology is not going to penetrate the social structure evenly and neutrally. It will penetrate some areas much faster than others; it will be blocked and subverted at certain points.

The most controversial, the most far reaching, and indeed the most "futuristic" genetic screen (even though it is with us now) is the third and final form: screening for carriers of a gene that can produce an inherited disorder, or *carrier screening.* This kind of genetic screening is in its infancy. While approximately two million blacks have already been screened for sickle-cell anemia trait (carrier status), these programs have been embarrassingly unfocused and inconsistent on a national level. It has been noted how, in the early years, some states screened black school children before puberty, others attached the screen to a marriage license, and still others have tried to make screening a condition of hospital admission and treatment (Powledge, 1974; Reilly, 1977; NAS, 1975; Bowman, 1977). From an earlier discussion of the Air Force Academy and the airline industry, it will be recalled that carrier status was used to exclude from the academy, flight training, and flight personnel positions. Reversals came only after political mobilization.

The official purpose of such screening is to alert individuals to their own genetic makeup so that they take this into account in mating, or in the choice of a mate. Etzioni (1973:89-92) early on noted some personal and political implications of this development. At the rate of discovery cited in chapter 2, it is possible to envision a world only two decades away in which many persons have been "identified" as carriers of genes for a variety of specific inheritable disorders. Once this information is available, the social and political issue arises: to whom should this information be limited? A fanciful futuristic image that sells glossy magazines off the newsstands is of a prospective couple with their respective decoded gene belts. Each scans the other's genetic makeup for matching and mismatching of autosomal recessive genes. Far short of the sensationalism of such speculation is the current reality of a national or state registry of carriers of identified defective genes. The registry classifies disorders, and designates who has them. It also designates carriers. Those who control it will determine under what conditions such information will be given out. The complexity of the various kinds of disorders leads me to a deep concern for the category "multifactorial" genetic disorders.

When is a Multifactorial Disorder a "Genetic" Disorder?

When is a disorder a genetic disorder, and when is it something else? We know from our review of materials presented above that some of these disorders are caused by a single dominant gene. However, for hundreds, even thousands of "genetic disorders" it is far from definitive and even misleading to categorize them as *genetic* disorders.[27] For example, a small industrial town in southern Wales has the highest rate of spina bifida in the world. Spina bifida is a disorder of the central nervous system with both a genetic and an environmental component. On the scientific grounds alone, this disorder could as easily be named an industrial-environmental disorder as a genetic disorder. But if spina bifida was characterized as an "environmental disorder," the policy injunction for social planning and the scientific work "to address the problem" would be quite different than what we see today. If it is an "industrial-town disorder," we think instead of (a) moving from the industrial town, or (b) cleaning up the toxicity in the environment, or (c) controlling or shutting down the factories producing high toxic levels.

To characterize spina bifida as a genetic disorder enjoins us to move in the direction of gene screening or gene therapies and other high technologies aimed at handling or preventing the "genetic" problem. By contrast, one of the most recent studies indicates that extra doses of multi-vitamins during pregnancy reduces the risk of neural tube defects (spina bifida is one such) by more than 60 percent (Mulinare et al., 1988). We have long known that babies with neural tube defects are more likely to be born to women of lower socioeconomic status and poor diets. In the United States, there was a rash of such births during the Great Depression, with a steady decline since. There is currently screening for this disorder in Great Britain and several major jurisdictions in the United States.

Since so many disorders are multifactorial, the key question is: under what conditions is a disorder characterized and treated as if it were more genetically than environmentally induced? If there were some kind of scientific precision in our measurement, then one could say for example that when a disorder is 51 percent or more "genetic," it will be called a "genetic disorder," and when a disorder is 51 percent or more "environmental," it will be called an "environmental disorder." But there would still be the basis for a good argument about what this could mean. For the vast majority of human disorders, the best evidence available informs us that genes and environment are in continuous interaction. Therefore, any such characterization (51 percent or more) would be arbitrary, problematic, and fluid. But at least we could "name" these disorders with the idea that the name does indeed predispose thought and ameliorative action along the more "dominant" path that would then make a kind of cost- or energy-effective sense. Current practice lacks even this rationale (McKusick, 1988).

It is important to distinguish between a birth defect and an inherited genetic disorder. During pregnancy, a woman may have experiences that alter the genetic code. For example, methyl mercury is an industrial chemical by-product which polluted Minimata Bay in Japan. Women who ate fish from this bay gave birth to babies with severe neurological damage, similar to cerebral palsy. There is the infamous drug Thalidomide, given to pregnant women in Germany and the United States for a brief period in the 1960s. Babies born to women who took this drug tended to develop limb growth abnormalities. In these cases, "environmental factors" almost certainly altered the genetic expression. Still, there is an overwhelming tendency to characterize a number of multifactorial disorders as "genetic" and thus give shape to and order possible ways of thinking on these matters, both inside scientific disciplines and in the general public.

> Despite the absence of identifiable genes, more emphasis is generally placed by medical researchers on the hereditary (genetic) components of heart disease, cancer, schizophrenia, and a host of other diseases than on the environmental factors that may contribute to the initiation and progression of these diseases. (Edlin, 1987:47)

It is not just a matter of personal linguistic or conceptual inclination as to whether one calls these *genetic* disorders, *multifactorial* disorders, or *environmental* disorders. Career choices and related organizational, institutional, and ultimately political forces also help determine the naming. Edlin (1987:48) notes that the "increased overemphasis on 'genetic factors' and 'genetic tendencies' in human disorders has serious consequences in allocating federal research funds and in formulating public health policies."

The decision to fund particular types of research on such matters as heart disease, cancer, and enzyme deficiencies depends upon who frames the issues. This is generally understood to be true if we see these as areas competing with each other for funding. It is less well appreciated that this is also true within a line of research. Whether one pursues a line of work that emphasizes the genetic component of cancer, or whether one moves towards nutritional studies, or attempts to intercede by focusing upon the larger immunological system by shifting chemical balances, depends upon who is framing the questions and problems (Fujimura, 1988).

To conceptualize these problems as primarily genetic is to chart a range of other actions set in motion by the purported explanatory power of the genes. That is, to avoid the "genetic" disorder, one must either change the genes or set up a genetic screen to prevent those affected fetuses from being born.[29] It is hardly neutral, unpackaged scientific "facts" that are influencing whether one heads down one path or another. Yet, once the research is under way, both the scientific and conventional wisdom begin to be overwhelmed by the use of the nomenclature of genetic disorder. It is precisely the multifactorial character of these disorders that makes the appropriation of genetic explanations so deserving of closer examination. It is important, rather, to identify the real and significant developments in molecular genetics that are informing health and medical practices and separate these from the unwarranted appropriation of the halo from these real developments.

Summary

In contemporary social science, we can find a general advocacy of attempts to integrate studies of local scenes with analysis that comes from our broadest understandings of cultural, social, political, and economic forces. This advocacy could possibly have greater persuasive powers if it were accompanied by an articulation of how such an integration might be achieved. For a study to achieve the kind of integration described, there should be inclusion of separate levels of entry into the empirical world, buttressed by a strategy of vertical integration.[30]

In regard to the possible adversarial positions that will ensue when mass genetic screening is available, several commentators have addressed the inevitable conflict between the individual and the social interests (Blank, 1981; Wertz and Fletcher, 1988), the private versus the public, and the "rights" of the unborn fetus as opposed to the interests of the state that may become its ward (Hilton et al., 1973; Dunstan, 1988). For individuals who suffer the consequences of inherited disorders, and for their families and friends, the new technology offers hope for treatment. In this area, developments in human genetics research may have some very positive effects. What appears at one level to be a "genetic" or health issue is at another level enmeshed with social, political, and scientific concerns. Key analytical distinctions include single-gene determinations of inherited disorders versus multifactorial determinations, and what is socially inherited in a family or group versus what is genetically transmitted. The current classification of "inherited disorders" takes outcomes that are a result of complex multifactorial (even an interaction between genes and environment), and by naming them "genetic disorders" inadvertently shapes a way of seeing and understanding diverse conditions including diabetes, alcoholism, heart disease, breast and cervical cancer that favors a genetic approach to medical intervention.

This and related developments reduce the likelihood of other solutions to multifactorial disorders, even though extant data suggest that such current, already available solutions are cheaper and more consequential in terms of health benefits for a larger population.[31]

Where gene screening overlaps ethnic and racial groups, it can mobilize those already socially identified into a political force. However, it can also isolate and further fragment a work force, for example, of persons aggregated only by a privately held bit of information about their genetic makeup.

Such facts sharpen the difficulties which decision-makers face in answering questions about how scarce national and state resources are to be spent: Which disorders are most important? Which groups are most deserving, or most needful, of government-supported action? Decisions about such issues are very much subject to the forces of political manipulation. In very concrete and specific ways, genetic screening is inevitably joined to the matter of power and control over that screening, and to the issue of which groups exercise it.

4

Dilemmas of a "General" Genetic Disorder Control Policy

Between the suffering of a victim of a genetic disorder and the impassioned rhetoric on the floor of Congress, there stands a large faceless buffer, distiller, interpreter, and reasoned constructor of genetic disorder policy: the state health bureaucracy. It is easy and comforting to make the mistake of thinking that bureaucracy is something that happens over there, in another building, to government employees in Washington, or in the state capitols. In fact, bureaucracy everywhere touches and often deeply infuses our lives. If by chance we don't work in one, we have to work around or through such an organization almost daily. It has led one commentator to prophesize the bureaucratization of the world (Jacoby, 1973), a contemporary update to the gloomy futurism of Max Weber. But if it is a mistake to divide people into bureaucrats and nonbureaucrats, it makes a lot of sense to divide the institutions that envelop us into bureaucratic and nonbureaucratic. For example, the family is an institution, but few families take it as their central task to treat everybody with whom they come in contact with neutrality and dispassionate detachment. Families, to the contrary, divide people into friends-of-the-family and enemies or strangers, and the rules of behavior bend and shift accordingly.

A state health department is quite another matter, and the Constitution leaves to the states the task of guarding the public health of its inhabitants. Particular health department employees or staff may be hot-blooded, intense, emotionally feeling, warm, and sensitive human beings. Some may have strong feelings about hemophilia as opposed to Down syndrome. But the institutional setting sanctions the public expression of these preferences over time, muting or subduing the passionate or expressive formulations. There is neutral universalism in the language of the following passage from the California Department of Health:

> The Genetic Disease Section conducts surveillance of newborn testing to safeguard the right of each newborn child to be tested. Additionally, a

registry of confirmed PKU cases is maintained by correspondence and telephone to ensure that affected persons receive appropriate management through community and State resources for the prevention of mental retardation. The registry also provides data for analysis to promote better understanding of PKU and its treatment. All records are kept confidential. . . .

In 1978, laboratories reported performing initial screening tests on 339,340 newborns, 333 of which were positive, a rate of 1.0 per thousand initial tests. The regulations require that newborns with positive screening tests promptly have a confirmatory test. Of the 333 newborns with initial positive tests, 318 (95.5%) had the test repeated in 1978 and of these, 32 (10.1%) were again positive. (Report to California State Legislature, January 1, 1980, by the Genetic Disease Section, Department of Public Health)

This gray, colorless reportage should not lull us into the belief that neutrality prevails. In a health organization, everyone has their "favorite" disorder or ailment. Sometimes this most favored status may be as fortuitous as a key actor having a deformed birth in the family. Sometimes it may be fed by special-interest lobbies like insurance companies that have no interest in paying claims for victims of chronic disorders that skew the actuarial tables, and take a big bite out of the profits.[1] In any event, state public health policy is the big buffer. It mutes and transforms personal and special interests into the grand chasm where the rhetoric is "the public interest."

Law, Lobbying, and Screening

In the United States, federal law often sets the tone and frames what occurs in state law. But health is one of those residual matters left up to the state.[2] In the area of genetic screening, action by the states preceded that of the federal government. Not only did the various states have earlier laws mandating genetic screening, but some of the mistakes that they made were avoided by those that developed into national legislation. For example, many states had made genetic screening compulsory (National Academy of Sciences, 1975). The National Sickle-Cell Anemia, Cooley's Anemia, Tay-Sachs, and Genetic Disease Act of 1976 required that any federally funded screening programs be "voluntary." But it is necessary to go back to the first national legislation on sickle cell to understand how and why the latter bill developed into such a conglomerate.

In 1972, the National Sickle-Cell Anemia Control Act was signed into law, with an authorization of over one hundred million dollars for the establishment of screening and counseling programs, and for research. While state laws mandated screening, and sometimes provided limited funding for these programs, this level of support at the federal level engendered interethnic group competition, envy, rivalry, and an increasing demand for "our fair share" of concern and money from other ethnic and racial minorities (Reilly, 1977:79–83). People from the Mediterranean, especially southern Italy, are at greater risk for Beta-thalassemia (Cooley's anemia). As it became clear that blacks were going to get "their" disease control funded, the Mediterranean constituents of Congressman Robert Giaimo persuaded him to introduce a bill, also in 1972, for a National Cooley's Anemia Control Act. That bill passed. Ashkenazi Jews are at greater risk for Tay-Sachs, and within a few months, a Jewish constituency put pressure on Senator Jacob Javits to secure passage of a national Tay-Sachs control act. At this point, a very interesting controversy surfaced. Should there be a proliferation of specific laws and programs tailored to specific inherited disorders, or should there be a centralized program, with one omnibus law? Initially, Javits and others moved to introduce and support a separate bill for Tay-Sachs. Later, they became persuaded that a single comprehensive bill covering all disorders should be developed. From a review of testimony at congressional hearings on the bills, it is clear that blacks almost uniformly testified in favor of keeping the national legislation for sickle cell separate (U.S. Senate, 94th Congress, 1975). They argued that a composite bill would dilute the interest, concern, and funding for sickle cell. They feared that control of the sickle-cell program would shift more and more away from blacks. But the medical establishment brought out all of its artillery to these hearings, and argued the language of *efficiency* quite effectively. They won, and Congress passed the comprehensive law in 1976.

Compulsory screening has had an uneven history in the United States, even in the short space of two decades. Most programs currently in effect are voluntary. However, "voluntary" means different things in different times and circumstances, in different places among different groups of people from different strata. This position will be developed later, but the specter of mandatory screening remains:

> While the federal law eliminated compulsion, it has also brought mass genetic screening into the sphere of routine public health activities. Given the fact that many screening laws have not actually been repealed and that compulsory screening programs might survive a court test, it is not frivolous to suggest that the current popularity of voluntary laws is no guarantee that mandatory programs will not someday be resumed. (Reilly, 1977:82)

Reilly became something of a prophet because in less than a decade, newborn screening was again mandatory in seven states by 1987 (Townes, 1986:1192).[3]

Federal Support for the Local Genetic Screen

In the early and mid-1970s, the federal government set up over a dozen sickle-cell centers around the country. Among the varied purposes of these centers were biomedical and epidemiological research, and counseling services. Specifically, the centers would engage in broad-gauged testing and screening, basic research on the sickling process, clinical research on patients with sickle-cell disease (to obtain more information on the natural history of the disease), and some form of educational outreach and counseling service (with high variability in both strategy and in the amount of social research to determine impact and effectiveness). They were appropriately named "Comprehensive Sickle Cell Centers."

Each of the centers had unique problems of adjustment in cities as varied as Augusta, Chicago, Los Angeles, Washington, and Detroit. Nonetheless, there are some basic commonalities in what they tried to accomplish, which can be garnered from the annual reports that each center is required to submit to the federal agencies responsible for their administration. In the section that follows, I have focused upon the Detroit center because it is a modal center in a number of ways.

During the single year of 1980, the Detroit center sponsored a combined educational and testing program in thirty-five grade schools and five high schools, distributing printed literature to more than 11,000 students and their parents by this method. The center also distributed 32,000 informational pamphlets and 26,000 fact sheets on sickle cell throughout the black community. Like all the other centers, Detroit made considerable use of the media, with scores of spot announcements on radio and television, active participation by center staff on radio talk shows and public service television stations, the release of public information articles to newspapers, and features for newspaper supplements.

In addition, a mobile unit was dispatched throughout the black community, both for the distribution of information (flyers and pamphlets at shopping centers, banks, and schools), and for on-the-spot testing, screening, and laboratory diagnosis. At a major hospital, all newborn blacks are routinely screened to determine if the child has the disease or is a carrier. Consent forms are required, but they are routinely signed, and it is rare to find a refusal. Carrier screening in the community is more complex. The educational outreach program offers the screening service, and those who show up at the center to be screened do so voluntarily. The same is true of the mobile unit, which spends one week at high schools, elementary schools, churches, and shopping centers. For those under eighteen, a parent must accompany the potential screenee, or there must be a written consent form. Otherwise, since the subjects are appearing voluntarily, the center takes the position that no formal written consent form need be used.

The procedures are the same for the center and the mobile unit. There is registration, a fifteen-minute slide show on sickle cell, and a blood test with laboratory analysis performed within thirty to sixty minutes. If the test is negative, the client is usually informed within that first half hour. A positive result, with cross-checks, takes approximately a full hour. From January 1 to December 31, 1980, the center processed 16,075 laboratory records and approximately 5,100 clinical records for sickle-cell screening.

The Detroit center at Wayne State University engaged in basic research that ranged from the construction of highly abstract mathematical models about the amounts of oxygen uptake and release for selected cells all the way to statistical associations of sickle cell with kidney failure, leg ulcers, and strokes. In 1980, the clinical aspect of the research program included a study of ninety-two sickle-cell patients, with particular concern given to the psychosocial adjustments of these patients to their employment status. Another part of the study included therapy sessions designed to evaluate and mitigate negative self-conceptions of these patients.

While carrier screening was an important feature of the early stages of sickle-cell screening, it has steadily declined in significance and has given way to testing of the newly born.

A State Policy on Prenatal Diagnosis

In order to get a good picture of how the state bureaucracy operates to buffer, interpret, and shape genetics policy, it is worthwhile to take a look at how the amniocentesis program started in California. The technology of amniocentesis is such that a single private physician working alone can rarely afford or manage the laboratory work involved. Thus, the state provides funding for consortia in order that such laboratories can be maintained. This power to fund or not fund a laboratory shapes genetics research and technology.

In the late 1960s, the state's Genetic Disease Section chose to fund nine amniocentesis centers. The criteria for funding these centers included such requirements as having a medical geneticist on the staff, laboratory facilities already available for doing the karyotyping necessary for analysis of the amniotic fluid, and considerable experience with amniocentesis. Provisions were made for adding new centers, but these new centers had to attach themselves as satellites for a period to one of the established funded centers. If they performed approximately one hundred amniocenteses under the auspices of the parent center within a year, these new centers could be independently funded and operated.

By the mid-1970s, ten centers were granted Class A status, namely, they were fully independent centers judged capable of performing amniocentesis on their own. They each received state support. One of the ten centers served a constituency of people of color, primarily blacks, but some Latinos. This was Martin Luther King Hospital in East Los Angeles. King Hospital was the only one of the ten centers to serve a predominantly nonwhite constituency, and it was the only one of the centers to lose Class A status and be dropped from full support. In the spring of 1978, I interviewed the chief of the Genetic Disease Section and asked why this occurred. He gave the official account that "insufficient numbers of women were coming in for amniocentesis."

That terse statement provided the grounds for closing the center, but broader explanations of why there were insufficient numbers of women coming in for amniocentesis eluded the state bureaucracy, or at least did not stall the decision to close down a center. The bureaucracy is the buffer and executor of rules and regulations. It did not matter to those in the organization charged with following the rules that the one center in ten that served mainly the people of color in the state was also the center with insufficient usage to warrant sustained funding. State policy was unambiguous: to support amniocentesis centers only in places where they would be used. Where there is insufficient usage, the policy is clearly reasonable, and using these narrow bureaucratic guidelines couched in terms of cost-effectiveness, reasonably defensible before the state legislature. The earliest consumers of amniocentesis were primarily white middle-class females in their middle thirties. Without for the moment addressing the larger causes for this development, we can say that the relative social homogeneity of this group, and the relative homogeneity of their interests in consuming the new technology, account for much of the pattern of use in the first decade of parental screening via amniocentesis.[4]

It became clear from an interview with the head of the Genetic Disease Section (and two other officials in the state health bureaucracy) that the prevailing wisdom, sense, and understanding of the situation as to why King Hospital was closed was that the black community was relatively uneducated in these matters, relatively unaware of the availability of the new technology. It followed that the solution proposed and pursued would be an intensive public education program in the black community. Churches, schools, libraries, and public political meetings were to be the focus of an intensive educational campaign. Prospective parents were to be "made aware" of the facilities, and were to be informed that the state actually paid for a good percentage of the tests.

This strategy assumed that once the black community was more fully informed, its members would be receptive to the new technology. But

Table 4.1 California Women Receiving Amniocentesis By Income Level

Income Level	% Distribution of for California	$ Distribution of Women Receiving Amniocentesis in California Prenatal Diagnosis Program, 1977–1978
$ 6,000 & under	1.2	6.5
7,000–10,000	12.7	9.9
11,000–15,000	21.3	14.7
16,000–20,000	28.9	22.0
21,000–35,000	27.8	30.6
36,000 & over	8.1	16.4

California State Franchise Tax Board 1976 Annual Report for the 1975 income tax year (from report to California State Legislature, Genetic Disease Section, January 1980).

there is an important reason why this assumption is not warranted. Whether the consumers are black or white, they are more likely to come from the more privileged socioeconomic strata. It is a feature of the American landscape that there are many more working-class black women than there are middle-class black women; but conversely, there are more middle-class white women than working-class white women. Consumption patterns for the new technology are clear (see tables 4.2 and 4.3). In short, class position and age in combination explain most of what is happening here. No matter how much information is provided to working-class black women or to working-class Italian women concerning amniocentesis, they are far less likely than middle-class black and Italian

Table 4.2 Last Paid Occupation of Mothers Receiving Amniocentesis Compared With 1970 Census Figures for California Women

Occupation	Number	%	% of 1970 Census
Professional, technical	1,992	30.0	15.8
Managers, officials	274	4.1	4.4
Clerical, sales, and related	1,458	21.9	44.2
Craftsmen, foremen, and skilled workers	134	2.0	1.5
Operators, semiskilled	234	3.5	9.9
Service workers, farm owners	351	5.3	17.0
Farm laborers, foremen	52	0.8	0.6
Members of Armed Forces	2	0.1	—
None	781	11.8	—
Not reported or declined to state	1,365	20.5	6.5
TOTAL	6,643	100.0	99.9

From Report to California State Legislature, Genetic Disease Section, January 1980.

Table 4.3 *Age of Mothers Receiving Amniocentesis Compared With California Births,*
1977

Age	Number	%	California Births*
15	0	—	0.20
15–19	43	0.6	15.20
20–24	241	3.6	34.30
25–29	417	6.3	30.50
30–34	730	11.0	14.70
35–39	4,206	63.3	4.10
40 & over	943	14.2	0.80
Unknown or Declined to State	63	0.9	.01
TOTAL	6,643	99.9	99.90

*California Vital Statistics Birth Records, 1977

From report to California State Legislature, Genetics Disease Section, January 1980.

women to have amniocentesis. The latter overwhelmingly tend to bear
children in their twenties, or even teens. The more typical Latino, black,
or working-class white women who bear children well into their thirties
do so not because of a delay of the first pregnancy, but as a continuation
of their already well-established childbearing.

The state's gift of "more information" and subsidized payment as an
attempt to even up public resource distribution was doomed to failure.
Such a strategy did not address, much less alter, the *social* circumstances
that explain patterns of use (and nonuse) of the technology. The major
issue is not ignorance of that technology, but life situations shaping the
timing of reproductive decision making.

State Funding for Amniocentesis

In 1976, the California State Legislature passed a bill requiring the
Department of Health to set up a three-year pilot program of prenatal
testing for inherited disorders by means of amniocentesis. Thirteen medical centers joined the program, each affiliated with a medical school.
Because amniocentesis provides some risk to the fetus (perhaps 1 in 150,
depending upon the study cited, and related to the experience of the
physician), the procedure is restricted to women with select characteristics
which place them at greater risk for having a child with an inherited
disorder. The state health department set out the following criteria,
restricting amniocentesis support to:

1. Women 35 years of age or older.
2. Women having had a previous Down syndrome child or a child with any other genetic disorder.
3. Pregnancies where one parent is a translocation carrier.
4. Women who are carriers of a sex-linked disorder.
5. Pregnancies where both parents are carriers of an autosomal recessive trait.
6. Pregnancies where the parents have a previous child who has a neural tube defect.

In the first two years of the program, 6,643 amniocenteses were performed, resulting in the detection of 171 genetically abnormal fetuses, or 2.6 percent. However, thirty of these "abnormalities" were not expected to show clinical symptoms. Of the remaining fetuses, approximately 80 percent either spontaneously aborted or were aborted with the conscious decision of the prospective parent(s).

Who Uses Amniocentesis?

As noted, most of the women who have used the state-supported program for amniocentesis are over thirty-five. A review of table 4.3 reveals that only about 5 percent of women who bear children in California bear children after the age of thirty-five. Those who do so tend to come from families that have delayed childbearing as a matter of choice. Women who show up for amniocentesis tend to be much more likely to come from the higher social and economic strata (refer to tables 4.1 and 4.2). A research team from a well-used amniocentesis center in northern California at the end of the seventies reported the following patterns it had uncovered from an analysis of more than 3,000 amniocenteses. The excerpt which follows refers to a one-year period of the study, but we have seen from the previous chapter that there are other data that support these findings.

A survey of the patients seen from July, 1976, through June, 1977, reveals that 56.2 per cent of the mothers and 78.6 per cent of their mates had some college education, including 25.9 per cent and 35.5 per cent, respectively, who had done graduate work. The average gross annual income for all families was $25,271. These statistics suggest that the lower socioeconomic groups have yet to use prenatal diagnosis facilities as fully as those in the higher socioeconomic groups. (Golbus et al., 1979:158)

At the time, the average cost per patient was approximately $550. Generally, the state bureaucracy asked that each person contribute about

$200 to this figure. The average family income of women using prenatal diagnostic services in California during the two-year period under discussion was $26,300, while the median income of a family of four in California at that time was $18,900. Table 4.1 indicates the more precise utilization of services by income distribution. Now comes the language of the bureaucracy, the self-consciously sensitive language of those who know the virtue of neutral, detached, equality of treatment (appearance) in the utilization of public funds:

> It is the intent of the Genetic Disease Section to encourage a more equitable distribution of prenatal diagnosis services. As special program efforts are made to direct outreach, educational and genetic counseling to high-risk but less informed, less motivated and lower income groups, it is anticipated that the average family income will fall and average family size increase in the population served over the next few years. More families will be seen from the lower middle income classes who, while not being eligible for Medi-Cal coverage, nonetheless experience great difficulty in paying for medical care, particularly that of an elective nature. Thus, it must be expected that substantial financial support will be required to achieve this equity and to encourage acceptance of preventive services. (California Department of Health, Genetic Disease Section report, January 1980, p. 30).

The next chapter addresses directly the emerging professional ideology of genetic counselors. A primary element of that ideology is the commitment to the idea that the patient has the right to choose the option best for him or her. The counselor primarily provides information, elaborates options, answers complicated genetic questions, explains risk figures and probabilities, and offers a measure of emotional support and understanding. The counselor, according to the ideology, does not hint, cajole, or try to influence in a direction that is against the indications of the counselee. But the state department of public health "is in the business" of justifying itself to the legislature, of constructing an account of the health benefits of its policies and procedures and practices. Note the following passage from the report to the legislature:

> About half the families who are so counseled refuse to accept services. When a financial obligation is implied the decision is further weighted away from accepting services. Indeed, centers have found that, even in the presence of clear medical indication, families decline the procedure when asked to pay more than $100 to $200. These families continue their high-risk pregnancies. Approximately 3% of these pregnancies will result in the birth of a child with a genetic disorder which could have been diagnosed prenatally. This is definitely contrary to the Department's recommendation that primary prevention programs should emphasize incentive to clients to accept preven-

tive services. (California State Department of Health, Genetics Disease Section report, January 1980:32)

This is hardly the language of neutrality on the matter of refusal of services. Add to this the fact that four of five women who learn of a diagnostic test that produces positive indications of a genetic abnormality that will manifest symptoms choose abortion, or have spontaneous abortions, and it is apparent that the state is not just idly standing by.

The Third Party in the Medical Triangle

When prenatal diagnosis becomes more widespread (for women under thirty-five as well) and more routinely available, there will be the problem of what might best be termed the intrusive role of the third party in the traditional doctor-patient relationship. In order to make the argument, I will have to shift grounds and leave genetics, while remaining within the larger medical context.

In the history of medicine, the one-to-one relationship between doctor and patient is primarily characterized by voluntary association of each of the two parties (Arney and Bergen, 1984:78-97). In the classical market relationship, the physician is "on the market" and can have his or her services purchased by the patient. Should the patient be unhappy with the doctor's services for any reason, the patient is then free to change doctors. Similarly, a physician, in such a free-market relationship, is free to disentangle from a relationship with a patient. A wide variety of devices are available to the physician to accomplish this, including shifting services to some other physician who is "less busy" or who has a greater specialization in the area or a more sympathetic style (Rosen, 1983).

This voluntary association between the physician and patient, where the patient is paying out of his or her own pocket, usually means that the patient is from the more economically privileged sections of society. In nineteenth-century Europe, the bourgeoisie often grafted the family doctor into the family social scene, as the plays of Ibsen and Strindberg, and the novels of Tolstoy and Balzac reveal. For the poor, social historians and analysts have documented how the delivery of medical service was quite another matter (Starr, 1982; Rosen, 1983; Szasz, 1961). The public hospital was for the poor, and "treatment" there could often be as motivated by experimental as by therapeutic concerns.

Under conditions where the poor cannot pay, some third party, usually the state, employs the physician to deliver health care. When the third party breaks up the classical conception of the one-to-one doctor-patient relationship, a new set of social and political forces reshape patterns of diagnosis and treatment. Perhaps the best-known example is the emergence of notions of hypochondria and malingering, two ideas that rarely surface in the traditional one-to-one relationship. Indeed, the whole field of functional theorizing in psychiatry is deeply indebted to the role of the third party as it intruded upon the diagnosis of "illness" in the nineteenth century. The French neurologist Charcot got his "practice" on poor people at the state hospital at Salpiêtre (Szasz, 1974).

Employers and kin sometimes suspected the poor of faking illness ("malingering") in order to avoid work. Charcot, suspecting a neurological basis for the inability of these malingerers to act normally, performed autopsies on their brains to try to discern the pathology. When he could discover no such abnormality, he laid the groundwork for Freud and Breuer to develop the concept of "hysteria" as a functional, not organically based explanation of mental disturbance. This kind of question would never have surfaced so long as the well-to-do were employing Charcot, or any other physician, to attend to their needs directly. Ibsen's family doctor sometimes suspects hypochondria or malingering, but it is rarely in the interests of the doctor to dwell upon the real versus the imagined character of the illness. As explanatory hypotheses, malingering and hysteria could hardly surface so long as the physicians were in attendance to those who paid them directly, and who found it in their (the physicians') interest to indulge a bit of hypochondria, perhaps with placebo. Here is yet another instance of the emergence of a kind of knowledge from one social circumstance, propelled by sets of social and economic forces in a direction that is only comprehensible from a stance that permits one to uncover the social basis of initial knowledge formation.

The Power of the Third Party

Once the third party steps in to pay the physician for delivering health care to the patient, the interests of the third party will typically supersede those of the patient. A few examples will illustrate the point. Let us take the three cases of the army, the factory, and the professional sports franchise.

When a country institutes a military draft, especially in times of war, the physical health of recruits becomes an important interest of the military. The army, as third party, employs physicians to give medical examinations to potential draftees. In this situation, the interests of the "patient" and the doctor are now basically transformed by the interests of the third party. The medical examiner may now become suspicious of those who would try to fake illness in order to avoid the draft. This kind of concern for discerning the fake illness has no strong base if the patient is paying the physician directly to diagnose and treat a problem. If the medical examiner "excuses too many" possible inductees, the army will simply choose to find another medical examiner, who obtains a "better" number or proportion.

A second example of the phenomenon is the factory worker in the Soviet Union. The state employs a medical doctor to examine those who claim physical ailment as the legitimate grounds for missing work (Field, 1953). The physician is placed in a situation of potential interest conflict. If there is a genuine flu epidemic, but the factory has a work output quota, the physician must weigh the conflicting interests of the two parties served. Again, the central purpose of this portrayal is to illustrate how such a situation can surface most dramatically only when the physician is in the employ of the third party.

The last example is of the professional sports franchise. The team physician in professional athletics must often examine an athlete to determine the extent of an injury, and make a medical judgment about whether to permit him to continue playing. While most would err on the side of caution, consider how much more so this would be the case were this the personal physician of the athlete, in a one-to-one relationship. In a recent case, a National Football League player was awarded $2.3 million damages against a franchise that kept him on the playing field despite foreknowledge of substantial injuries that had already been sustained.[5]

There are powerful ethical considerations in a doctor-patient relationship that turn, in large measure, upon the symmetry of the connection. Confidentiality, trust, and the interest of the patient are often cited as primary among these concerns. This is predicated on the simple notion that the two parties are engaged in a relatively equal and free human exchange—fee for services. In cases where the poor can not afford these medical services (in corporate capitalist countries) or where even the more privileged do not have private physicians (party officials in socialist countries), the symmetry is disturbed by the introduction of the third party.

However, our ways of thinking about the "ethics" of the doctor-patient relationship are grounded in an often unwarranted presumption of the two-party symmetry. Let us examine more closely the notions of confidentiality, trust, and the patient's interest. When the third party enters as employer of the physician, what happens to "confidentiality"? Whether in the U.S. or the U.S.S.R., the employer becomes the receiver of information about the patient's health status for the purposes of further action in behalf of the employing party. What of trust? It is a structural imperative that it be violated. As for the interest of the patient, the empirical cases above suggest that the medical examiner's suspicion is an emergent but organizationally required intrusion into the new, tripartite relationship between the doctor, the patient, and the third party.

In all of this, a clear pattern is to be found, and a lesson to be learned, about the relative weights of factors that we might predict to influence the course and development of genetic screening. It is a direction that can be accounted for by reference to the weighing of ethical and sociological emphasis in the clarification of the issues.

The Bearing of the Third-Party
Analysis on Genetic Screening

Whether the genetic counselor is a physician, a licensed and certified genetic counselor with specialized training, or a paraprofessional, when payment for services comes from the third party (in this case, the state), the interests of the third party will often supersede that of the patient. This means that the poor are at continual risk that their interests will be given a low priority. Nothing new about that. But with a general genetic screen, paid for by the state, even the more privileged classes, who have been more accustomed to direct fee-for-service relationships with the medical profession, may find themselves in a position of greater vulnerability in this three-way connection.

From the figures in table 4.1, we can see the proportion of women from various income categories who have used amniocentesis, a service in California substantially funded by the state Department of Public Health. It is the wealthier women who have availed themselves of this service, not the poor. These women are more accustomed to discussions and challenges to their physicians and genetic counselors than are the poor (Rapp, 1988; Sorenson et al., 1981). Consider the implications when the new genetics technology for prenatal diagnosis is made more generally available across the class structure, and across age levels. Younger women, younger couples, the working class, the poor, and the unemployed will confront the third party (the state, usually) from a quite different position, attitudinally and structurally. They will be more vulnerable, as a rule, than older (over thirty-five) professional women who presently are likely to have lots of information buttressed by a strong ideology about an egalitarian relationship with health professionals (Sorenson et al., 1981).

Perhaps the clearest indication of the power of the third party as employer of a genetic "information giver" comes from industry. Dow Chemical Company employed a doctor on its staff to conduct studies of the effects of exposure of its workforce to benzene, a chemical that is in wide use, and a known carcinogen. After several months of collecting data and reviewing it, and subjecting it to analysis, the physician and geneticist, Dante Picciano, found strong evidence of chromosome damage in workers exposed to benzene. He said:

We wanted them to tell the workers what we had found, reduce the levels
of benzene to which workers were exposed, and inform the appropriate
government agencies and the rest of the petrochemical industry.[6]

But Dow management took the position that the evidence was not
sufficiently convincing to set off an alarm in the workers. The management argued that the data were complicated and difficult to interpret in
any singular causal direction. This is certainly true in any multifactorial
explanation, as noted in chapter 2. But the issue was drawn on the
workers' right to know what evidence did exist. Dr. Picciano resigned his
position at Dow soon thereafter.

The conflict over the distribution of information in the Dow case
throws into relief the role of the third party as employer of one with
genetic information. If the union had employed Picciano, we would of
course have predicted a different outcome. The important point is less
the distinction between management and labor than the role of *any* third-
party intercession. The compelling contrast would be with a worker
himself or herself employing Picciano directly, one-to-one, to provide
information about chromosome damage and benzene exposure.

Unions, as organizations of workers taking up the "collective interests"
of their constituents, may well trivialize the relative importance of the
substantial health of a few isolated members with "genetic predispositions" to disease under sustained exposure to a chemical in the workplace.
There is evidence from a related sphere that, given the importance of
holding down a job for economic survival, concern for the chromosomes
of some other workers will be regarded as a luxury to be indulged in
only after general security of employment has been established. The
suggestive parallel comes from the debate over nuclear versus solar
power. Radiation leaks may well be demonstrated to cause genetic defects
in the offspring of those exposed to them, but labor has generally sided
with corporate capital more than with the environmentalists on nuclear
power, for the simple reason that management has been able to successfully frame the issue in the most immediate terms: that the choice is
between nuclear power and no jobs.[7] Since this has been the case with
respect to the collective representation of the interests of workers, it will
be all the more compelling when a workforce is fragmented by the
individualized determination of "at risk" susceptibility by genetic
makeup.

Workforce Genetic Screening and the Government

In workplace genetic screening, what of the possibility of the state as
the third party? For those who would look to the state to act as a more

progressive force on matters of worker health and safety than the corporation, there is the caveat that the occupants of government offices bend with strong political winds, or break.

As soon as the Reagan administration took office in 1981, the new director of the Office of Management and Budget recommended a thorough overhaul and reduction in the regulatory apparatus of the Occupational Safety and Health Administration that would affect standards on worker safety. It was recommended that new standards on worker exposure to asbestos, chromium and cadmium, and grain elevator dust control be deferred or drastically modified. The government can hardly be counted on to protect worker safety on a consistent basis. In a three-way relationship with the state, the interests of industry and management are likely to win out in a battle with the interests of fragmented and atomized workers who have individual chromosome breakage, or long-term genetic damage of a variety of sorts.

It is this last element of genetic screening that may be unique and new, and which is to be distinguished from screening for sickle cell or Tay-Sachs or other genetic disorders linked to racial and ethnic groups. Namely, it is possible to see political mobilization of blacks and Jews and Italians around a disorder that is "their own"—a risk population that is identifiable because of social and cultural factors like language, heritage, race, and so forth. It is quite another dimension when a genetic screen is erected that does not coincide with already established social groupings, but which is socially "random." When there is overlap, there is the likely formation of interest groups and the increased social awareness and capacity for mobilization. It is equally significant what happens when there is *no* overlap between the genetic screen and socially identifiable groupings. There is some evidence that people with northern European ancestry, among them northern Germans, Danes, Swedes, and Norwegians, are at much greater risk than the rest of us for an inborn deficiency of serum alpha$_1$ antitrypsin, and are vulnerable to chemical agents in the industrial workplace that could trigger emphysema and chronic bronchitis (Lappé, 1988).

If in the next decade the new technology for detecting such inborn errors was to permit such a genetic screen, a social analyst would have solid basis for predicting a quite different pattern of mobilization than we have seen for sickle cell, Tay-Sachs, or beta-thalassemia. European-Americans of north German and variable Scandinavian ancestry do not comprise a social grouping identifiable and known to each other. At the workplace, they are, for purposes of interest-group potential mobilization, far too isolated and fragmented. When a few percent of them are identified as vulnerable to emphysema due to a genetically related deficiency, neither the workers as a collectivity nor the individuals identified will see it as in their interest to mobilize as a group. The victims will be seen as isolated and particular cases with a personal problem. There is an interesting dialectic here, for the particularization, or isolation, or fragmentation of this phenomenon of the genetic screenee is explicable by social and cultural development.

Rather than seeing a social reaction to the new genetic screen, then (as with blacks over sickle cell), the wave of the next period could well be the passive, individualized acceptance of a "personal" problem of a genetic deficiency that does not permit one to work on certain jobs. This would be a reversal of the trend of the last decade of the genetic screen, where many could take personal problems and turn them into social problems. The new genetics may help take social problems and turn them into personal problems.

Vertical Integration and the Variable Meanings of "Consent"

A set of issues that cuts across all levels[8] is the combination of concern for voluntary participation in the screening process, informed consent, and confidentiality. One way to insure continuity between levels is to follow issues that obviously surface at every level of empirical inquiry. For the purposes of illustration in this area of work, we can take the three related issues mentioned above. Each taps a quite different political and conceptual problem. The matter of confidentiality takes us into the interests of giant international insurance conglomerates,[9] but it is also a matter of an exchange and trust in the relationship between the individual and the physician. In sharp contrast, "informed consent" is simply an ideal set up by a number of quite different interests at many levels, but it is quite difficult to monitor.

If viewed as an isolated problem, informed consent seems hardly an issue that could generate much concern or interest. However, it is tied up with a vital nerve of all genetics controversies between the state and the individual—the degree of voluntarism in participation. Federal law and government regulations insist on the noncoercive assurances built into many genetic screening programs (Capron, 1973; Kilbrandon, 1973). The primary device for insuring that voluntarism is the requirement that participants be fully informed (sometimes verbally, usually in writing) that they have the right to refuse a fully explained screening detection procedure.

But while federal and state laws are clear and unequivocal on this matter, the implementation of the ideal is fraught with almost insurmountable problems for the administering agency, the clinic, and the physician. Regulations call for standardization, yet the populations being screened are infinitely variable. In the State of California, how does one individual achieve the assurance that a recently-arrived Asian from Hong Kong or Cambodia, a recently arrived eighteen-year-old black from rural Alabama, and a Hungarian professor of engineering each gets "standardized" consent forms that insure informed consent? Implicit in "giving" consent is the background assumption that the individual feels or senses no hidden coercion and expects no negative sanction if he or she says no. The forms may require that the person be "read a passage" that tells them how participation is totally voluntary, but individuals from certain groups come to the bureaucratic setting with widely varying expectations of what will ensue once one rejects or refuses what are described as routine procedures (Rapp, 1988).

Summary

The state health bureaucracy is the apparently neutral and rationalized force that stands between the local clinical and community activity around genetic disorder treatment and screening, and the state and federal laws designed to protect the public health. Yet, this surface neutrality masks important features of the way the state health department operates.

First, the wide variability between genetic disorders and variation within any given disorder means that a singular policy will benefit some, and harshly penalize others. It is virtually impossible to develop a plan attuned to specific disorders, with close attention to specific local situations, cultures, cultural mistrusts, education levels, and the social and economic circumstances of those affected. Here is an inherent contradiction, because a "policy" that calibrates to specific interests and needs is not policy that can be administered with standardized bureaucratic rules, but is rather the opposite—responsive, adaptive, even particularistic. But since the public monies pay for these services, differing interest groups come along, see that certain groups are being served more than others, and lay strong claims to "their share" of the state budget. Ethnic and racial groups with "their own" disorder are socially positioned to mobilize political and economic support. However, different groups have differing access to the levers of power, to legislative hearings that produce legal change, and even to the medical profession.

Second, there are some genetic disorders that are not tied to any particular social grouping (ethnic, racial, religious) ripe for collective mobilization. If and when screening for these disorders reveals individuals at greater risk for illnesses such as cancer or birth defects in the offspring, the victim has no ready-made or socially prefabricated allies to generate social and political support. Such persons, atomized and isolated, can be barred from occupations or vocational and educational programs and denied insurance, without redress. Screening for these disorders can transform what in many ways should be a general health problem or a cost problem for the state into a personal problem for the individual.

Third, and possibly most significant, there is a powerful undercurrent of state genetic disorder control that needs to be more directly addressed. When the state pays for genetic screening, counseling, and treatment, it becomes the "third party" in the transaction. Without regard to intentions or personal style, the cost-benefit justifications of state-funded programs require that the interests of the state supersede that of the individual client, the physician, or the genetic counselor. Here is the final inherent contradiction: the state cannot both (a) insist that such genetics disorder control programs are designed to assist the individual, *whatever his or her choice*, and then (b) argue cost effectiveness of service utilization on the grounds that such services as utilized in the aggregate cost the public less money.

The experience of the State of California during the 1970s was that upper-income women availed themselves more of the new technology than lower income women. These more privileged women are able to confront the medical establishment with a fuller sense of equality and dialogue as professionals. As the new technology moves along, it will become more available to all women. We should stay alert to the problem of the state as the third party and the implications for genetics control policy.

I do not therefore conclude that the state should extricate itself from the role of the third party, and abandon any role in genetic screening as monitor and protector of the public health. The state has an important role to play, but it is more complicated than the disclaimers of neutrality and rationality that emanate from the state bureaucracy, or from the newly emerging profession of genetic counselors whose training is underwritten by state support.

Genetic counselors are probably, as professionals, indeed neutral, if this means that they do as much as possible to not communicate their personal prejudices and opinions about whether a couple should take a chance or not or whether they would recommend living with a disability or not, etc. However, the individual neutrality of the counselor is not the issue. It is the fact of the machinery of a screen that has been erected. Even if one is neutral about whether one uses the advice or technology, etc., the simple fact that the screen is in place communicates a powerful message that something is wrong with the disorder for which the screen is in place.

5
Neutrality and Ideology in Genetic Disorder Control

Imagine, for a moment, that the genetics technology of the 1990s was available in the 1930s. Turn the clock back sixty years, and reflect upon these three images: First, try to conceive of Tay-Sachs screening programs for Jews during the latter part of the Third Reich, with prenatal genetic screening widely available as a possible tool, controlled by the German state apparatus. Second, try to imagine a new sickle-cell anemia screening program suddenly made available in the rural South of the United States, controlled by the states of Mississippi, Alabama, and South Carolina, in the year 1938. Finally, consider a gene screening program in Scotland during the same period, set up and administered because of the discovery of a genetic disorder found to have relatively high incidence in the Scottish population.

Consideration of these extreme hypothetical cases sharpens the issues and focuses attention on the matter of how and why different groups can be expected to respond differently to the "neutral technology" of the new genetics. While the Scottish people might conceivably have accepted the presuppositions of the health-giving features of such a genetic screen, the Jews and blacks might understandably wonder about the motives and hidden purposes. Implicit in the current professional ideology of genetic counseling is the assumption that political tranquility and social equality either prevail, or that these considerations are secondary. The basic structural underpinnings of the professional stance require that genetic counselors downplay the social and political frame, and instead emphasize the technical competence and skill that, they would say, *should* be the foundation of a genetic counseling credential.

There is a basic difficulty with an attempt to characterize "the central problem" of genetic consultation. The objective of the profession cannot be summed up as preventing the production of babies seriously impaired by genetic disorders (Sorenson et al., 1981:42). If this were the major issue, we could at least expect that some substantial agreement would be forged around what constitutes the far end of the continuum of serious health- or life-threatening debilitation. But, as has been noted previously, (a) there is a wide range of genetic disorders, and (b) what is "serious" in one racial group, social class, or economic circumstance or culture may be rare or nonexistent in another. To make matters even more complicated, for a "single" genetic disorder such as sickle-cell anemia, there is wide variability in its clinical expression. Some persons with sickle-cell anemia will live to be sixty or seventy, while others may die at an early age; some will live with recurrent painful crises, while others may have only minor ailments (Bowman, 1977).

Given this high variability in genetic disorders, and the tendency of these disorders to be attached to socially identifiable groups which have their own (socially patterned) ways of coping, it is not possible to advocate a single method or a particular style of genetic counseling that is most effective. What would it mean, for example, for the genetic counselor to be "directive" to a client with a one-in-four chance for the next-born to have sickle cell, when no one can know the full extent or nature of the expression of that disorder before the child is three or, in some cases, thirty-three?

In spite of such complexities that confound our capacities to make straightforward assessments, the nation has embarked upon a path to screen for inherited disorders, and to train professionals to counsel those who are so screened. Under these circumstances, it was inevitable that the new profession would craft its own version of its legitimacy and mission, and develop a protective armor of technical neutrality (Rollnick, 1984). The social patterning in the selection process is dramatic: of the more than six hundred genetic counselors practicing in the late 1980s, *99 percent were women.* Moreover, for the same period, *more than 95 percent of practicing genetic counselors were white* (Rapp, 1988:145).[1]

The Professional Ideology of the Genetic Counselor

The current professional ideology of genetic counselors is heavily weighted by the quite palatable characterization of their role as sympathetic, nondirective purveyors of information. A major study of genetic counseling corroborates this (Sorenson et al., 1981). Those in the vanguard who are setting the ethical standards for this group say that the task of the genetic counselor is to lay out the options for clients, but not to cajole, press, advise, or "counsel" in one direction or another about whether to have a child with a high potential for (or even a fetus diagnostically determined to have) a genetic disorder (Kelly, 1977; Hsia et al., 1979). For many individual genetic counselors, this is an accurate description of how they try to relate to many of their clients. In legal terms, it is imperative that the genetic counselor provide all such information to a client that would constitute an "informed decision-maker" (Capron, 1973:230). But in social terms, the mere existence of a screen assures that the "idea of a screen" will penetrate the consciousness of lay persons, and communicate that the screened-for characteristic is undesirable.

However simple or complex, however subtle or blatant, a screen is, nonetheless, a screen.[2] This elementary observation can also be elusive, since one need not confront a screen directly to experience its force. This came to our attention inadvertently, as a consequence of the decision to interview a number of women who *refused* to undergo prenatal screening by amniocentesis. The purpose of these interviews was to find out why some people refuse the new technology. However, we soon discovered that the mere existence of the new technology, and the social distribution of knowledge about its availability act together as twin pressures on a potential client.

> It seemed that all my friends wanted to make sure I knew about amniocentesis. Everywhere I went, acquaintances of only a few months would "inform" me of this device for detecting if my pregnancy were "normal." At first, I just politely responded that I knew about it, but didn't want it. Then I started getting angry, because I began to realize what they were implying . . . that any sane woman over 35 with an ounce of brains would have amniocentesis. "Do you have religious objections?" they'd ask. As if being crazy or stupid or religious were my only options.

This personal account is corroborated by interviews with women from several countries in which prenatal testing is available. Commenting on work in Germany, Hubbard (1986) reports that

> once a test is available and a woman decides not to use it, if her baby is born with a disability that could have been diagnosed, it is no longer an act of fate but has become her fault. (p. 227)

The genetic counselor, part of the larger apparatus of screening, has two sides that are frequently in tandem, rarely side-by-side, and sometimes in direct conflict. On the one hand, there is the neutral "information giver" who as specialist simply provides the prospective parents with data and risk considerations. On the other hand, since the information provided can be very disturbing, there is the "counselor" side of the genetic counselor which is needed to provide the emotional support and the human professional service that makes for an adjustment to the news or information about a child with a genetic disorder (Kelly, 1977).

What is the proper role of the genetic counselor when she or he sees the client very emotionally upset by the received information about the probabilities of having a child with a serious birth disorder? People are too varied in their class, cultural, and racial heritages, too varied in their religious and secular commitments, and too varied as personalities (in response to the counseling mode, especially) to expect that general guidelines will charter any singular path of confidence and competence for the genetic counselor. There are no formulas, and no list of ethical guidelines from a professional's manual which can adequately define the correct role.

The emotional upset of a thirty-seven year old professional in her first pregnancy, or the way she gives expression to that upset, will be quite different from the parallel upset of a twenty-two-year-old housewife or single parent in her third pregnancy.[3] But the matter is far more complex than just the nature, experience, and expression of emotional upset. If one of these women has a deep structural dependency upon kin, bounded by a religious orthodoxy, apprehension of her social situation becomes a feature of the assessment of the genetic counselor. It is likely that, within the next decade, genetic counselors will have to deal with a much wider band of the social and cultural spectrum. At that point, the attempt to assist the prospective parent(s) in the decision about prenatal diagnosis, or in the decision to think explicitly about pursuing some abstract probability (one in every four live births) will be fraught with "land mines" of interethnic, interracial, interclass, intergenerational "misunderstandings."

It is one thing to know about the devices for dealing with momentary displays of disturbance. It is another to try to attend to the "chronic" structural features that may be the source of that upset, and to offer good counsel about the long-term consequences of having a child with a debilitating disorder. The most obvious consideration that comes to the fore is the great differences between people in their capacities to live with adversity. There is not only diversity in the ability or willingness to acknowledge and deal with emotional upset, but there are large differences in clients in the amount of strain upon their financial resources that would result in having a child with a health problem requiring great amounts of time, attention, and care. Further, there are great differences in social contexts, in levels of stigma, isolation, or support that are both tolerable and available (McCollum and Silverberg, 1979:245-252).

Genetic counselors will always face a monumental tax upon their abilities to sort confidently the complex ways in which the personal, the economic, and the social are intertwined as they "counsel" a prospective parent. A black working-class woman may be able to call upon a network of social supports that are not indicated by her income (Stack, 1974:); an upper-middle-class white Presbyterian may have the financial wherewithal to deal with Down syndrome or spina bifida, but might be wracked with a sense of personal guilt or personal failure. A devout believer might leave it all "in God's hands" and disengage from the faithless intrusion of high-technological fix.

But beyond these surface responses, the genetic counselor will discover in one thirty-to-sixty minute session only the very tip of the iceberg of intricate personal and public policy dilemmas. Capron (1973:229) noted early on that, unlike the bedside physician of another era who knew the patient and family well, the genetic counselor will routinely have only the most fragmentary knowledge of the larger frame and circumstances. If the genetic counselor comes from a very different social and cultural background, as in the case of new counseling programs for recently immigrated Southeast Asians (Stein et al., 1984), should she or he encourage a client from another cultural tradition (with a penchant for suppressing emotional expression) to more fully experience and express emotional upset, or to assume that the providing of information from a health professional is "neutral"? While psychiatrists have had to deal with such matters at the level of the individual, the genetic counselor may have more of a burden requiring several levels of competence and knowledge, moving in the direction of cultural and medical anthropology. In short, the requirements of the role of the genetic counselor force psychological, sociocultural, and economic analyses. There is the high potential for role conflict embedded in the structure of requirements that start as early as the first bit of training in the educational career of the genetic counselor.

Two Sides (at Least) of the Genetic Counselor

Two sides of the genetic counselor (information giver versus sympathetic supporter) come into conflict in decisions on how to construct the curriculum for those who are to be certified to practice in this new field. In the early 1970s, the University of California at Berkeley set up a graduate degree-granting program designed to train genetic counselors.[4] Members of this advisory board argued among themselves about the best course of study for genetic counselors. On one side were those who saw the problem as essentially one of technical expertise. They took the position that students should get a first-rate genetics course offered by professors in the university's graduate program in genetics. They wanted "no dilution" of the curriculum. Those on the other side objected, pointing out that a sympathetic communication between counselor and counselee was the central concern of good counseling. They observed that the university's graduate programs were designed to train students to become researchers, indeed, premier researchers at the forefront of the field of genetics. This was hardly a relevant training, they argued, for a person who was destined to be a practicing counselor with a master's degree.

It is important now to set the context for the battle. Recall from the two previous chapters that sickle-cell anemia education and counseling programs were funded by the State of California during this period, and jobs were awaiting "certain" students with the master's degree. Many of these jobs would be located in the black community, delimited both geographically and demographically. Behind the battle between the two sides of the board was the unstated tension and disagreement about the degree of importance attached to the race of these prospective counselors, i.e., whether or not these counselors would or should be black.

One faction of the advisory board argued for a training program whereby "the best students" (defined by technical and standardized measures) would be exposed to the best in technical training in genetics. But the opposing faction argued that genetic counseling does not occur in a hermetically sealed vacuum, where technical knowledge is the major source of good communication, advice, and counsel. Sorenson and his colleagues (1981:137), even though not addressing racial and ethnic diversity explicitly, concluded that there is "room for improvement in the interactive process between counselor and client." Only when a society is relatively homogeneous with respect to racial and ethnic distinctions, and to privilege, can technical competence be the "neutral" first principle.

The three hypothetical cases that opened this chapter are admittedly "limiting cases." However, the notion of a neutral technology in a society that is completely egalitarian is equally extreme. But while social analysts are usually quite willing to admit to the primarily heuristic use of the Third Reich,[5] the purveyors of science and medicine as neutral are far less willing to acknowledge that, in a socially stratified world, the socially neutral communication of genetic disorder control is also a hypothetical extreme. All societies are differentiated and stratified, some groups having more power and privilege than others. While that is the nature of social order, societies differ in the extent and degree of stratification. The more stratified, the more it is an "extremist position" to argue that there can be such a thing as technical neutrality in providing genetic/health consultations that incorporate advice about adjustments to social and economic life (Donovan, 1984).

The costs, benefits, and meaning of genetic screening vary not only with location in the social structure, but with proximity and relationship to the group screened. Unlike previous general public health screens for contagious diseases, there is little possibility for consensus around a single correct stance in favor of, or opposed to genetic screening. An enlightened perspective gives recognition to the variation in interests and perspectives (Murray et al., 1980). Carrier screening has two major health purposes. First, it can be used to inform someone who has a health risk because they possess a particular genetic variant. The client could then either avoid exposure to certain triggering elements in the environment that would be a high health risk (e.g., barbiturates should be avoided by those with the dominantly inherited porphyria phenotype), or receive treatment. An example of the latter would be drug treatment for the regulation of cholesterol metabolism, for which some persons appear to have a specific genetic vulnerability (Scriver, 1979:19). Second, of course, heterozygote screening is carried out to determine those at risk for passing a genetic disorder on to their offspring.

Any gene screening program promotes some interests over other programs (Stein et al., 1984; Lappé, 1988). Resources are used and energies are expended, and those with "other" health and welfare agendas vie for both. This cannot be avoided, but it should be acknowledged. Trust of medical professionals and the Public Health Service is not evenly distributed in the population. When we get to such technical matters as the kinds of genetic screening just mentioned, it is predictable that some segments of the population will be resistant, skeptical, sometimes even hostile. The following passage from an overview of the scientific proceedings on the topic of prevention and detection of health risk requires that the audience have faith and trust:

> The public is being apprised, sometimes inaccurately, of the value of genetic services, and the clamor will increase. So to my mind, the way that shift in emphasis will occur is through the spread of preventive services in which people with special hereditary qualities will be found and advised, whether to adopt some new mode of living or to avoid some particular experience. (Childs, 1979:10)

The tendency towards the panacea of education is almost inevitable, but some deep-rooted suspicions can be accounted for by experience, and cannot be easily attributed to ignorance or paranoia. This is illustrated in the following case from the history of American science and medicine.

The Tuskegee Syphilis Study

In 1932, the United States Public Health Service authorized a study of untreated syphilis in black males, a study that was to last forty years. Medical journals reported the progress of this study beginning as early as the mid-1930s, but neither the American Medical Association, independent medical professionals, nor the federal or state government officials ever blew the whistle during these four decades (Brandt, 1981). In 1972, as a direct result of national press attention, the research was finally halted. To understand more fully what happened, it is necessary to delve more deeply into the social history, which Brandt (1981) and Jones (1981) do quite admirably; the following brief discussion is indebted to their work. For our purposes here, we need only tell a small part of the story.

A few years before the study began, the Public Health Service had conducted a survey of the prevalence of venereal disease in the rural South. One of the highest rates of incidence was uncovered in Macon County, Alabama. This county contains the city of Tuskegee. It also has a high proportion of blacks. Here is what the nation's surgeon general had to say about conditions there in the early 1930s:

> The recent syphilis control demonstration carried out in Macon County, with the financial assistance of the Julius Rosenwald Fund, revealed the presence of an unusually high rate in this county and, what is more remarkable, the fact that 99 per cent of this group was entirely without previous treatment. This combination, together with the expected cooperation of your hospital, offers unparallel opportunity for carrying on this piece of scientific research which probably can not be duplicated anywhere in the world. (Brandt, 1981:188)

The study called for the selection of four hundred black males, aged twenty-five to sixty, with latent syphilis. Each of the subjects was given a thorough physical examination, and were then deliberately given the false impression that the government was going to help them get treatment for the disease, to improve their health. The men were administered a mercurial ointment, a treatment that the attending physicians knew had no bearing upon syphilis. The mercurial treatment was a device just to keep their interest up, to keep them in the study—just to fool them into thinking they were getting help. In the neutral language of science and medicine, one might be tempted to call the mercurial ointment a "placebo."

Yet, at the time, even in 1931, every major textbook advocated treatment of syphilis in its latent stages. It should be added here that each of the subjects was given a spinal tap to detect evidence of neuro-syphilis.

In addition to the four hundred subjects with latent syphilis, there was a control group of two hundred black men who did not have the disease:

> Reports of the study's findings, which appeared regularly in the medical press beginning in 1936, consistently cited the ravages of untreated syphilis. The first paper, read at the 1936 American Medical Association annual meeting, found that "syphilis in this period (latency) tends to greatly increase the frequency of manifestations of cardiovascular disease." Only 16 per cent of the subjects gave no sign of morbidity as opposed to 61 per cent of the controls. Ten years later, a report noted coldly, "The fact that nearly twice as large a proportion of the syphilitic individuals as the control group has died is a very striking one." Life expectancy, concluded the doctors, is re-

duced by about 20 per cent. A 1955 article found that slightly more than 30 per cent of the test group autopsied had died directly from advanced syphilitic lesions of either the cardiovascular or the central nervous system. (Brandt, 1981:191)

The Tuskegee Syphilis Study has some lessons about selection procedures for those who would counsel others about their health. In 1930–1932, there was no affirmative action that intervened in the selection procedures for technically competent medical people to carry out this study of venereal disease. I am sure that the Public Health Service was using the most neutrally meritocratic procedures for the selection of personnel then available. The surgeon general of the United States, the staff at the Public Health Service for forty years, and the many middle- and high-level bureaucrats at the Department of Health, Education, and Welfare and the National Institutes of Health who later monitored the study were probably drawn from among the "best students" in their cohort.

When these individuals were selected for medical school or graduate studies in the sciences, they were chosen because of their high grade-point averages, and for the judgmental equivalent of high Scholastic Aptitude Test scores, or high Graduate Record Examination scores or high Medical School Aptitude Test scores, had they been available during this period. In any event, these men who conducted and/or read about the Tuskegee Syphilis Study for forty years (1932–1972) undoubtedly had better technical grasp of the medical and health issues than their "ignorant" subjects. But as late as 1971, these technically competent scientists, researchers, scholars, public health service bureaucrats, and their legal advisers, and the American Medical Association never found it in their collective wisdom to advise these black men about the true nature of their health (Jones, 1981). In fact, they did the opposite by deliberately deceiving them.

There are implications of the Tuskegee Syphilis Study for a discussion of the selection of genetic counselors. Technical expertise is only one element of what is involved in health counseling. A second element, certainly equal in importance, is the social and political relationships that provide the context in which counselor and counselee communicate. Those who argue for "the best expertise" as the only legitimate selection procedure for genetic counselors fear, with some justification, that there will be a political abuse of any other grounds for selection. Their fear fantasy is captured by certain practices of the Chinese Cultural Revolution, where a fundamentally political criterion about the "correct line" on health problems could often be more important than knowledge about health and medical care.

But both the excesses of the Chinese Cultural Revolution on the one hand, and the relatively pure, unstratified, homogeneous society on the other, are extreme situations rarely encountered in human society. If the Chinese erred on the side of an unbalanced political criterion in excess, then the American medical and scientific professionals err no less on the side of excessive and even obsessive emphasis on neutral technical expertise. We cannot even imagine that the Tuskegee syphilis experiment could have been the Harvard-Yale-Stanford syphilis experiment, carried out on upper-middle-class professors of medicine at Harvard and Stanford, or on corporation lawyers recently graduated from Yale. We cannot imagine that these white male professionals might be treated with a completely useless mercury ointment when the medical staff had full knowledge that "treatment" would have absolutely no effect.

The clear medical and health aspects of venereal disease in this case are also framed by the social status of the diseased. Genetic disorders are distributed unevenly through the class structure, and vary with racial and ethnic groupings. There is strong evidence to suggest that genetic counseling will, in a similar fashion, always find itself immersed and entangled in the prevailing social and political relationships of the period. Mastery of some technical genetic knowledge is obviously essential for a genetic counselor, but this knowledge does not stand alone, apart from the social and political fabric by which it was generated, and through which it must be communicated. Lunsford (1982) and Rapp (1988) both make this point in an analysis of how "informed consent" takes on different shapes and means different things, depending upon the variable class positions of the pairing in the doctor-patient or counselor-client relationship.

Zola (1966) found that the patient's background is highly related to the kinds of symptoms individuals report to their physician, even to the point of ignoring or repressing pain. Woo (1983) and Scheper-Hughes (1979) report considerable variation along ethnic and racial lines with respect to ways communities respond to imputations of mental illness. While physical pain crosses over all ethnic and racial categories, and while "mental illness" in some form is present in all cultures (Yap, 1951; Edgerton, 1976; Wegrocki, 1954), we have noted that genetic disorders can cluster around socially encased groups.

Since it is well established that members of various racial and ethnic groups respond to mental and physical illness (with respect to reporting and reacting) with patterned variation, there is every reason to believe that there will be even more systematic patterns in racial and ethnic variation when it comes to responses to genetic disorders. The latter, after all, are claimed as "their own disorder." In short, as attempts at genetic disorder control move further along one should expect a multiplier effect of what Woo (1983), Zola (1966), Yap (1951), and others have identified as a patterned group response. Indeed, we should anticipate different forms of mobilization by those groups who find themselves being screened and counseled by those not at risk for the genetic disorder in question (Blank, 1981:19).

A substantial amount of good work has already been completed on genetic counseling (Rapp, 1988; Biersecker et al., 1987; Sorenson et al., 1980, 1981; Kelly, 1977; Hsia et al., 1979; Sissine et al., 1981; Pearn, 1973). We know that it takes many forms and can be fruitfully approached for study in a variety of ways. One important way of looking at genetic counseling, both theoretically and politically, is in terms of the stage or time in which it occurs.

The Genetic Counseling of Screened Carriers

As noted in chapter 3, screening for an inherited disorder can occur at three stages: (1) soon after birth, to aid the family and the physician in the assessment of symptoms and the determination of possible intervention; (2) early in the pregnancy, to determine whether the fetus has the disorder screened for, with abortion as the implicit option; and (3) before conception, called "carrier screening," where a prospective mate is screened to determine if he or she simply "carries" a gene (autosomal recessive) that, if matched with its counterpart in a mate, would produce a child with the disorder.

As we move further back in time, the social and political issues in screening and counseling become more complex and controversial. In neonatal screening, the die is cast, and the major choices for the parents are in kinds of treatment, sometimes nutritional intervention, sometimes the psychological "handling" of a *fait accompli*, sometimes the decision to give the child up to a different home.

With screening during early pregnancy, a host of new sociopolitical problems surface, including the self-selection of certain groups to the (sometimes) publicly supported and funded programs, and the imbalance in the distribution of resources to genetic screening programs identified with socially distinct groups who are at greater risk for a particular genetic disorder. To add to all this, there is the knotty matter of the social controversy over abortion itself (Luker, 1984). Screening for genetic disorders during pregnancy inevitably engages a large arena of potential and real controversy with the new technology and the newly emerging profession of genetic counselors.

At the third level, screening those who are simply carriers of autosomal recessive genes, the social issues multiply. First, there is the matter of two carriers potentially meeting, either as acts of will, or by chance. Second, there is the matter of "personal choice" by a couple, or even by one party to the couple, to try to have a normal child "despite the odds." Remember that when both parties to a couple are autosomal recessive, the chances for a normal child (i.e., without the genetic defect screened for) are 75 percent, at each birth. Finally, there is the socially and politically volatile issue of some agency of the state discouraging a socially identifiable risk population from "taking a chance" in pursuing childbirth, when such discouragement is easily translatable into a sociopolitical attack.

In the United States, since African Americans are at greater risk than any other identifiable population for sickle-cell anemia, there is such an overwhelming association of blacks with sickle cell that Americans are generally unaware that European Americans can have it as well. For comparative purposes, it will prove instructive to take a look at a population of whites who are at greater risk for sickle cell than African Americans. With this in mind, let us briefly turn out attention to a small village in rural Greece where the likelihood of a resident having the disorder is twice that of American blacks. A review of these two populations will permit us to get a better handle on which aspects of the experience are inexorably genetic and biomedical, and which aspects are social, cultural, and political.

Screening in Orchomenos, Greece

Orchomenos is a rural town in central mainland Greece. The population is approximately 5,400, and the location, near the ancient city of Orchomenos in the fertile valley of Kopaida, is central to the genetics of this case. The fertile valley is the scene of a large lake that dried up. However, when the lake was there, it was apparently the source of a malaria-carrying mosquito. The best evidence from studies of West Africa suggest that to be a carrier of the sickle-cell gene is to provide protection from malaria (Edelstein, 1986:44-64). Indeed, 23 percent of the population of Orchomenos are carriers of the sickle-cell gene. (This is more than double the incidence of sickle-cell trait in the black population of the United States.) In the late 1960s, approximately 80 percent of the population were screened for both trait and disorder (Stamatoyannopoulous, 1974). Ten percent of the Orchomenos population are settled Gypsies, but no incidence of sickle cell was found among them. Before 1950, the disorder was unknown, and occurrence of illness and death were attributed largely to supernatural causes and the fates.

In 1973, a follow-up study was done of 354 married couples. From this study, it was learned that parents of carriers, almost without fail, instructed their children to avoid carriers as mates. This, in spite of the "only" one-in-four chance of any single birth from such a mating producing a child with sickle-cell anemia. Moreover, one-fifth of all parents of noncarriers advised their children to avoid carriers, and 10 percent of the parents of carriers advised the offspring of noncarriers to avoid a carrier mate:

> Because few carriers talked freely about their status, the courting couple lived in anxiety up to the moment that the hemoglobin status of the prospective spouse was revealed. This anxiety arose because social stigmatization occurred subsequent to the collapse of engagements. Almost one-fourth of all families, independent of carrier status, considered that having the sickle cell trait meant restriction of freedom and the risk of social stigmatization. All parents with carrier children taught them to avoid a carrier mate. In addition, however, *normal* children were advised by 10% of carrier parents and 20% of normal parents to avoid marrying a carrier. In both situations, this reaction could be attributed to the social embarrassment of the carrier state. (Hollerbach, 1980:170)

One of the striking findings from Orchomenos is that some noncarriers admitted avoiding carriers for reasons of social stigma; they knew that there was no risk of their offspring having sickle-cell anemia. But while social stigmatization played a role in avoidance of a potential mate, actual carrier status (and foreknowledge thereof) did not play a decisive role in avoidance of mates.

> The carriers, however, did not consistently exercise caution in mate selection. One-quarter reported that they had concealed their carrier status from the spouse, and one-quarter stated that hemoglobin status had been unimportant in spouse selection—they were ready to accept the risks. Only one-half of the carrier spouses had conscientiously avoided marrying a carrier and had inquired premaritally about the carrier status of the future spouse; among these, 20% stated that they had broken a marital engagement when they learned that the future spouse was also a carrier. (Hollerbach, 1980:170)

This study throws light upon the role of the genetic counselor at the earliest stage of genetic screening, the screening of carriers. At this early point, the genetic counselor has to be something of the anthropologist, psychiatrist, economist, and sociologist. To try to give advice about mate selection in some "neutral" genetic/health realm is quickly to come full flush up against obdurate realities that have more to do with the clients' social, cultural, and economic concerns.

Field Interviews in Orchomenos

In June 1982 I visited the community of Orchomenos and interviewed the mayor, the local medical doctor and genetic counselor (who had lived and practiced there for more than two decades), and several members of the community whose lives were variously affected by the disorder and the screening program. Everyone agreed that the community was suspicious and noncooperative in the 1950s, when the first attempt was made at a large-scale medical intervention of sickle cell. There was no consensus about the level of acceptance of the current medical version of sickle-cell trait and disorder as a purely health or genetic issue, free from social stigma.

The mayor of Orchomenos was quite receptive to the interview. In the most recent election, the town had voted quite heavily in favor of the new socialist regime, and the mayor strongly favored the notion that the public sector should actively support the health and medical assistance programs for the general public welfare. He spoke with considerable knowledge about the early period of sickle-cell screening, noting the high levels of hostility and suspicion that greeted the 1950s attempt. Now, he surmised, there was a general acceptance that the disorder was transmitted via inheritance of the genes. According to the mayor, there is no longer substantial stigma attached to either being a carrier, or to having the disorder.

Next, I interviewed the medical doctor of the town who perhaps had the greatest amount of experience with the screening program during the preceding twenty years. In a similar vein to the mayor's account, the doctor characterized the early period of screening as difficult and unharmonious. Many residents refused to come forward to be screened. In response to my inquiry as to why a genetic screening program was initiated in this small village thirty years ago, he provided the following brief social history.

Prior to 1950, Greece and several other countries on the Mediterranean reported incidents of birth defects concentrated in select regions, or small pockets of these regions. Often, these were rural areas where there had been little demographic mobility, and where there had consequently been very little intercommunity intermarriage for centuries. In Greece, several communities are known by the medical profession to have such high incidence, such as Thessaly and Macedonia. However, until quite recently, no systematic medical records had been kept, and so there have been no risk figures available, nor had rates of incidence been documented with any confidence. By the late 1940s, only word-of-mouth knowledge was passed among various medical and health professionals. It was in this context that an interested medical doctor and medical researcher in Orchomenos (the mentor of the doctor that I was interviewing) decided to conduct a study of incidence rates. He set up a small clinic, and asked the community members to come forward for preliminary screening interviews, and some blood testing. In this first study, less than

20 percent of the 5,000 members of the community voluntarily came forward. However, this was sufficient to establish a high enough incidence to trigger interest in a more substantial and successful study that was to occur fifteen years later.

In 1967, a new study was begun with American private foundation economic support. A research team was assembled, heavily staffed and directed by American technical assistance. In order to increase the responsiveness of the community, the new study team enlisted the support of the local medical doctors. These local doctors were encouraged to participate actively in the plan for research, and in the collection of data for the study itself. The strategy paid off. In the three-year period from 1967–1970, as was noted earlier, nearly 80 percent of the population was screened for sickle-cell trait and disorder. This "success" (in terms of the population voluntarily coming forward to be screened) is in sharp contrast to early attempts in the United States, circa 1967–1970, to screen American blacks for sickle cell (Bowman, 1977).

As with white Greeks in Orchomenos in the early 1950s, American blacks frequently were suspicious of genetic screening. The American researchers had come a long way by 1967, at least in muting the suspicions of the Greeks in Orchomenos. A common explanation for the reluctance of blacks to come forward is that blacks, relative to American whites, are less well educated and more "traditional." But by any measure, the people of Orchomenos are more "traditional" than American blacks. Blacks in America are more urbanized, more literate, more formally educated, and in general have a higher standard of living.

This calls into question a central premise of much public policy thinking on how to deal with reluctance or resistance of a population to new technological developments. That is, rather than assuming that more information, more education, or more "modernity" will make people more receptive, we can begin to acknowledge the importance of frame and setting of this knowledge as crucial. The key to the success of getting the population of Orchomenos to volunteer for screening was the participation of local health and medical staff who had the confidence of the local population, coupled with substantial funding. These are the main reasons why Ashkenazi Jews in America come forward for voluntary Tay-Sachs screening (Goodman and Goodman, 1981; Kaback, 1974), not the fact that the mean number of years of those Jews screened is a year of post-graduate education. The amount of education or the degree of modernity would not be the key ingredients in the responsiveness of the Jewish population to such a screening program. The level of trust, not the level of education, better explains such compliance.

When it came to genetic screening in the 1970s, American Jews had good reason to trust. American Jewish doctors were among the key architects of voluntary Tay-Sachs screening programs (Goodman and Goodman, 1981). They visibly and vocally argued in favor of this kind of screening, and made sure that it was voluntary (Kaback, 1974). Since Tay-Sachs is a far more devastating disorder than is sickle cell, it is clear that the respective experiences of the frame and the social and political context of the *meaning* of such screening is a major ingredient of the risk-population's response.[6]

The level of trust in a social setting between prospective counselor and counselee is thus an important social frame to help us better understand the initial responsiveness of a population to the genetic screen. There are also powerful social forces that help explain the outcomes and consequences of genetic screening once it is in place. Here, the amount of education or the degree of "modernity" of a population do play significant roles. For some, the shift from the inexplicable ("God's will") to the known (genetically transmitted) has highly positive outcomes, especially around a sense of increased personal control. For others, the social consequences can be devastating. By locating the problem in the genetic code of specific individuals, this increase in genetic knowledge can isolate those identified and victimize them in ways far more difficult to cope with than when everyone in the community simply assigned God's will as an explanation. Once again, whether this new genetic knowledge is an advantage or a cross depends only partly on how the genes are arranged. It depends as well upon where one is located in the social order.

6

The Increasing Appropriation
of Genetic Explanations

In the mid- to late 1970s, both the popular media and scientific journals published an explosion of articles that staked a renewed claim to the genetic explanation of matters that the previous two decades had "laid to rest" as social and environmental. A review of the *Reader's Guide to Periodical Literature* from 1976 to 1982 revealed a 231 percent increase in articles that attempted to explain the genetic basis for crime, mental illness, intelligence, and alcoholism during this brief six-year period. Even more remarkably, between 1983 and 1988, articles that attributed a genetic basis to crime appeared *more than four times* as frequently as they had during the previous decade. This development in the popular print media was based in part upon what was occurring in the scientific journals. During this period, a new surge of articles (more than double the previous decade) appeared in the scientific literature,[1] making claims about the genetic basis of several forms of social deviance and mental illness.[2]

At first glance, it would appear that this was an outgrowth of what was happening in the field of molecular genetics. As noted in chapter 1, many important breakthroughs were occurring during this period, including the increasing ability for intrauterine detection of birth defects. However, the resurgence of genetic claims just noted was not coming from those working at the vanguard laboratories in molecular biology or biochemistry. Indeed, given the requirements of up-to-the minute monitoring to keep abreast of technological and scientific breakthroughs in these fields, it is of special interest to note that the major data base for the resurgent claims was a heavy reliance upon Scandinavian institutional registries dating back to the early part of the century (Kety, 1968, 1976; Kringlen, 1968; Fischer, 1971; Mednick, 1984, 1985; Jensen, 1969). If the new claimants were not the researchers responsible for the new developments described in the previous chapters, who were they?

Who is Making the "Genetic Claims"?

It was noted in chapter 1 that the field of genetics is a combination of very different strategies of research and analysis. The population geneticists were from the start concerned with explaining evolution from a statistical determination of how much observed patterning could be attributed to heritability. Mendelian geneticists were concerned with the search for their own patterns of observed traits that might be attributable to genetics if and when they conform to certain laws of inheritance. A dazzling array of problems confront each strategy, since many things "run in the family," including wealth, crime, and occupational choice; and many things also "run in large population aggregates." In chapter 2, we looked at ways to explain which of the many human attributes, characteristics, traits, or behaviors that "run in families" or "populations" become prime candidates for a genetic treatment, and the subject of a program of research. To paraphrase Gould (1985), the size of the toe is also inherited, but the size of the toe has little to do with the stratification system. It is not the subject of investigation. Skin color does have to do with stratifying practices, as does the imputation of mental deficiency.

The metaphor of the shifting prism that rotates to refract upon a central issue in the stratification of groups can better help us understand the angle at which the prism is tilted to determine which matters are to be investigated and researched. This works as well for the subject matter of the newer molecular genetics as for analyses of family trees and population statistics. An understanding of the prism is less available when discussion turns to the new technologies in molecular genetics, in part because of the complete hegemony of the health and medical and science banner, in part because the technical laboratory issues are out of reach and scrutiny of much of even an informed laity. However, it is the halo from the molecular work of the last decades that has helped provide the new legitimacy to the old claimants who have continued to use twin studies and IQ test score differences to assert genetic explanations, and which is the major subject of this chapter.

Those making the claims about the genetic component of an array of behaviors and conditions (crime, mental illness, alcoholism, gender relations, intelligence) come from a wide range of disciplines, tenuously united under a banner of an increased role for the explanatory power of genetics. Relatively few of these claims come from molecular genetics. Edward Wilson is an entomologist who made his reputation studying insect societies (Wilson, 1971). Yet, he got the Pulitzer Prize for publishing a book applying a genetic theory to social life of humans (Wilson, 1978). Then, in *Genes, Mind, and Culture* (cowritten with Lumsden, 1981), he went on to argue that culture itself springs largely from genetics.

Arthur Jensen (1969), who vaulted to national fame with a claim on the relationship between genetics and intelligence, is an educational psychologist. Seymour Kety (1976) is a psychiatrist, and is one of the leading figures in the world espousing the genetics of schizophrenia. David Rowe (1986) and Sarnoff Mednick (1984), who argue the genetic basis of crime, and Eysenck (1975, 1971), who argues the genetic basis of psychopathology and intelligence, are all psychologists. Richard Herrnstein (1971) is a Harvard psychologist who has not only argued the genetics of intelligence, but has even speculated that someday "the tendency to be unemployed may run in the genes." Herrnstein recently teamed with James Q. Wilson (1985:103), a political scientist, to write a book that asks for a more sympathetic reading of the possible "biological roots of an individual predisposition to crime." And it is a sociologist, Robert Gordon (1987), who argues that race differences in delinquency are best explained by IQ differences between the races, not socioeconomic status. Each of these men lays considerable claim, and most have achieved considerable attention in the popular media postulating the importance of heredity in the explication of human behavior.

Molecular geneticists, whether specialists with humans, animals, or plants, are themselves typically wary of making claims about the genetics of these forms of human behavior.[3] How can the relative modesty, scientific tentativeness, even quietude of these laboratory geneticists on these subjects be explained, while researchers in these other traditions of genetics tend to be the most passionate advocates for the biological or genetic component? It is the rare molecular geneticist who would stake his or her professional reputation on the genetics of "altruism" or "intelligence" or "crime" or a host of other human concerns and behaviors.[4] Yet, these *other* researches have made remarkably effective claim to the territory. Before turning to a closer examination of the nature and substance and credibility of the claim, it will be instructive to review some of the halo effects of some of these "genetic explanations."

Is the Issue Really "Hard" vs. "Soft" Science?

In the conventional wisdom and the popular media, genetics is "hard" science with a precise data base and clearly defined empirical referents for its concepts, while sociology is "soft" or, perhaps, not science at all.[5] That depends. If one compares the prediction and control in plant or animal genetics with prediction and control in affective social relations, this is unequivocally true. A basic difference, of course, is the availability of far more tightly controlled experiments in plant and animal genetics, unthinkable in human genetics or human behavioral research (Edlin, 1987). However, in the construction of a knowledge base about such matters as the causes of mental illness, crime, intelligence, and alcoholism, the distinction between the explanatory power of genetics and sociology fades completely. In the language of science, the dependent variable is equally complex for those seeking a genetic explanation as for those seeking a social structural account. However, the social scientists have been far more sophisticated in analyzing the contingencies and patterned variations that render a one-dimensional version of these "dependent variables" scientifically meaningless. To illustrate this point, I will contrast the basic flaws in the assumptions around the "genetics" of the three multidimensional phenomena: crime, race/intelligence, and mental illness.

The Problematic of the Genetics of Criminals

In early January 1982, Sarnoff Mednick, a professor of psychology at the University of Southern California, presented results of his research on "crime and heredity" to the annual meeting of the American Association for the Advancement of Science. Mednick reported on a study of 14,237 Danish men from the Danish adoption records for the years 1924–1927. He found that the rate of criminality among men whose natural parents had been criminals was nearly three times higher than it was among men whose natural parents were law-abiding. He said he found this to be the case even when the sons of criminals were raised in law-abiding families.

On the recurrent theme from those who report such results from twin studies, Mednick also reported that identical twins are more likely to both be criminals (if one was a criminal) than were fraternal twins, even when reared apart.

Here is the print media's account of Mednick's claims of findings on the "biology of crime":

> Criminals Mednick has studied also show strong biological "markers" associ-
> ated with their criminality, he said. Their "galvanic skin responses"—the
> kind of response typically elicited by liars in lie detector tests—show a marked
> difference from non-criminals, Mednick said. Their brain wave patterns
> are different from non-criminals, and so are several other nervous system
> responses, he said.[6]

Mednick is then reported to have stated the following:

> "If this small, active and highly disturbing group could be identified early it
> would have a marked effect on the crime rate," Mednick said. "But the form
> of intervention would have to be attractive and non-punitive."

This concern for identifying criminals early has had the strong endorsement of a president of the United States. When Ronald Reagan was governor of California, he strongly supported those at the University of California at Los Angeles who wanted to establish a Center for the Study and Prevention of Violence. An important feature of the proposed center's work, which Reagan endorsed, was the early identification of violent-prone individuals (Nelkin and Swazey, 1985).[7]

The major methodological strategy in twin studies and related work comparing adopted children to blood relatives is based primarily upon already existing *institutional* records.[8] These institutional contacts with the criminal justice system almost universally represent the population from which one can take and make generalizable statements.

However, there are three basic reasons why studies of crime and genetics are so problematic that it is almost impossible to have much confidence in them. First, the very definition of what constitutes a crime is highly socially variable, depending upon the passage of law, on policing practices and the judicial system of a society, on the point in history, etc.

In 1764 Parliament decreed that the death penalty would apply to those who broke into buildings to steal or destroy linen, or the tools to make it, or to cut it into bleaching-grounds. But the penalties were contained in an incidental clause in an act passed to incorporate the English Linen Company, whose proprietors included Lord Verney and the Right Honorable Charles Townsend (Hay et al., 1975:21)

Even inside a single culture, at a given moment, the social status of the offender is central to the process of determining whether a "crime" has been committed. It is the social scientists of crime who have best articulated, researched, and documented this problem (Currie, 1985).[9] Moreover, studies of crime and genetics are based upon police records, but the records simply record the local customs. For example, if one looks at the record in 250 years of U.S. history, no white man ever committed the crime of rape on a black woman in twelve southern states. If a Scandinavian came to the United States to study crime and genetics (to parallel Mednick's study) and the research was based upon *records,* this whole population of "criminals" would be missed.[10]

Second, the term *criminal* lumps together the one-time offender with the career criminal, the professional and isolated con artist with a bureaucrat in organized crime; it lumps together the hit-and-run driver with the rapist; it even lumps together the inadvertent poacher on the land of the gentry with a deliberately adulterous member of the gentry (Hay et al., 1975:189-253). What it typically does not do is lump together the crimes of corporate executives with the crimes of the common thief and burglar. The implications of this for a genetic explanation of crime have not escaped the Supreme Court of the United States. It was noted in chapter 2 how in *Skinner v. Oklahoma,* the Supreme Court ruled in 1942 that the sterilization of a man because he was a third-generation criminal was in violation of the equal protection clause of the Constitution, unwarranted because the prosecution had not demonstrated that the more privileged classes could not similarly be prosecuted. The State of Oklahoma's *Habitual Criminal Sterilization Act* provided that one convicted of three felonies could be "rendered sexually sterile."

> Skinner had been convicted of stealing chickens in 1926 and had been found guilty of armed robbery in 1926 and 1929. . . . [The U.S. Supreme Court] chose to overturn the law because it violated the Fourteenth Amendment's guarantee of the equal protection of the laws. Oklahoma had exempted certain kinds of felons from its reach. Offenses against prohibition, revenue laws, embezzlement, and political crimes were deemed insufficient for sterilization. This clear bias in favor of white-collar criminals was judged by the Supreme Court to be "unmistakable discrimination" (Reilly, 1977:126–127)

I shall return shortly to this very matter of systematic distortion in the scientific literature on crime as it relates to privilege, power, and genetic explanations.

Finally, what constitutes a criminal is not as straightforward as it appears. One way of defining a criminal is to simply say that it is someone who has committed a crime. However, there is a competing definition, which characterizes a criminal as someone who has been *convicted* of a crime. Not all those who commit crimes are convicted.[11] Only a small percentage of such persons are arrested, fewer still are prosecuted, only a fraction of these are convicted, and even a smaller percentage incarcerated. Serious students of the topic have reported for at least the last three decades that, for the bulk of crimes committed (reported and known to the police), the fall-away rate can be as high as 80 percent. In Skolnick's (1966) earlier study of a police department in a major city of the United States, less than 25 percent of the burglaries were cleared by arrest and prosecution (much less conviction and incarceration). The figure was only slightly higher for robberies, a repeated pattern in reports from around the nation (President's Commission on Law Enforcement, 1967), and this has not changed in the last two decades (FBI Uniform Crime Report, 1988).

To understand the sieve of the criminal justice system that produces the remarkable skew of human subjects that show up in prisons, it is necessary to move from the commission of the act characterized in law as a "crime" to the point of conviction. Starting with the arbitrary figure of 1,000 burglaries, it is generous beyond the best empirical research now available to say that 700 will come to the attention of the police (Reiman, 1984). Of these, at most 300 will be "cleared by arrest," and a maximum of 180 would go to trial. Of these, at most 120 would be convicted (often plea bargaining lessens the "crime" to a different category). Of these, no more than 75 will ever spend any time in prison. To designate this the "criminal population" for purposes of research is obviously not a sound procedure. Yet, it is from these records that researchers come along to obtain their data on the "genetics" or "biology" of criminals.

The assumption lodged in the genetic explanation of criminals based upon prison incarceration studies is that the population "in hand" (in contact with the institutional sieve) can be related to the putative genetics of the phenomena. Rates of incarceration vary from country to country, as indicated in the following European rates of incarceration:

When reviewing the incarceration rates in the United States, the striking figure is the difference by race. For whites, 65 per 100,000 are locked up, which comes close to the European figure. But for blacks, the rate is an astonishing 544 per 100,000 (Dunbaugh, 1979). In certain states, the racial breakdown and difference is even more dramatic. In Maryland, from 1973 to 1977, the imprisonment rate for whites went from 42 to 69 per 100,000; for blacks, however, the leap for the same period went from 467 to 823 per 100,000 (Dunbaugh, 1979).

If one were doing a correlational study looking for the "genetic component" in imprisonment, one could find a "significant" statistic that would show the importance of "genes" (in this case, race). If one were to use the data presented above on incarceration rates with correlational studies, by race, one would have far more significant correlations than any previously reported in all the studies of IQ and genetics, crime, kinship and genetics, or in any of the adoptive/biological relative studies of schizophrenia. If one were looking for the "genetic" evidence, using the same theoretical approach and methodological techniques of reviewing institu-

Table 6.1 European Incarceration Rates Per 100,000

England and Wales	81.3
Denmark	69.8
Sweden	61.4
France	61.1
Italy	51.2
Spain	39.9
Norway	37.1
Netherlands	22.4

Dunbaugh, 1979

tional records, such a correlational study must conclude that there is a high probability of a "criminal gene" and that it is related to "race." Yet, that is precisely the kind of erroneous conclusion that Bohannan (1960) "laid to rest" some three decades ago in his study of African homicide patterns. The African rate is lower than the American rate of murder, and much closer to the European rate (Bohannan, 1960:237). In fact, a review of the homicide rates of seventeen different tribes in Africa revealed that most had a rate that was less than half that of the U.S. population (158). At one point, he notes:

> If it needed stressing, here is overwhelming evidence that it is cultural and not biological factors which make for a high homicide rate among American Negroes. (p. 237)

The racial domination of blacks in U.S. prisons has only occurred in the last part of this century. The problem with genetic interpretations is that they are routinely based upon institutional practices at certain historical moments. During the last decades of this century, with blacks constituting about 12 percent of the U.S. population and committing about 60 percent of the reported homicides, and with the incarceration rates reflecting the racial patterns noted above, and with our prisons getting darker and darker, it is only a matter of time before there is a convergence of the halo of the new genetics and the appropriation of that halo by other researchers. Robert Gordon (1987) concluded his research on race and delinquency as follows:

> black-white IQ difference exists even before pupils enter school, that it holds for tests whose content is related to the school curriculum only remotely at best, that it is not changed in the course of schooling, that it has not decreased over time despite the substantial reduction of black-white differences in the amount of schooling attained, and that the difference has been demonstrated not to depend on differences in the same underlying *g* that accounts for individual differences within each race. It is time to consider the black-white IQ difference seriously when confronting the problem of crime in American society. (Gordon, 1987:91–92)

Many years ago, two scholars enjoined social scientists to spend more of their time studying the deviance of those in power, to at least bring some balance to the study of those without power. In the late 1960s, Martin Nicolas coined a popular phrase when he said that sociologists of deviance spent too much of their time with "their eyes down, and their hands up." He called attention to the warped imbalance of the vast amount of time, resources, and energy social scientists spend looking at people at the bottom of the social order (prostitutes, traditional criminal gangs, organized crime, drug addicts, etc.). Noting that these researchers were being funded to engage in such research by federal and state governments, and by private foundations, Nicolas pointed to the sharp contrast of the relatively few studies done on the deviance and criminal behavior of those in power.[12] Laura Nader (1972) made a similar point when she enjoined anthropologists to balance their studies of tribal peoples and do more research on power and privilege, what she called a requirement to "study up."

There has been a plethora of data collected and published in the last decade documenting the pervasive character of crime among the most privileged strata of the society (Simon and Eitzen, 1982; Simpson, 1987; Clinard and Yeager, 1980; Mokhiber, 1988). These crimes range from criminal homicide prosecution and conviction to the knowledgeable continued pollution of workplace air with a substance known at the time to be cancer-causing (Brodeur, 1985). Other researchers have documented the increasing routinization of illegal practices among the most privileged sectors of the society (Mintz, 1985; Jackall, 1988; Hochstedler, 1984; Braithwaite, 1984; Fisse and Braithwaite, 1983).[13] The issue is often crime, often resulting in death to innocent victims, not only the violation of regulatory statutes. Yet, the implicit injunction from the culture is so powerful that when researchers summarize the data on "crime and genetics" (Wilson and Herrnstein, 1985:90:103), there is no conceptualization of the upper strata of the society as the subject matter. Indeed, the one time that Wilson and Herrnstein refer to white-collar crime is to note that blacks make up about one-third of those arrested for fraud, forgery, and counterfeiting, and for receiving stolen property, and one-quarter of those arrested for embezzlement. They note that blacks are therefore overrepresented even in these categories. But they follow this with an insidious conclusion that white overrepresentation in securities violations and tax fraud schemes is mainly a function of the fact that blacks lack access to high-status occupations (Wilson and Herrnstein, 1985:462). In other words, when whites commit more crimes at the top, they attribute this to opportunity structures; when blacks commit more crimes, it is implicitly more a feature of their race.

In all of the adoption and twin studies around crime, none addresses the possible criminal genetics of the privileged strata (Marsh and Katz, 1985). Indeed, it seems a jarring concept to even consider. And that is of course the point. "Genetic explanations" of crime are appropriated to account for those at the base of the social order.

Appropriation of Genetics for IQ and Race

The problem with trying to define something called "intelligence" with a written IQ test has been substantially critiqued by others (Schiff and

Lewontin, 1986; Lewontin et al., 1984:83–129; Kamin, 1974). Jean Lave (1983) finds children on the streets of Brazil very skillful in their verbal and quantitative transactions, but these same children "fail" the exact same questions once rephrased and adapted into the style of the classroom. These criticisms are independently important, but adding the genetics of race substantially undermines the whole formulation. It is precisely in the United States where 250 years of interbreeding between whites and blacks during slavery makes problematic any scientific rendering of the racial makeup of American blacks, yet most of the empirical work on black-white differences has been done in the U.S. It is fundamentally a social definition that converts a child into a "black" when that child has any traceable black ancestry. Thus, one could be anywhere from 1/32 to 32/32 black, and both stand for black in America.[14] Obviously, while this is genetic nonsense, it is powerful social and environmental reality.

The pursuit of the ideal scientific study of race[15] and intelligence would specify the empirical referent for each concept in ways that are culture-free, and either is an impossible task. The researcher would first have to find a location where there was almost no "race-mixing" and yet where the different races experienced similar environments. The United States has had the opposite experience. As Goldsby (1985) and many others have pointed out, blacks and whites are increasingly segregated residentially, with great differences in educational, cultural, and occupational experiences. Meanwhile, slavery, an institution that predominated for nearly two-thirds of the nation's history, produced substantial "race-mixing." Second, the empirical referent for "intelligence" would have to have some focus that requires the demonstration of "intelligence" in an appropriate and relevant situation. That is elusive, of course, and contingent upon the interests and motives of those who frame the test and define the situation.

One of the criticisms of social science generalizations by those who adopt the physical science model is that there is relatively little control over a vast array of variables in human affairs. This criticism can hardly suddenly dissipate in the realm of the "genetics of intelligence," where indeed it becomes the most overpowering criticism of all. Indeed, this is exactly where the appropriation of genetic explanations is on the weakest scientific grounds. Every criticism leveled at the social sciences for not being able to control the myriad of variables *comes back around on these genetic inference studies.* Just because one of the variables, the single gene, is treated as if it were one-dimensional, there is an illusion of precision in other controls:

> Limitations of the power of nongenetic factors are also apparent from a
> study of IQ scores of children raised from infancy in an orphanage under

relatively uniform conditions. In spite of the nongenetic uniformity, the children of parents from upper occupational groups on the average scored higher than those from lower groups. Methodologically none of these studies on adopted and orphanage children are beyond criticism but in the aggregate they leave little doubt as to the existence of genetic differences in the mean endowments of different socioeconomic sub-populations. (Stern, 1977)

This is an extraordinary statement. Children raised in an orphanage are "under relatively uniform conditions"? A host of social, economic, personality, ethnic, birth-order, etc., factors that are in continuous variance and interaction fall away and are suddenly "relatively uniform." Race is not explicitly the subject of this quotation, but socioeconomic status and race have high enough correlations so that the leap would not be significant.

An important study that has attempted to assess the importance of class and environment on IQ was completed in France by Schiff and his associates (1982). The research team found thirty-two children from working-class families who had been adopted before six months of age by upper-middle-class families. They compared the IQ scores of these children with that of their twenty biological siblings who had remained with their working-class families. By school age, the adopted children had an average IQ of 111, sixteen points higher than the average IQ of their siblings.

In the earlier discussion, it was noted that most of the data bases for larger correlational studies come from institutions, and rely upon an assumed, even socially neutral contact with those institutions. That is true for studies of crime and genetics, for IQ studies where the two major institutions are the family and the school, and for research (and the resulting available data) on patterns of mental illness. In this realm, institutional factors play a formidable role in skewing these data along socially patterned lines. As the data are reconfigured by the convenience of a collection strategy mandated by an empirical research design, researchers looking for the genetics of the phenomena may not even be aware of these intersecting institutional forces. We have an abundance of data indicating that select parts of a population do not bring their families and friends to mental health facilities for social and cultural reasons. Woo (1989) indicates that the low rate of utilization of mental health facilities (the very backbone of these "genetic-schizophrenia" correlations) among many Asians is explained partly by strong negative cultural sanctions against giving up a family member to a care-taking institution of the larger society. Admitting that one cannot "take care of one's own" *(pao tin* in Chinese) is a fate worse than living with the problem (Tong, 1971). Yet, the positivistic approach to data on schizophrenia and ethnicity based upon the kinds of correlations used in registry studies (data collected from institutional records) would skew any understanding of mental health issues among Asians.

A plausible methodology would have to address the prior research issue of how institutional rates were constructed (Kitsuse and Cicourel, 1963). This is hardly possible with studies based upon the Scandinavian registries from the first part of the century. Yet, these correlational studies from already-constructed rates of contact with an institution and the resulting records are the very foundation pegs of the dominant methodological and theoretical claims for a connection between genes and "crime" or genes and "mental illness."

Appropriating the Genetics of Mental Illness

For a number of reasons, then, claims for a larger role for genetic explanations in the previous two areas of crime and intelligence have met with considerable resistance. There is greater resonance among both the informed laity and more consensus among researchers and their critics concerning the genetic explanation of certain forms of mental illness, especially schizophrenia. *There may well be a considerable genetic component in mental illness.* However, close scrutiny of the basic research in this area reveals that the claim is much weaker than one would have guessed, given the relatively strong consensus.

The first problem is the variation in the definable entity. For most of this century, psychiatrists in the United States have been twice as likely to make a diagnosis of schizophrenia as European psychiatrists (McGuffin and Sturt, 1986). As we shall see, much of the baseline data used to make putative judgments about the genetic component of schizophrenia are from institutional records compiled on two continents before a consensus was forged in the last two decades. Because of this, some analysts have voiced serious cautions about any generalizations about the genetics of the phenomenon (Abrams and Taylor, 1983).

In a review of the literature on twin and adoption studies, Hoffman (1985) effectively criticizes these studies for their fundamental method-ologically flawed assumptions.[16] Most adoption studies have little or no biological data on one crucial set of parents, and must therefore rely on the differences between the biologic and adoptive families to infer the genetic effect. There are so many other possible variables that could explain observed differences[17] that to leap to the genetic explana-tion requires more faith than commitment to scientific rigor and controls.

I will briefly review three classical sets of studies which present evidence that genetic factors are important in the explanation of schizophrenia. It must be kept in mind that there is no known gene for schizophrenia.[18] Thus, in the epistemology of science, the genetic studies that I am about to summarize are based upon correlations, and are entitled to scientific status equal to that of any correlational study where the researcher must try to control for a wide range of potentially important variables. Further, as the researcher approaches the problem for study, this range of variables can appear infinite, limited only by the theory or perspective employed, or clues in the body of research previously reported on the topic.

A landmark study that purports to show genetic predispositions to schizophrenia is the work of Seymour Kety and his associates (1968). This work dominates the literature, and is often referred to as a centerpiece of such research.[19] Kety et al. used the records of all adoptions in Denmark from 1924 to 1947. From these records, they identified 33 "schizophrenic index cases." Next, they selected a control group of normal adoptees, and matched for sex, age, age at time of adoption, and the socioeconomic status of the adopting families.

For these 66 cases, the researcher identified 463 "biological" relatives. They then went on to contrast the biological relatives of the adoptees who were schizophrenics with the biological relatives of the controls, who were "normals." They reasoned that "if schizophrenia were to some extent genetically transmitted, there should be a higher prevalence of disorders in the schizophrenia spectrum among the biological relatives of the index cases than in those of the controls" (Kety et al., 1968:353).

For the 150 biological relatives of the 33 schizophrenic index cases, they found that 13, or 8.7 percent had "schizophrenia spectrum disorders," while only three, or about 2 percent of the 156 biological relatives of the controls, were so categorizable. They report this difference as highly significant. It is very questionable whether this difference is to be taken as "significant," as a cursory review would lead us to believe. The way in which the researchers defined the "schizophrenia spectrum" is worth noting. For the biological relatives, they distinguished three categories and rated the subjects as (1) acute or chronic schizophrenic, (2) borderline, or (3) having inadequate personality. They then lumped these three categories together and entitled this "schizophrenic spectrum disorder."

Next, looking only at biological half-siblings, Kety et al. found a 10 percent incidence of schizophrenia among the biological half-siblings of the controls. Again, they find this to be statistically significant, and suggest it as evidence for the biological transmission of schizophrenia. In this particular case, the reference is to a maximum of 3 people, in Denmark, between 1924 and 1947.[20]

If this were a correlational study trying to show the relationship between cigarette smoking and some illness, it would be soundly criticized for such methodological problems as the small number, the retrospective character of the data, and the clear problematics in the construction of the categories. Were the biological half-siblings of the schizophrenics immersed in an environment (family) productive of difficulty in coping with the world? When Kety et al. found that the adoptive parents of schizophrenic children were more likely to suffer from some psychiatric disorder than the parents of nonschizophrenics, they did take this to be evidence of powerful environmental forces.[21]

A second classical study that claims to show how genetics explains mental illness more than does environment is also based upon Danish data, taken from the Danish Twin Registry from 1870 to 1920 (Fischer, 1971). Two sets of children are compared. The first set were the offspring of 21 monozygotic (identical) twins who had been diagnosed as schizophrenic. There were 47 such children. The second set of children were the offspring of the 21 identical twins who were "normal." There were 25 such children. Fischer found six cases of psychosis among the offspring, equally distributed between the two sets of children. She reports the data as follows:

> In group 1, consisting of 47 children, three schizophrenic cases and one suicide were found, giving a morbidity risk of 9.4 percent after age correction.
> In group 2, consisting of 25 children, they were also three schizophrenic cases. The morbidity risk after age correction was 12.3 percent (not a significant difference from group 1).
> The present investigation gives no support to the hypothesis that environmental factors, associated with being reared by a schizophrenic parent, should cause more schizophrenia in the offspring, since controls reared by a non-schizophrenic had the same morbidity risk. (Fischer, 1971:51).

Then she makes the remarkable statement:

> The result could be explained as due to factor(s) equally present in the schizophrenic MZ twins and their normal co-twin. As a pair of MZ twins are genetically identical, a hereditary factor is the most likely explanation. However, the present material is of such limited size that no conclusion can be drawn. (Fisher, 1971:51)

The final study in this set also comes from Scandinavia (Kringlen, 1968). Kringlen's data comes from the Norwegian birth register, from 1901 to 1930. His final sample contained 342 pairs of twins. Seventy-five pairs were identical twins (monozygotic), and 257 pairs were fraternal twins (dizygotic). Among 55 pairs of identical twins, 14 pairs (about 25 percent) were found where both twins had a severe mental disturbance as reported by the hospital register.[22] In contrast, among 142 fraternal twins, they found only 14 pairs (about 8 percent) where both twins had a diagnosis of severe mental problems. These data are interpreted cautiously by the author, but when cited in the literature, these studies are treated as compelling evidence of a genetic cause of mental illness.[23] Yet, since the overwhelming proportion of even identical twins is reported as discordant for serious mental disorder (i.e., where one had such a diagnosis, the other did not), one could as easily read these very data to compel the conclusion that environment is dominating the genes (Dworkin and Lenzenweger, 1984).[24] This is in sharp contrast with current concordance figures for autism, where over 95 percent of identical twins are concordant for autism, while the figure for fraternal twins is 23 percent (Ritvo et al., 1985). That kind of evidence is by far more compelling as requiring a genetic explanation of autism than of any parallel research on schizophrenia.

Since the three sets of studies summarized above, there have been scores of publications using the same underlying logic, and similar methodological strategies (Baron et al., 1985a, 1985b; Kendler and Gruenberg, 1984;[25] Soloff and Millward, 1983; and Loranger et al., 1982). In addition to a comparison of concordance rates for twin pairs, a basic assumption is that if schizophrenia or related mental disorders (schizophrenia spectrum disorder, schizotypal, even borderline personality disorders) are found in higher proportion in the blood relatives of those with a mental problem than in the relatives of controls, this is evidence for the genetic component of the disorder. While it is the structure of the argument that is being addressed, I should also point out that not all the research reaches this conclusion. A more recent study found no schizophrenia in 199 first-degree relatives of 39 schizophrenia patients (Pope et al., 1982). Two other studies found much lower rates than previous reports of morbidity risks of schizophrenia in first-degree relatives of schizophrenics (Abrams and Taylor, 1983; Tsuang, et al., 1980).

This summary critique of a set of studies arguing for a genetic component of mental illness is not intended to dismiss such claims. A growing body of work in this area makes a possible link suggestive. Rather, the strength of the claims so far outstrips the strength of the evidence that one must wonder why so much passion is generated in discounting or discouraging other approaches to the problem of schizophrenia.[26] Some critics and analysts have wondered aloud how researchers can feel so strongly and confidently in this area, given the state of the evidence (Lewontin et al., 1984:227). Part of the answer may lie in the notion of *penetrance*. The working assumption for the typical pattern for the display of a single-gene trait is that the individual manifests the trait determined by the genotype. However, since in reality the environment (biological as well as social) interacts with the genes, there will be variation in the ways in which individuals manifest their genotype. Even single-gene autosomal dominant traits can show irregularities in expressed transmission patterns. When this occurs, the trait is said to be *incompletely penetrant*. It is therefore possible to better understand why observational work in this area, even when confronting confounding evidence, can fall back (often legitimately) on the notion of incomplete penetrance.

A somewhat different line of work has attempted to get at the genetics of schizophrenia by examining the presence or absence of particular chromosome structure (HLA antigens) thought to be associated with the disorder. One group (Smeraldi et al., 1986) has examined the associations in family members, but the evidence was not conclusive. Authors of a recent summary of the literature on HLA antigens and schizophrenia were more hopeful than the summary seemed to warrant (McGuffin and Sturt, 1986).

One of the driving forces behind a better understanding of what causes schizophrenia is the desire to come up with an effective treatment.

A different kind of correlational research finds that the state of the economy and the amount of mental illness in the population have some relationship: hospitalization for mental disorders varies significantly with the rate of unemployment. Using admissions data to New York state mental hospitals from 1842 to 1967, Harvey Brenner (1973) found that when employment levels went down, the rate of admissions to mental hospitals went up. He employed a technically intricate method to help account for the time lag between a downturn in the economy and the variable rates of entry. Moreover, with a base of more than 6,000 cases, he was able to stratify with a number of important theoretically informed controls to show systematic variation by age, sex, marital status, and socioeconomic status. Brenner found that people of higher socioeconomic status seem more sensitive to downturns in the economy.

The most recent long-term correlational study is by Warner (1987). He shows that the recovery rates from schizophrenia are related to the condition of the economy. Warner reviewed 68 follow-up studies of schizophrenia in Europe and North America since the turn of the century, and found a strong correlation between complete, symptomatic recovery and levels of employment. With respect to the central question of treatment, Warner documents that

> recovery rates from schizophrenia are not significantly better now than they were during the first two decades of the century. The arrival of the antipsychotic drugs shortly before 1955 appears to have had little effect on long-term outcome. (Warner, 1987:70)

Then there is the classic work on social class and mental illness by Hollingshead and Redlich (1958). Reviewing data from mental hospitals, clinics, and private psychiatrists in New Haven, Connecticut, Hollingshead and Redlich found a startlingly high correlation between class position and diagnosis of psychosis. The relationship is inverse. That is, when a diagnosis of personality disorder is made on persons at the bottom of the social order, nine times in ten it will be a serious psychosis. Conversely, psychosis was infrequently the diagnosis for members of the highest social class. The data are no less striking from a more recent study of depression and social class (Brown and Harris, 1978). The researchers found that middle-class women living in a predominantly working-class area of London were far less likely to experience severe depression than working-class women. The rate of this and related mental health problems among the working-class women was approximately 25 percent, but only 6 percent among the middle class.

In these social science studies of mental illness, the researchers are clearly making inferences about the causal nexus in the association between mental illness and the economy on the one hand, and mental illness and social class position on the other. Any such correlational study has a superabundance of methodological problems. As I have already indicated, the analytic status of the leap from correlation to explicit and patterned "nexus of association" to implicit "antecedent conditions" implying causation places the work on genetics of schizophrenia and unemployment and mental illness on the same footing in the epistemology of science. Both kinds of studies reveal a "relationship" to mental illness with some variable empirical support, but neither controls enough of the many variables to demonstrably get at the causes. Still, there is something plausible here.

Suppose these researchers had looked instead at the association between "genetics" and poverty or (un)employment. They might well have combed the Scandinavian registries and found a higher incidence of concordance for identical twins working (or unemployed) than for fraternal twins. Would this higher rate of concordance for employment have permitted these researchers to have concluded (statistical significance notwithstanding) that there is a genetic predisposition to employment, or a genetic transmission of employability? It is rather the social and theoretical framework in which questions are asked that generates the body of empirical literature on the topic, and which in turn inclines "treatment" towards either the biological destiny or the social order.

"Appropriation" and the "Genetics of Depression"

Correlational twin studies have dominated the methodological strategy to impute a genetic base for human behavior (in sharp contrast to a clinical manifestation of an "illness"), and the search for harder evidence is multifaceted. Weitkamp and his associates published an article (1981) in which they claim that they may have *located* a contributing agent to explain depression. Indeed, they named Chromosome 6, and postulated that a susceptibility-to-depression gene might be lodged thereupon. These researchers did not, however, make a discovery of some chromosome abnormality or genetic marker, then observe its clinical manifestation. Rather, they were working backwards from a diagnosis of "depressive" towards the hypothesized susceptibility:

> If an increased number of susceptibility genes in a person results in an increased probability of illness, it follows that in nuclear families that are ascertained through affected offspring, the higher the proportion of offspring affected, the higher the probability of more susceptibility genes in the parents. Increased HLA haplotype sharing among affected siblings is most likely to be evident when the genetic susceptibility that could be contributed by either parent is limited to a single allele at an HLA-linked locus. Increased HLA haplotype sharing is less likely when either parent has two HLA haplotypes containing genes that confer susceptibility, or possibly when a parent has susceptibility genes on other chromosomes. (Weitkamp et al., 1981:1,302)

To provide a sense of the number of controls that might have been done to check for spurious correlations, we need only cite the very small number of subjects involved. Quoting again from the study:

> Of 120 families studied, 20 met the criteria of containing at least two affected members, either siblings or a parent and offspring, and consented to participate. These families were not intended to be representative of the occurrence of depressive disorders in relative probands; they were selected for constellations of affected and unaffected family members that would be useful for the analysis described below. Within the 20 families there were 30 sibships with two or more siblings, at least one of whom had a depressive disorder. (Weitkamp et al., 1981:1,301)

I would like to call close attention to the way in which the Weitkamp article on inheritability introduces the subject matter. Following is a quotation from the very first two paragraphs. Note the careful phrasing of how "well established" is the data base indicating that depressive disorders are "at least in part" attributable to the transmission of vulnerability genes (Weitkamp et al., 1981:1,301).

> An increased concordance for disease in monozygotic twins (57 per cent versus 14 per cent, respectively) and the correlations between adopted per-

sons and their biological relatives indicate the well-established familial incidence of primary depressive disorders can be attributed at least in part to
transmission of vulnerability genes. (Weitkamp et al., 1981:1,301)

There is a fundamental fallacy in this "well-established" base of data,
constructed as it was on correlational data from twin studies and biological and adoptive relative data already critiqued. Kamin (1974) called
attention to this with an analogy, and even though his critique was aimed
at the genetics/IQ controversy, it is apt here:

The fallacy can be illustrated by an analogy. There was a sense in which
black slavery had a clear genetic basis. The black man's color is determined
by his genes, and there was a strong tendency for slavery to run in black
families. The black man was a slave "because" of his genetically determined
skin color. We do not conclude from these observations that the black man
carries slavery genes. We cannot conclude from twin studies that there are
"IQ genes," although we recognize that in an indirect sense genes are involved in determining twin IQ resemblance. (Kamin, 1974:100)

The controversy around the genetics of depression, or of intelligence,
will continue, but not so much upon the terrestial firmness of a well-
established set of correlations plagued with heretofore insurmountable
barriers to the most elementary scientific controls.

Why are there "appropriated genetic" studies of these three phenomenon, while no "appropriated genetic" studies exist for the crimes of the
privileged, i.e., of white-collar and corporate crime.[27] The answer lies in
the cultural frame of the questions to be asked, not in the compelling
evidence gathered on the three issues for which there is such appropriated genetic study. That is, just as the Rubik's cube is a useful metaphor
for thinking of a wide array of possible DNA combinations, it is also
useful for thinking of how certain pathways of knowledge get developed
in these appropriated genetic studies. For those who work on these
studies, there is a tendency towards "normal science" and not substantial
concern in the published work with discussion or reflection on the problematic character of the paradigm itself (Fujimura, 1988).

The nature of the evidence is sufficiently problematic as to make the
claim no stronger than in any other line of work in which an appropriation of genetics would make equal theoretical sense. That is, the task is
to demonstrate that the central issue here is not the genetics of the
phenomenon, but the commonsense world of social action that generated
the cultural and theoretical frame to pursue this line of research in the
first place.

7

Eugenics by the Back Door

If in the First Act, you hang a gun upon the wall,
by the Third Act, you must use it.
                    Chekhov

The front door to eugenics is closed. Hitler's *Lebensborn project*, the most infamous attempt in this century to produce "good babies," cast a chilling pall over the frontal assault, the direct route.[1] While we have witnessed the development of sperm banks, *in vitro* fertilization, and artificial insemination, only a small fringe will take the public stage and argue for eugenic aims. Shockley and a few others have espoused a kind of selective breeding of the "good" genetic ("eu-genic") stock, but would-be human breeders remain a tiny node on the periphery of the current genetic revolution. They are likely to remain so. The romantic imagery of Romeo and Juliet is deeply rooted, and shopping at a sperm bank is not something we are likely to see in 1994, or the year 2000. Rather more indirectly, our late twentieth-century Romeo and Juliet will still take their chances of making a good baby, but if they can get a boost from the new technology to insure that they won't have a "defective" baby, a personal head-on confrontation of the eugenic issue need never occur. But what of the social policy concern of disease prevention? Here, I believe, a subtle and subliminally compelling idea is starting to penetrate the collective conscience, namely, that the "defective fetus" can be eliminated.

This book has been aimed at stimulating a general public debate, rather than advocating a single or specific policy. Insofar as I have public policy suggestions, they are made in the spirit of advancing that debate. Accordingly, there is a need to clarify the central issues *converging* on the horizon. Indeed, it is the convergence that I mean to emphasize. As isolated issues, they hardly present grounds for a eugenic concern. For example, there is nothing particularly disturbing about the search for genetic markers for susceptibility to a disease. Indeed, it can be applauded as providing one more piece of weaponry in medicine's arsenal against disease. However, when placed in a larger framework of related developments, the picture is less benign.

In chapter 6, it was noted that the achievements and the promise of the new technologies relevant to human genetics extend a halo of legitimacy to resurgent appropriations of genetic accounts. Among the most consequential of these achievements for public policy is the burgeoning prenatal detection of inherited disorders, which has spawned an array of gene screening programs and registries at the state and national levels. Even more significant, these gene screening programs serve risk populations that overlap ethnic and racial groups. At the same time, recent successes in molecular genetics have shifted the prism to a search for genetic markers of susceptibility for multifactorial disorders, such as heart disease, diabetes, and mental illness—that is, disorders which are caused by a yet unknown interplay of genetic and environmental factors. It is my contention that the foregoing issues coalesce with three developments which, while on the surface only peripherally related, converge to dramatize the political direction in which genetic programs are headed. These developments include: (1) higher rates of cardiovascular disease and major cancers among major ethnic and racial grouping, especially blacks; (2) the increasing domination of racial and ethnic groups among convicted criminals and the mentally impaired; and (3) under the banner of health, medicine, and science, the appearance of the Human Genome Project. I begin with a discussion of the context in which any disease prevention model needs to be examined.

Sylvia Tesh and the Notion of "Hidden Arguments"

In a recent work that reviews competing theories of disease prevention policies over the last two centuries, Sylvia Tesh (1988) provides an astute analysis of the subterranean political ideologies that undergirded each position. Cholera epidemics and other contagious diseases frequently devastated segments of the population during the nineteenth century. There was no consensus on how to best address these problems, and there was often open and bitter conflict. Proponents of supernatural theories argued that prayer, penitence, and piety were an important bulwark against disease.

> Because epidemics took a greater toll on the poor than the rich, the healthier rich could employ the supernatural theory as a justification for berating the poor for sinful behavior. . . . One New York minister assured his flock that cholera, which first appeared in the slums, served to "promote the cause of righteousness by sweeping away the obdurate and incorrigible." (Tesh, 1988:18)

Those who held this position were political conservatives locked in a struggle with Jacksonian democrats; who saw poverty as the villain and democracy as salvation. A first major combatant of supernatural theory was "contagion theory." Those who believed in this theory argued that by cleaning, fumigating, and avoiding contact with victims and their waste and garbage, diseases could be avoided or contained.

Contagion theory ran up against two formidable obstacles. First, not everyone who was in contact with the diseased got sick. This was strong evidence to fuel the beliefs of those with alternative views. Second, and more significant for Tesh's formulation, contagion required quarantine and restrictions on travel. But this was the period of great industrial development and increasing regional, national, and international trade. It was crucial to the economy that there be open ports and waterways, with continuous movement along railways and open roads. Quarantine would be an economic disaster. And the merchant class steadfastly rejected contagion theory.

> It was impossible to separate the scientific debate about disease causality from the economic consequences of its application. . . . Hence the theory was opposed not only by the new industrialists, but by a vociferous group of politically liberal physicians who argued against contagionism on economic and political grounds. (Tesh, 1988:15)

If the merchant class rejected both supernatural theories[2] of disease prevention and control, and contagion theory, they had yet an alternative: the belief that personal behavior, personal cleanliness, or what we now term "lifestyle" was the answer. The echo into the twentieth century is clear, in that the premium was placed upon personal hygiene, proper diet, exercise, and emotional health and well-being.

The poor and the workers lacked the combination of resources and will to just change their styles of life. Most lived close to subsistence and had persistently poor health. It was left to yet another theory, a fourth and winning version of disease prevention, to come along. In England, the home of the Industrial Revolution, there emerged in the mid-nineteenth century a utilitarian viewpoint. Its principle advocate and author was Edwin Chadwick, a disciple of Jeremy Bentham himself.[3] In his *Report on the Sanitary Condition,* Chadwick argued forcefully and persuasively that the government was spending too much money on the poor with relief, and that instead it should help them stand on their own. Heavy expenditures in the short run for public health and sanitation measures would more than pay off in the increased health, and therefore the increased productivity, of the workers. The argument was articulated in precisely those terms. The report proposed a sewage system that carried waste from every home, and a water system that pumped water into every home. Its crowning achievement was the passage of the Public Health Act of 1848.

Ultimately, this environmental theory (known as miasma theory) would prevail, at least insofar as public policy was concerned. It suited the new merchant class well enough, in that there was no closing off of trade avenues. The major point is that disease prevention policy lies on the surface, and lying beneath it are "hidden arguments" that reflect political choices and political differences. That is no less true today. In industrialized nations, chronic disorders take the highest death tolls. Heart disease is the biggest killer in the United States, accounting for about one-third of the deaths. It is followed by cancer, which accounts for about one-quarter. In the late twentieth century, the major battle lines are drawn around how much to direct health policies towards the behavior of individuals, and how much to clean up the environment. This debate is not just a matter of difference of opinion about health matters, nor is it merely a disagreement about the scientific state of knowledge. On the latter, there is no decisive victor, and considerable humility. At this level of the debate, we are where we were 150 years ago: there are no cancer breakthroughs, no cure for AIDS; heart disease is the leading cause of death, and there is no consensus as to how to best employ a public health policy to address these issues.

Despite the lack of data that might inform the wisdom of such a commitment, the United States Government is setting aside at least three billion dollars, to fund the Human Genome Project, so that the entire gene map of humans can begin (Palca, 1988:467). Moreover, the twenty major biotechnology companies are shifting their research agendas towards a search for genetic markers for susceptibility to heart disease, diabetes, major cancers, and major mental illness (Nichols, 1988:62). As noted throughout this book, genetic disorders have overlapped racial and ethnic categories. So do environmental and multifactorial disorders. Here, however, is the ominous turn. In the 1930s, blacks were only half as likely as whites to die of lung cancer. Things are now almost reversed. Since 1950, the rate of lung cancer deaths among black men has increased at three times the rate for white men, and age-adjusted rates reveal that the current figure is actually 40 percent higher among black men (Cooper and Simmons, 1985). By some margin then, blacks now have the highest rates of lung cancer and coronary disease.

It will hardly come as a surprise that blacks were increasing their consumption of cigarettes in the last few decades just as whites were decreasing their consumption.[4] Forty percent of black males now smoke, compared to 31 percent of white males. Thirty-five percent of all spending for urban billboards in the black communities of this country is for advertising cigarettes.[5] And yet the top twenty biotechnology firms are *shifting their research efforts to search for genetic markers of susceptibility* to cardiovascular diseases, cancer, and diabetes (Nichols, 1988:62).

As noted, heart disease is the biggest killer of all. At the beginning of the 1980s, blacks were dying from heart disease at more than double the rate of whites, and there is every indication that the trend is worsening.[6] Given the nature of this epidemiology, it is not at all clear that the molecular level is where the nation should commit its limited resources as the most effective attack on its greatest health problems. There are of course competing theories of disease prevention, but the scientific evidence does not point decisively in any one direction. On balance, to the extent that it points anywhere, as I will demonstrate in the next section, it is more towards what we know now that we can affect in the environment, not to some hypothetical, very expensive and mortgaged future.

Disease prevention policy is the surface, says Tesh, and just below the surface is the political ideology which underpins it. She is correct, and the analysis extends to disease prevention as it relates to molecular genetics and the century-old debates from population and Mendelian genetics. Just as in the nineteenth century, the way in which this debate is framed today is of great consequence. What is the question? Or, more to the point raised in the first part of this book, who is posing the question? Is heart disease an individual problem, or is it, as the Jacksonian Democrats argued about disease prevention, to be explained and reduced by addressing risk groups, caught in the vice of some great social transformation and therefore best attacked by a collective assault on poverty? Or, as we move toward the twenty-first century, with the tools of molecular genetics, is it a matter of the *genetic susceptibility* of some individuals, more than others, to get heart disease or lung cancer?

The ahistorical view would lead one to say that since there are competing theories, since both genes and the environment are important, and since both are in interaction, it is only a matter of sitting back to see which has the greater success, or the greater explanatory power. But that is to ignore a recent history rich with suggestive answers. The lung cancer rate among blacks has soared in five decades, and since human gene pools cannot change so rapidly, no one can argue that this is a function of a changing genetic susceptibility. Rather, the 39,000 blacks who died in 1986 from smoking-related diseases did so in large measure because the black smoking rate is higher than the white smoking rate, and in part because blacks are more likely to be employed in occupations and industries with high levels of environmental pollutants, and four times more likely to live in poverty—a combination of factors that just happen to "coincide" with the last half-century of shifting race-related cancer rates. Even so, there are models of successful public policy intervention in public health areas with monumental health problems, to which we now turn.

Successful Models of Prenatal Intervention, Low-Cost and Low-Technology

In 1967, the U.S. Office of Economic Opportunity established the Atlanta Southside Community Health Center, in Fulton County, Georgia. While 40 percent of the county had some form of private medical insurance, in the area in which this center was established, only 1.9 percent had any form of private medical insurance. Only a single physician was serving the area of eighty thousand inhabitants. The center embarked upon a program of information dissemination and prenatal education, identifying high-risk factors such as reducing smoking and alcohol consumption, and communicating basic information about diet and nutrition to women during the first months of their pregnancies. In the first period, infant mortality rates did not change much (Sogurno, 1987). But between 1977 and 1982, the comparative rates of decrease in infant mortality rates were dramatic:

(a) For the U.S., a 19 percent decrease;

(b) for the State of Georgia, a 21 percent decrease;

(c) for Fulton County, Georgia, a 22 percent decrease;

(d) but for the study area, a 47 percent decrease.

When the results of this study appeared in a journal, they did not command front page coverage in the *New York Times,* and the Associated Press ignored them. Contrast this treatment with the front-page stories in the *New York Times* about a possible location of a genetic marker on a designated chromosome, with only the "possibility" that one had discovered a genetic component to multifactorial clinical depression (see the Weitkamp article cited earlier in this chapter). Nelkin (1987:33–52) has recently provided an analysis of how the media covers science news, in which she notes how the sensational big promises command attention, week after week after week.

One of the most striking findings from public health and poverty research on the relative roles of class and race comes from another study begun in the 1960s. In 1965, the Human Population Lab study of Alameda County, California, began with a cohort of 1,811 adults aged 35 and over, randomly selected from a federally designated "poverty area."[7] This group was contrasted with those who lived in the more affluent tracts in Oakland. As in the Fulton County, Georgia, study, a high proportion of the study group had no health insurance. The researchers found a higher proportion of mortality among white males in the poverty area than among white males outside that area. The authors concluded that "poverty area residence" was as good a predictor of mortality rates as individual risk factors (Haan et al., 1987:996). That is, there is something about just living in a poverty area that increased one's health risk. Still, there are some success stories in how to deliver health care to the urban poor. It does matter whether one looks at this concentration with a prism of environment or biological inheritance.

The most important health risk for newborns in the United States is not genetic defects, but low birthweight stemming from environmental factors. Low-birthweight babies can be born too soon (preterm births), or even if carried to full term, these babies can be too small (intra-uterine growth retardation). Diet, smoking, alcohol, and drug use are all well established as strongly related to mothers having low-birthweight babies (Korenbrot, 1984; Berhman, 1985). Thus, changing the habits of pregnant women, with elementary shifts in prenatal care in the first and second trimesters, would have a dramatic impact on this problem. This is firmly established in the literature (Gortmaker, 1979). Two studies have demonstrated both the health improvements and the cost savings of early intervention prenatal care.

The first is a national study carried out by a special committee appointed by the Institute of Medicine in the early 1980s. The target population was a national cohort of women 15 to 39 years of age who receive public assistance, and who have less than twelve years of education.[8] Using data from the 1980 census, the study group estimated that about 12,800 live births (about 11.5 percent) would be low-birthweight that year (Behrman, 1985:214). Using such factors as initial hospitalization costs and select but routinely required repeat hospitalizations during the first year following birth of low-birthweight babies, the conservative estimate placed the cost minimally at $13,000 per infant, for a total of well over $170,000,000. In contrast, it was estimated that it would cost approximately $400 per pregnant woman to provide adequate prenatal care, for a total of about $12,000,000 for the full national cohort (Behrman, 1985:227). Thus, just a small percentage decrease in the low-birthweight rate would result in savings of several million dollars during the first year alone. Later savings were not even included here, and the health factor itself is beyond a straightforward cost-effective analysis in terms of dollars expended.

The second study is from California. The Maternal and Child Health Branch of the state's Department of Health Services carried out a thirteen-county study from 1979 to 1982, aimed at reducing perinatal mortality rates for low-income mothers. One-third of the fifty-eight counties in the state had no resident obstetrician in the Medi-Cal program in 1977, and "the proportion of obstetricians who accepted Medi-Cal patients actually declined from 65 per cent in 1974 to 46 per cent in 1977" (Korenbrot, 1984:36).

The state lawmakers approved a bill authorizing a pilot project to increase access to obstetrical services in the Medi-Cal program. The strategy was to reimburse health departments and other health providers for prenatal care services on a capitation basis. In a carefully matched control study, a 33 percent reduction in the low-birthweight rate was recorded for those participating in the pilot program (Korenbrot, 1984:40). The study was an unequivocal demonstration of substantial cost savings, since low-birthweight infants need initial hospitalization requiring expensive intensive care, and frequent visits, as reported above in the description of the national study from the Institutes of Medicine. The calculation of the cost-benefit ratio to Medi-Cal budget alone was 1:1.7. "For every dollar Medi-Cal reimburses for expanded prenatal care, the state should save reimbursement of $1.70 in neonatal intensive care" (Korenbrot, 1984:42).

If the health of the population and cost benefits to the taxpayers are the paramount concerns, why has there not been a clamor for great savings by instituting a national program of maternal health care with prenatal services to reduce low-birthweight rates? Why has there not been a Chadwick Report for the twentieth century, showing the cost-benefit analysis of prenatal intervention, focusing upon maternal care in the first trimester? It is because there is a competing, very effective, and seductive lobby. This time around, the lobby is the medical establishment, premier research interests, powerful biotechnology lobbying, and insurance companies (Nichols, 1988). Recall from the two studies summarized above on prenatal intervention in impoverished areas that almost none of the poor had private medical insurance. High rates of infant mortality among the poor and uninsured are of little interest to insurance companies. But a screen for genetic disorders, with a computer registry, might well pique the interest of insurance companies. Recall from the discussion in chapter 3 how most of the major insurance companies even raised the rates of *carriers* of sickle-cell in the early 1970s (Bowman, 1977).

Registered Prenatal Detection as Disease Prevention Policy: The Gun on the Wall

Anton Chekhov once made this observation as an injunction to playwrights: "*If in the first act you place a gun upon the wall, by the third act you must use it.*" In chapter 4 we noted that the California State Department of Public Health must justify its budget requests to the legislature in terms of the cost effectiveness of its health programs (Act I?). At this level, we have merely a flexible administrative accounting principle, the local and empirical manifestation of which is subject to a wide variety of interpretations and strategies. In chapter 5, we noted that the professional ideology of the genetic counselor is that of the neutral provider of information, leaving open to the client the choice of options (Act II?).[9] The "gun in the *third* act" reminds us to keep a close watch. Once this machinery is erected, with the inexorable march of technology, it will be used.

The California study of successful prenatal intervention with maternal education reported above is competing with another California story. In April 1986, California, by far the largest state in the union, with a population of over twenty-seven million,[10] put in place the nation's first fully *mass* screening program for prenatal detection of a birth disorder. The social and political implications are enormous. Because of the significance of this development in California, it is important to provide a brief review of how this program came to be and the rationale behind it.

About two babies in every thousand are born with neural tube defects. Family histories are not predictive, and there are no good guesses or theories as to why or when the disorder will occur. Some unknown combination of the genes and the environment is involved. The effects are frequently devastating. Half the time, the defect is fatal. This occurs when the neural tube, which in the embryo forms the brain and the spinal cord, is arrested early in its development and does not close off at the top. In such a circumstance, the baby is born with either no brain or a very small one (anencephaly), and dies within twenty to thirty days. In the other half of the cases, the tube fails to close along the spine (spina bifida), leaving it exposed:

> Twenty percent of the time, the open spine is covered by skin, in which case the children generally have normal intelligence and, with surgery, have no physical handicaps or only minor ones. The rest of the time, however, the open spine is not covered and the spinal cord and nerve bundles protrude at the site of the defect, sometimes looking like a red lump on the baby's back. Often, these children with "open" spina bifida have an accompanying birth defect that prevents fluid from draining from their heads, a condition called hydrocephaly. This condition can be surgically ameliorated, but often irreversible damage to a child's brain is done before and just after birth by the increased fluid pressure.
>
> Children with open spina bifida usually survive, but many are mentally retarded, many have no bowel or bladder control, nearly all require extensive medical and surgical treatments, and most have some degree of paralysis, usually from the waist down. (Kolata, 1980:1,216)

The test for the detection of whether the fetus has a neural tube defect was first developed in 1972 in Edinburgh, Scotland. While all pregnant women have serum protein, David Brock discovered that there are elevated levels of this protein, called alpha-fetoprotein (AFP), in the blood of women carrying babies with neural tube defects. The problem is that there are other reasons for a woman to have high levels of alpha-fetoprotein, including multiple pregnancies. Moreover, some women with normal pregnancies have high alpha-fetoprotein levels. In any event, in alpha-fetoprotein screening, a blood test for AFP levels is administered between weeks 16 and 20 of the pregnancy, the optimum time for a first diagnosis.

At this time approximately 50 of 1000 pregnant women will have very high alpha-fetoprotein concentrations—above the 95th percentile of the normal range. The test is repeated on these women, and 30 will have a second high reading. These 30 are then given ultrasound scans to check for twins or triplets, for fetal death, and or incorrect gestational dates. The ultrasound will eliminate approximately 15 of the women from consideration. The remaining 15 are given amniocentesis to check for alpha-fetoprotein in the amniotic fluid and also to check for acetylcholinesterase, an enzyme that often is present in the fluid when the fetus has a neural tube defect. (Kolata, 1980:1,217)

California began its alpha-fetoprotein screening program in April 1986. During the first six months, 37,000 women, about half of those eligible, agreed to be screened. Of the first 316 who tested with high enough alpha-fetoprotein levels to warrant follow-up diagnostic procedures, 15 percent had fetuses with neural tube defects.[11]

According to the Center for Disease Control in Atlanta, the annual cost of screening half the pregnant women in the United States would be thirty million dollars. The center estimates that more than twice that amount of money would be saved by mass alpha-fetoprotein screening, including the costs of medical care for children with spina bifida, and work time lost by parents and guardians who must care for these children (Kolata, 1980). However, there are dissenting views from Great Britain. After reviewing the frequency rates and relative costs of a neural tube defect screening program in South Wales, British investigators concluded that, in some circumstances, a better expenditure of funds could be made for other medical and health needs:

[When the prevalence rate is at about 1.25 per 1,000,] spending money to avoid the birth of one surviving child with an open neural tube defect might require the denial of the chance of improved quality and duration of life to five patients needing coronary bypass surgery or 2500 women who might otherwise undergo screening for cervical cancer. (Hibbard et al., 1985:295)

The researchers go on to actively discourage such screening when the prevalence rate falls under 2.5 per 1,000. Since the rate of spina bifida is just about 2 per 1,000 in California, we can see the makings of a vigorous debate, if the public were informed. Rather, we have an articulation of the problem from the British medical approach, currently a much more socialized medical system (but under siege at the end of the 1980s), arguing that perhaps alternative expenditures might be the most effective. On the American side, there is the optimistic formulation about cost savings. Will the debate even take place?

Why, indeed, is there no late twentieth-century *Chadwick Report on Infant Mortality and Low Birthweight?* For one thing, the competition is big science and the more effective voices of elite scientists, driven in part by huge incomes derived from associations with the biotechnology companies (Yoxen, 1983; Wofsy, 1986). There is a greater potential profit to select private interests and individuals from the genetic prism. Unlike the environmental lobby, which is heavily weighted with public servants and private citizens, the molecular genetic lobby has vanguard research and Nobel laureates who will come forward to make the case before Congress or a national television audience.[12] Unlike the environmental lobby, genetics research has built-in cheerleaders from the media whenever there is even a hint of a possible genetic breakthrough (Nelkin, 1987). Finally, the environmental lobby is fighting against an era in which individualized solutions are popular, where attacks on government spending bring applause and votes. It may be short-sighted disease prevention policy; it may even be astronomically expensive in the long run, but three successive presidential elections have been won by the candidate who promised either tax reductions or no new taxes. In such a setting, how much more seductive is it to believe that molecular genetics will (someday) save the day. The infant mortality rate may be high in poor communities, and low-birthweight babies are considerably more expensive to keep alive during that first year, but there is no strong public advocate for this strong public interest. Center stage has been preempted by the search for high-tech, high-prestige suggestion of a solution.

Hidden Arguments and Multifactorial Disorders

In chapter 1, I emphasized the importance of the fact that certain disorders are sometimes arbitrarily labeled as "genetic" when they are really multifactorial, that is, where environmental and genetic factors interact to produce the disorder, as in the case of spina bifida. However, the label "genetic disorder" is usually what sticks, and it in turn becomes a charter for a narrowing kind of preventive action or treatment. This process can be seen to be forming with the way in which heart disease, diabetes, and mental illness are increasingly addressed through a genetic prism of susceptibility, and in the current search for genetic markers. Chronic obstructive pulmonary diseases, which include emphysema, asthma, and bronchitis, are the eleventh leading cause of years of potential life lost in the United States. It is fairly well established that genetic factors play an important role in determining age at onset and severity. Individuals who are homozygous for alpha$_1$ antitripsin are at greater risk for these lung diseases. That risk is greatly exacerbated by smoking, or by being in an environment with high levels of dust, welding fumes, and a number of other substances. Smoking is regarded as a dominant factor, and contributes as much as 50 percent of the known excess risk. The interaction of smoking with other factors is not well understood.

Lappé (1988) has argued that genetic screening for susceptibility for chronic lung disease is a worthwhile project. He bases his judgment on a careful reading of the material base of the interaction between susceptibility and environmental hazards, such as excessive dust in the environment, smoking, etc. Lappé's argument is that people who are at higher risk should be informed, so that they can adjust their personal behaviors and lifestyles to reduce the possibility of disease. With the focus on the individual, Lappé is compelling. So long as it remains a matter of personal choice and lifestyle, this kind of use of genetic screening lacks controversy. However, when it comes to earning a livelihood, there are echoes of "hidden arguments" from the nineteenth-century debates discussed earlier. Workplace genetic screening arguments are heavily saturated with political and economic ideology, much as were the nineteenth-century debates around disease prevention espousing contagion and supernatural theories. Workplace screening encounters old wine in new bottles: how much to we clean up the workplace, or what emphasis do we place on a genetic screen for the workers (Draper, 1986,1990)? However well-intentioned the motives, an orientation towards genetic susceptibility can easily begin to dominate our ways of thinking about disease prevention, until it becomes *the way* that we come to think about the problem. The kind of gene screening in these instances is currently of adults, but it is important to remember that phenylketonuria newborn screening was the wedge for legally mandated carrier screening in the 1960s. That history should be kept in mind with the search for genetic markers in full swing.

We are on the threshold of mass genetic screening for nearly every pregnant woman. With alpha-fetoprotein screening programs, there is a solid infrastructure for expanded prenatal screening. Add the search for genetic markers, with the attendant *tendency for reductionism* of multifactorial disorders, to the singular search for the genetic component of these multifactorial disorders, and we have the highest potential for a synergistic convergence of seemingly separate and isolated developments.

National and State Genetic Registries

In Scotland, where there is considerable racial and ethnic homogeneity, geneticists and public health officials developed a computerized genetic registry system which was already in use in the mid-1970s. The acronym RAPID stands for Register for Ascertainment and Prevention of Inherited Disease. The first step is the location of those at risk for having a child with an inherited disorder, accomplished either directly through carrier screening or through indirect reports and kin association data.

> Clinical and genetic data on individuals and their families are recorded on specially designed cards. Each family is allotted a code number (e.g. 247V—\) and each individual at risk in the family is numbered accordingly, starting with the individual first contacted (e.g. 247V1). Disorders are classified according to the ICD code with the addition of a 5th digit. For ease of storage and retrieval, this information, except for pedigree information, is encoded and then stored on computer file. The present file system can store data on 25–30,000 individuals. Access to the data is through a teletype terminal using the Edinburgh Multi-Access System on an ICL 4–75 computer. (Emery, 1976:16)

Those who have developed the system in Edinburgh are quite aware of the possible misuses or abuses of such a data bank:

> To maintain strict confidentiality of the information on the register we have incorporated a number of security checks in the system. Access to the system is possible only when a valid password A is used. If data are requested the request is first checked for its validity, i.e. correct family names, numbers, and disease codes, etc. Finally, a second password B allows data to be retrieved at different levels depending on the particular operator's password. The clinician or geneticist dealing with a family has access to all the genetic and medical information, but a genetic field worker concerned with tracing relatives may retrieve only pedigree data. Information in the register is released only to other physicians and medical geneticists directly involved in the management of the patient and his family. (Emery, 1976)

British and American geneticists have for some time advocated the development of "computerized genetic information banks" so that relevant data could be made available to those at high risk of transmitting a serious hereditary disorder (Kevles, 1985:277).

It was noted in chapter 3 that the Center for Disease Control began systematizing the collection of data on genetic defects of the newborn in the United States in the early 1980s. The Birth Defects Monitoring Program currently logs data from approximately 1,500 hospitals from around the country, on more than 150 disorder diagnoses. In the period 1981–1986, the program catalogued more than four and a half million births (Chavez et al., 1988:18). The role of the state in such a venture is emergent, and will be quite variable depending upon "archaic" customs, traditions, cultural inclinations, cultural "ethos," and, of course, the nature of the social organizations of various states and countries, their political orders, and their ethnic and racial heterogeneity (culturally defined, but ratified by "at-risk" figures for these identifiable populations for cost-effective screening).

What should be the role of the state and the individual in the utilization and application of this knowledge? The Chicago Bar Association has advocated a change in Illinois marriage laws to require premarital tests for "diseases or abnormalities causing birth defects." Looking down the road to further technological advances, they went on to suggest that

> Illinois might, if and when the feat became technically possible, require from applicants the correction of the genes for certain race-specific maladies—for example, Tay-Sachs or sickle-cell anemia—before it issued a marriage license. (Kevles, 1985:277)

If information about genetic makeup is made known to the individual, there may be a conflict between the state and the individual on the right to bear a child with that defect. Should there be a national registry of those with identifiable "defective" genes clustered in populations that are socially definable? Should the state have the right to inform any prospective mate (at the point of marriage certification, or when?) of the gene-belt information of the other half? Or perhaps, should there be a restriction so that only the person who is the carrier knows, with only the moral or ethical obligation to disclose the information to a prospective mate? Even in the early 1970s, the Danish government adopted a strategy of prohibiting marriage if both parties were carriers of a gene that might result in the fetus having a genetic disorder (Reilly, 1975:319–376). While some of these questions appear now to be only hypothetical, many are either real now or will confront us soon.

The Achievements and the Halo of Molecular Genetics

In the last few years, we have witnessed two remarkable and related developments around the new technology in molecular biology and genetics. The first is the scientific phenomenon itself, the discoveries, experiments, and possible applications of recombinant DNA; the partial successes, the regenerated hopes for cures or therapies for cancer, diabetes, genetic disorders, and the attendant market speculation (Nichols, 1988). These developments are real and consequential, and have moved hundreds of million of dollars into molecular biology laboratories, thereby altering the course of graduate education in the life sciences and redefining the relationship between the academy and the world of business (Yoxen, 1983; Cherfas, 1982; Wolfsy, 1986). Researchers have already isolated and cloned more than three hundred human genes. The hope for gene therapies is that someday it may be possible to target particular cells and insert the "correct" gene in place of the defective one. Fame and fortune await the successful scientist. Placing the focus on individual identification, personal culpability, and shifting lifestyles, in contrast to other forms of disease prevention, the major biotechnology companies in the United States are shifting to a search for DNA markers linked to heart disease, diabetes, and major forms of mental illness (Nichols, 1988:62). A major purpose will be to alert people to the fact that they must change their individual lifestyles, or their personal habits, or their work situations, to reduce their personal risk. We noted above a prime example—gene screening for those with a greater susceptibility to chronic lung disease.

The second development is the increasing receptivity of the population to genetic explanations to human behavior. Parallel to a great transformation of the economy from industrial to service, and the displacements and adjustments that have accompanied this shift, there is a new legitimacy to genetic explanations that the first development has assisted. Articles in the daily press not only suggest that newfound genetic explanations of heart disease, diabetes, and cancer are just around the corner (Nelkin, 1987), but also we find the laity being "informed" of new discoveries of genetic explanations of crime, depression, shyness, intelligence, and mental illness. In December 1981, the national meetings of the American Association for the Advancement of Science heard a presentation about the genetic basis of crime, based upon adoption files from Denmark, originally compiled in the early part of the twentieth century.[13] That same month, the *New England Journal of Medicine* reported a study that claimed new evidence for a genetic explanation of depression (Weitkamp et al., 1981). Both of these stories were front-page news around the United States. Undergraduate students trained in the social sciences refer to newspaper articles about these matters as if the reports provided compelling rather than tentative and suggestive evidence for a genetic explanation of crime and mental health problems.[14]

The promise and achievements in recombinant DNA research at the molecular level have made us vulnerable to (a) the unwarranted and dangerous leap to interpreting this first set of achievements as if it bore some direct relevance to breakthroughs in how we can better understand social life on this planet, and (b) a diversion of attention and resources from other solutions, although there is already evidence that we could make a larger and faster difference (and cheaper) in the reduction of human suffering. With machinery in place, and with this machinery developing and expanding into a national project to map the entire human genome, it is only a matter of time before elliptical eugenic uses are made of these new technologies.

The United States has embarked upon a project aimed at ultimately mapping and sequencing all 3,000 million base pairs in the human genome. The genome is simply the name for the full complex of genes in a species, in this instance, *homo sapiens.* The National Research Council issued a report in early 1988 endorsing the Human Genome Project, and estimated the cost at two hundred million dollars per year, for fifteen years (Palca, 1988:467). In the earliest phases of the project, the NRC report recommended against a single central facility. Instead, it suggested funding individual researchers and medium-sized multidisciplinary groups. The hope is that these individual projects can engage in work that will increase the speed of sequencing tenfold, which is believed to be necessary to move the project along.

In 1988, as an interim arrangement, responsibility for the project was with an interagency committee, chaired by the White House Office of Science and Technology Policy. The National Research Council report could not agree on where authority and coordination should ultimately lie. While most members of the committee that issued the report thought one agency should ultimately have the responsibility, such as the National Science Foundation, the National Institutes of Health, or the Department of Energy, others thought a separate body should be created, and still others favored an interagency committee.

Once again, the major banner for the Human Genome Project would be the prospective gains in health and medicine (McKusick, 1989; Heilbron and Kevles, 1988). Yet, already there are warnings that commercial interests and concerns for profits might cause some private companies to withhold key information. As noted above, here we have another costly exploration into potential and yet unknown health benefits while we already know enough to save millions by applying existing knowledge.

Backdoor Eugenics

Groups have different access to the levers of power that make for effective lobbying around their medical and health interests. Since the Third Reich, paranoia levels have run high when the state enters to screen a population for a genetic problem, especially when the population at risk coincides with the racial and ethnic designations. The political volatility of genetic screening is joined around this convergence, but it is only the first of a large number of new and emergent issues that we must confront.

The government, through federal legislation, state public health departments, and local clinical practices and policies, shapes genetic screening in the "public interest." But since genetic screening affects select groups in new ways of contagion (parents to offspring), the claim of the *general* public interest in shaping the bureaucratic structure of the particular genetic screen is demonstrably less compelling than with a contagious disease like smallpox, where all are considered at risk.

In the next decades, there will and should be conflicting interests voiced about who screens whom, and for what purpose. While some of that screening will be applied to existing social groups (race and ethnicity), genetic screening will also create new social aggregates, such as workers who could not have known before gene screening that they shared a problem, "a genetic susceptibility." Depending upon social factors, whether these persons are fragmented or aggregated by the screening process becomes the critical issue in their abilities to mobilize resources in behalf of their own health intervention.

Genetic screening is inevitable. Hysterical warnings of genocide will always be likely to fall upon deaf ears in a culture, because the "typical citizen" can hardly come to think of himself or herself as living in a society that could be so brutal in its selective extermination of a people. That was as true of the "good Germans" in 1937 as of the "good Americans" of 1830 who could crush human life and quell slave rebellions with Christian righteousness. The direct route to eugenics is not the issue, nor is it likely to be an issue. It is a more insidious situation about which I would issue a warning and venture a prediction.[15]

At the extremes there is a life-threatening genetic disorder, and it is not difficult to achieve a consensus about screening for it. But this is the far end of the continuum. But what should be a public policy, disease prevention stance towards genetic disorders that are not life-threatening, but which make for lifetime dependency, or which are simply unaesthetic? The power of the technological advances is such that there is now a possible new attitude waiting to be adopted—that "the defective fetus" can be eliminated.

The elimination or prevention of the "defective fetus" is the most likely consequence and ultimate meaning of a genetic screen. In a heterogeneous mix, the public forum for this debate needs to be vigorous and informed, not just by modest levels of technical knowledge about genetic or molecular biological developments, but about the role of power and the relative social locations of key actors in the determination of the knowledge, and its application.

Today, about as much as we get in the public sphere is a Nobel laureate in molecular genetics debating on public television (or some other ten-to-fifteen minute forum) a "critic" who wants to shut down the gears of the new science technology. The former is going to "win" every time. By win, I mean that the discourse is always in terms of the medical, health, and scientific benefits, skewing the grounds upon which an informed debate about other social, cultural, and political questions can arise. There are, as Tesh would have it, "hidden arguments" underneath the surface language of neutrality of disease prevention and treatment. These need to be examined and addressed. I do not mean merely a discussion among elites about how these technologies can and should be deployed. Those who will be consumers of the technology need to be part of the discussion. Out of this, an informed public policy could be generated and shaped.

The State of California now requires that all chromosome abnormalities be reported. The reasons, once again, are for the good purposes of health. But now someone else knows that there is an extra X or extra Y chromosome on persons A, B, and C. Many states will follow this lead. It is not just the opportunities for abuse abound; that is true for most human endeavors and achievements. Rather, I would emphasize that these bits of information will be used, for both good and evil, and that ordinary citizens have more choices in this than heretofore realized or exercised. If I have something to add, it is primarily that the hour is late, the technology is closer, and the public debate has not been vigorous. Chekhov's injunction about the gun on the wall simply tells us that it will be used, it does not say how, or at whom it will be pointed. That is to be decided.

8

Human Genetics, Evolutionary Theory, and Social Stratification

From its very inception in the latter part of the nineteenth century, the science of human genetics germinated in, was nurtured by, and was inextricably entangled with the social and political storm of evolutionary theory. There has been both strong continuity and notable change with today's human genetic inquiry. Most commentators have chosen to emphasize the sharp differences from the past when it comes to the danger of eugenics. For example, the esteemed historian of science Daniel Kevles has argued that in today's society, vulnerable and marginalized groups have greater access to strategies and mechanisms for fending off any eugenic resurgence. Despite this, there is a persistent search for "hard data," for a biological or biochemical explanation for homelessness, mental retardation and mental illness, alcoholism and drug abuse, even unemployment, crime, and violent and abusive behavior. The change has come in a thick disguise of the old concerns, the promise of untold health benefits and the lessening of human suffering. Some of these promises will be fulfilled, and some remarkable strides have already been made in the detection of genetic disorders.

Yet these successes have had an unwitting and inadvertent side effect. The demonstrable advances in biomedicine have produced a "halo" over a host of problematic claims about the connection between genes and behavior, so much so that we are witnessing the chameleon-like reincarnation of some of the more regressive formulations of late-nineteenth-century thought.

On the surface, the Human Genome Project, a program to map and sequence the entire spectrum of human genes, has as its primary rationale the improvement of human health. The major goal is the uncovering of

This chapter is based upon an essay of the same name in Mark S. Frankel and Albert Teich, eds., *The Genetic Frontier: Ethics, Law, and Policy* (Washington, D.C.: American Association for the Advancement of Science, 1994), 131–53 (reprinted by permission of the AAAS Directorate).

genetic disorders and susceptibility to disorders . . . and ultimately, the hoped-for development of gene therapies to treat or cure those disorders (Kevles and Hood 1992; Proctor 1991; Bishop and Walholz 1990). But no matter how one slices it, just underneath the talk of a paradigmatic shift, we as a society seem inexorably pulled back to the ancient concern for what could be called "trouble at the bottom, virtue at the top." The fact that the banner of health, medicine, and science waves over the new biotechnologies has lulled us into a complacency, even a receptivity, to a re-hearing of claims made a century ago when the science of human genetics, in its infancy, was most seductive.

From Biological Darwinism to Social Darwinism

One of the most enduring truths in the study of human social life is that all societies are stratified. The unequal access to valuable resources can be based on something as simple as age or as complex as claims to spiritual or intellectual power. But as far back as recorded history permits us to garner evidence, we also know that humans have always tried to justify that stratification. The notion that power and privilege are inherited has a longer and wider history than the notion that power and privilege are achieved. The link between a theory of human biology and social theory has always been a significant force in the history of ideas, but only in the last 150 years has the connection donned scientific clothing. At the core of this relatively recent development is the direct link between biological Darwinism and social Darwinism, and the direct but underappreciated implications for the birth of human genetics. In order to appreciate the subtle, sometimes subterranean continuity between the past and the present, we must go back to those early beginnings.

Charles Darwin's *Origin of Species* is the bible of evolutionary theory, at once a meticulous classification system of organisms and a theory of the evolving relationships between them. In its simplest form, the implications of the taxonomy are known even to grade-school children: At the bottom of the rung is the single-celled amoeba; at the top of the heap is the magnificently complex human. In between are all the combinations and permutations that form an intricate hierarchy of organisms. It is intricate. It is most decidedly a hierarchy.[1]

What of humans? Once we get to the top rung of the ladder of species evolution, biological Darwinism trails off, and like a relay sprinter in a race, huffing and puffing and tired, hands the baton on to the runner in the next leg. The baton was passed from biological Darwinism to social Darwinism.

In the biological version of adaptation, species are ranked along a hierarchy of complexity in evolutionary adaptation, but what about rankings within species? Within, between, and among human groups, was there not also an evolutionary tree? As Darwin had done for biological Darwinism, the English social theorist Herbert Spencer (1820–1903) would issue the canon of social Darwinism. To better understand the climate in which scientific genetics germinated, it is necessary to rescue and restate two important features of late-nineteenth-century thought that have been largely forgotten. The first feature is that Spencer dominated the social thought of his age as few have ever done. By far the most popular nonfiction writer of his era, his ideas were so popular that he sold more than 400,000 copies of his books during his lifetime.[2] In the United States, by the turn of the twentieth century, Spencer had attained the status of a dominant cultural figure among a wide range of American politicians, intellectuals, educators, and public policy advocates (Hofstader 1955). Indeed, he was so influential that Oliver Wendell Holmes once sardonically turned to his colleagues on the Supreme Court to remind them that "Herbert Spencer did not write the U.S. Constitution" (Seagle 1946).[3]

Although Darwin would ultimately distance himself from the more regressive social implications of Spencer's social evolutionary theory, Darwin once called Spencer "about a dozen times my superior" (Darwin 1959, vol. 2, 239).[4] Perhaps more significantly, Francis Galton, the man who both coined the term *eugenics* and who was the founder of the eugenics movement, deeply admired Spencer and was influenced by Spencer's thinking on social evolution (Carneiro 1967, xxix). Not so coincidentally, Galton was also the father of human population genetics, a statistical method designed to study patterns of inheritance as a way of explaining evolutionary developmental stages within and between humans.

The second feature is that while Charles Darwin set the stage, it was Spencer, not Darwin, who would develop the key concepts that would apply evolutionary theory to humans. It was Spencer, for example, who coined the phrase "the survival of the fittest."[5] Herbert Spencer was not focusing his ideas on the animal kingdom, but on social life, human behavior, and the internal differences of evolution among humans.

"As Humans Can Be Stratified in Evolutionary Development, So Can Cultures"

Spencer's influence upon the newly emerging field of anthropology, the new scientific study of human groups across all human societies, was also overwhelming.[6] Not only are humans to be arrayed along a continuum of evolutionary development, but so are the races and the cultures, societies, tribes, and nations in which they live. Just as the idea of a "savage" or a "primitive" was at one end of that continuum, and the "civilized person" was at the other, so, too, was the notion of a primitive or savage society at one end, and a civilized society at the other.

The fundamental basis of the continuum from savage to civilized, wrote Spencer, was the developmental stage of the brain. This was demonstrated, in turn, by the way in which humans adapted to nature and, in particular, to the seasons and the passage of time. The primitive peoples had a sense of time relevant only to such natural events as when birds migrate, or when fall or winter or spring begins. The more advanced and more civilized could encompass decades, even centuries into their thinking, planning, and accumulation. Thus, their brain capacity was vitally stimulated and literally enlarged. The longer the time sequence a human could encompass, said Spencer, the higher the level of intellectual development. At the bottom of the heap were the Australian Aborigines. Just above them were the Hottentots, who were judged one notch superior because they could use a combination of astrological and terrestrial phenomena to make adjustments to time sequences and changes (Spencer 1899). Next on Spencer's social evolutionary ladder were the nomads, just a rung below the settled primitives who lived in huts. Since they stored goods for future use, their conception of and relation to time was thought to be more developed.

Anthropology was born in this same period of evolutionary theory and was saturated by it. Just as humans can be stratified according to their social evolutionary development, it was argued, so too can their cultures. It followed that, once selected individuals from "inferior" cultures came to live in "superior" cultures, there would be a limit as to what their brains, of lower development capacity, could handle. Writing exactly a century before this claim would be made again by Arthur Jensen (1969), Spencer noted in 1869 that black children in the United States could not keep up with whites because of the former's biological and genetically endowed limits, "their [blacks'] intellects being apparently incapable of being cultured beyond a particular point" (Haller 1971, 124).

This viewpoint reached its logical culmination in the work of James George Frazer (1854–1941), who produced a prodigious six-volume work, *The Golden Bough*, that formally stratified cultures and societies along a continuum from simple to complex, from savage to civilized. Frazer posited a three-stage hierarchical theory, that human societies evolve from magic, to religion, and finally, to science.[7] At the bottom of the hierarchy, of course, were primitive cultures.

It is well known that Darwin's biological evolutionary theory was not accepted among Christian clerics at the time.[8] Equally important for the birth of nineteenth-century scientific human genetics, the church had not only fiercely contested the biological evolutionary theory of the ladder from lower creatures to humans, but also had a strong vested interest in attacking the stage theory of social Darwinism. The idea that, over time, humans ascend to higher and higher forms of linguistic complexity, moral reasoning, and spiritual existence was counter to prevailing Christian theology. Four years before Darwin published the *Origin of Species*, Bishop Richard Whately published *On the Origin of Civilization*. Whately invoked a modern-day version of sociolinguistics to provide empirical evidence that humans had declined, not improved, over the millennia (Fraser 1990, 13). In the late eighteenth century, scholars had turned their attention to the origins of European languages. A body of work had developed indicating that there was probably an original common tongue that mothered the Indo-European languages and some Asiatic languages.

This theory resonated with the idea that the fate of humans was to fall away from basic religious truths (Fraser 1990). A fundamental tenet of Christian theology was that humans had declined, not ascended, over time.[9] It must be recalled that Christianity posited an early state of perfection and a "fall from grace." Thus, it was not an uncontested position to argue that in the beginning, there was savagery and primitivism and terrible warfare and sacrifices. To place science at the apex of the evolutionary development of human cultures was at odds with a strong strain of thought among theologians. There was thus popular and clerical resistance to these ideas. Many groups had to be persuaded. Enter social Darwinism.

This was the social and political context in which James Frazer's *The Golden Bough* was published. We can now see some of the reasons for the author's fervid assertions of counterevidence that early man was a primitive, barbaric, savage being. Wittgenstein understood this well. He cast suspicion on Frazer's motives for recounting stories of how terrible things are among "primitive peoples" in the following way:

> Frazer (tells) the story . . . in a tone which shows that something strange and terrible is happening here. And that is the answer to the question "why is this happening?": because it is terrible. (Fraser 1990, xiii)

Wittgenstein was hardly alone in his attack on Frazer's tautological and self-serving presentation of data. The eminent French social theorist Emile Durkheim also dissected the key architecture of Frazer's argument. Durkheim held that there was nothing primitive about totemic organization among the so-called primitives, but that instead, this served complex social functions parallel to what occurs in advanced societies (Durkheim 1957; Moret and Davy 1926).

The search for empirical evidence to document social evolution within homo sapiens is superbly documented in Stephen Gould's *The Mismeasure of Man* (1981). Gould reveals the painstaking care with which nineteenth-century scientists sought to prove that the size of the skull could be arrayed along an evolutionary continuum, with white males at the apex. When they failed, they improvised or compromised or finessed the data.

The Germination of Human Genetics in Social Evolutionary Soil: The Birth of Human Population Genetics and Human Mendelian Genetics

Galton and Pearson[10] were actively hostile to Mendelian genetics and derided this conception of genetic transmission in humans as "atomistic" (Wright 1959). Since Galton and Pearson were looking for variations in human intellectual ability in large population aggregates,[11] they found Mendel's laws on inheritance based upon dominant and recessive traits in family trees not only irrelevant, but a diversion to be attacked (Dunn 1962, 2). In sharp contrast, the eminent American geneticist Charles Davenport (1866–1944) was a "super-Mendelian" advocate. In the early years, until as late as World War I, there was considerable hostility and even open fighting between the population geneticists, mainly English, and the Mendelians, mainly American. Nonetheless, there was a remarkable, even stunning convergence in much of what some of these researchers and their followers in the eugenics movement considered to be wrong at the bottom of the social order. The social and political interests of the human geneticists were intertwined with the questions which would in turn constitute a fundamental building block of science.[12] Contemporary scientists are often drawn to make a separation between pure and applied science, and pure and applied genetics. But this is a distinction that is hard to sustain as one gets closer and closer to the decisions about what kinds of questions are to be investigated in human genetics.

Charles Davenport (1914), arguably the most influential American human geneticist of his day, was also a eugenicist. Davenport fused genetics and eugenics in ways that are, in retrospect, embarrassing. Most of the enthusiasts for human eugenics, then as now, were not formally trained, practicing geneticists. Davenport, an esteemed biological scientist and an unreconstructed Mendelian, was unabashed in his embrace of eugenics. He went so far as to count up the number of male offspring from his Harvard graduating class (141), and when he contrasted this with the number of males in his class (278), he sounded the following alarm:

> Assuming that a class matures half as many sons as it graduates and that their descendants do the same for six generations, 1000 Harvard graduates in the 1880s will have sixteen male descendants of the 2080s. These sixteen sons will be ruled by the scores of thousands of descendants of 1000 of the Rumanians, Bulgarians, Greeks and hybrid Portuguese of the 1880s. Such figures must make one fear for the future. (Davenport 1914, 11)

What Davenport feared was that these "lower forms of human life" would someday rule the "higher forms" from the old Harvard stock. In its crudest formulation, as we shall see, this idea would take an ugly political and public policy turn: both the strong advocacy for and the practice of forced sterilization of those at the bottom of the social order:

> The lowest stratum of society has, on the other hand, neither intelligence nor self-control enough to justify the State to leave its matings in their own hands. On the contrary, the defectives and the criminalistic are, so far as may be possible, to be segregated under the care of the State during the reproductive period or otherwise forcibly prevented from procreation. (Davenport 1914, 10)

The eugenicists wanted to impose harsher quotas on the nations of Southern and Eastern Europe because test scores were used to show that Italians, Slavs, Jews, and Poles came from inferior racial stock (Gould 1981, 232). The eugenicists won the fight, and—as noted earlier—a new, more restrictive law was passed in 1924, resetting the quotas at 2 percent from each nation recorded in the 1890 census. Since Northern Europeans and the British had predominated in 1890, this effectively shut off the flood of immigration from South, South Central, and Eastern Europe.

This was part of the first great social and economic transformation of America from rural agrarian to urban industrial society. The accompanying social problems and social troubles made for a receptive audience, among both scientists and laypersons, to the idea that the problems of poverty, crime, mental retardation, and mental illness could best be explained by reference to the qualities of the individuals who brought these problems with them, these "lower forms on the evolutionary tree" from "lower forms of cultural life." Even the infant mortality rate was explained by reference to "qualities inherent" in those so victimized:

> [T]he negro infant death rate is in every district higher than the white rate. Throughout the Austro-Hungarian and Russian districts, with very high density of population and great poverty, the infant mortality is exceptionally low. There can be no question that the low rate is due to the qualities inherent in the people themselves. (*Eugenical News* 1916, 79)

As the United States and other industrialized nations now move into their second great transformation, from industrial to service-sector–dominated societies, we are witnessing a similar set of social problems: high levels of endemic unemployment, high rates of homelessness, social dislocations, a sense of less safe streets, and the like. As in our past, we swing the pendulum back and forth between explaining these developments by reference to the qualities and characteristics of individuals (and the societies or cultures they come from) versus the social and economic forces that might also help explain these dislocations. Human genetics has always played an important role in the swing of this pendulum.

There are two fundamentally different approaches to the study of how knowledge gets developed in a society or culture.[13] In the first approach, the analyst looks at which kinds of questions get raised, and asks why. (The popular understanding of this is often illustrated with the apocryphal observation that Eskimos can differentiate more than forty kinds of snow, while most who live in temperate zones can distinguish only three or four.[14]) In the history of human genetics, we have seen how the saturation of social evolutionary thought prefigured many of the most important questions that would be raised for scientific inquiry. A second approach focuses on the internal structure of knowledge, namely, the rules of procedure for answering these questions, the canons of evidence, strategies and techniques of investigation, the systems of categorizing, and the arraying of answers. The philosophy of science literature is dominated by the second concern (Gutting 1980; Kuhn 1970; Popper 1962; Kaufmann 1958). These are widely divergent approaches with sharply different conclusions and implications for one's ultimate position on either the bias or neutrality of knowledge formation.

A concern for which questions get raised can be as fundamental as the concern for the rules of procedures for answering questions, with regard to the structure and outcome of knowledge development. An often cited example is the extensive knowledge about the biochemical aspects of reproduction and birth control among women, but the paucity of knowledge about these aspects among men. This has led some to the conclusion that a concern for the personal attributes of scientists might help explain what questions they pursue (the first approach cited above). Yet, this is a different order of concern than a focus upon the forces and laws and principles that account for why a bridge stands or falls (the second approach cited above). The latter has little to do with, for example, the race or gender of the engineer or physicist. In a similar vein, when it comes to medical training, there is something compelling in the argument that to perform a surgical operation, you have to know how and where to cut. However, if we back up a bit and raise a different order of question about the very foundation of medical research and training, we will see that the scaffolding of knowledge formation can neither be easily described, nor easily dismissed as constructionist.

For example, the United States has one of the highest rates of infant mortality of any industrialized nation, even though it has a very high standard of living. The issue of what is appropriate medical research and training suddenly gets complicated, because while there may be only one best way of removing gallstones or performing an appendectomy, the prior question is whether medical students get trained to remove gallstones or treat belly pain, or whether emphasis goes to primary prevention medicine. In another example, when Western-trained medical faculty introduced their curriculum for medical students in Nigeria, the African students were being prepared to treat ailments of the middle and late years, while primary medicine and the relevant research to support it were badly neglected (Ashby 1966). In knowledge development for a society, priorities, emphasis, and choice mean that it is always a decision as to where to place resources, time, and energy.

The two different approaches to knowledge development can now be recast. One order of question is, of course, how do we build a bridge, how is surgery performed, or how do we measure intelligence? Even the most rigid positivist would grudgingly acknowledge the point that it is quite another matter (political) as to whether we build a bridge here or there, perform surgery on the rich or the poor, or whether we measure the intelligence of group A or group B. The science of human genetics, deeply mired in the evolutionary paradigm, has always been poised to raise questions that address the explanation (and often) justification for human social stratification. The relative prominence of certain knowledge structures is related to the ability of specific groups, located variously in the social structure, to get their questions asked.

Trouble at the Bottom: Continuity and Persistence

While many are aware of the gross human rights abuses in the name of eugenics (Kevles 1985) of the early part of the twentieth century, most of the current advocates, researchers, and celebrants of the putative link between genetic accounts and socially undesirable behavior (or characteristics or attributes) are either unaware of the social context of that history, or they are too quick to dismiss it as something that happened among the unenlightened. Both attitudes miss the special appeal of genetic explanations and eugenic solutions to the most privileged strata of society.

Every era is certain of its facts. The heyday of the eugenics movement was no exception, with its certainty that feeble-mindedness, degeneracy, and criminality were inherited. In 1912 the American Breeder's Association, an organization of farmers and university-based theoreticians, created a "Committee to Study and to Report on the Best Practical Means of Cutting Off the Defective Germ Plasma in the American Population." It was a five-man committee, chaired by a prominent New York attorney and having among its membership a prominent physician from the faculty at Johns Hopkins. At the 1913 meeting of the association, the report was delivered and read in part:

Biologists tell us that whether of wholly defective inheritance or because of an insurmountable tendency toward defect, which is innate, members of (select) classes must generally be considered as socially unfit and their supply should if possible be eliminated from the human stock if we would maintain or raise the level of quality essential to the progress of the nation and our race. (Laughlin 1914, 12–13)

California had one of the longest-running involuntary sterilization programs in the country. In 1927 a team of prominent and respected citizens was assembled to consult on the effectiveness of this program. The team included Lewis Terman, the most prominent psychometrician in the country; David Starr Jordan, president at Stanford; and S. J. Holmes, a distinguished geneticist from Berkeley. Covering the period from 1909 to 1927, a series of reports emanated from this group that produced "the first comprehensive 'proof' that sterilization was cost-effective and posed no significant medical harm to the institutionalized persons at whom it was aimed" (Reilly 1991).

In the 1920s two major legal developments would shape and be shaped by increasingly dominant views of "race betterment" through biological science and its applications. The first would be new immigration laws, strongly backed by the old American stock, to close off the immigration doors to those from Southern and Eastern Europe. The second development was overwhelmingly popular among local politicians in several key states. For example, the Virginia legislature passed an involuntary sterilization bill (30 to 0 in the Senate, 75 to 2 in the House), noting that "heredity plays an important part in the transmission of insanity, idiocy, imbecility, epilepsy and crime." The law gave the superintendents of five state institutions the power to petition for the permission to sterilize selected inmates.

On May 2, 1927, the Supreme Court upheld Virginia's involuntary sterilization law, opening up not only a floodgate of sterilizations in the United States, but also a model that would soon be adopted, expanded, and forever made infamous by Hitler's Third Reich. In mid-July 1933 Germany enacted a eugenic sterilization law. The American eugenicists provided the intellectual and ideological underpinnings and were widely cited as the genetic authorities on behalf of this development. California was one of the leading states in the country in its use of involuntary sterilization laws. From 1930 to 1944 more than eleven thousand Californians were sterilized under these laws. The Germans cited the California development as a model (in 1936 Heidelberg University awarded honorary degrees to several key American eugenicists), but they took it much further. In the first year of the German program, fifty-two thousand were placed under final order to be sterilized, a development that was in turn hailed by American eugenicists. From 1933 to 1945 the best estimates indicate that the Nazis sterilized approximately 3.5 million people (Reilly 1991).

Today the United States is heading down a similar road with this faith in the connection between genes and social outcomes. This is being played out on a stage with converging preoccupations and tangled webs that interlace crime and violence, race, and genetic explanations. So-called genetic studies of criminality depend heavily on samples and subjects from incarcerated populations. Paralleling this development is the racial patterning of those arrested and serving time. African Americans are incarcerated at a rate approximately seven times greater than that of Americans of European descent. While the current incarceration rate of African Americans in American prisons is approximately eight times that of white Americans, this is a *very* recent development. If we are ignorant of recent history, and do not know that the incarceration rate and the coloring of our prisons is a function of dramatic changes in the last half-century, we are far more vulnerable to the seduction of a genetic explanation.

The Violence Initiative: Continuity with the Past via the Irrepressible Link

In September 1991 the National Institute of Mental Health issued a program announcement with the title *Research on Perpetrators of Violence*. The announcement was explicit in its aim to do further research on cost-effective measures, beginning with clinical assessment, that might "prevent" violence:

> The purpose of this announcement is to encourage investigator-initiated research on the etiology, course, and correlates of aggressive and violent behaviors in children, adolescents, and adults. Through this announcement, the National Institute of Mental Health (NIMH) expects to support research that will improve the scientific base for more effective and cost-efficient approaches to clinical assessment, treatment, management and prevention.

In specifying the priority areas of research interest, the Violence and Traumatic Stress Research Branch specified that "studies may focus on risk factors and procedures that contribute to the occurrence and influence the course of violent behaviors (e.g., neurochemicals and neuroendocrines, parent-child rearing practices . . .)." Here is the summary language of the major aims of one of the funded projects:

> This research seeks to contribute to the understanding of the origin of serious and chronic aggressive and antisocial behaviors so that preventive inter-

ventions can be more effectively timed and targeted. . . . The project involves a longitudinal design in which 310 parent-infant male dyads from low SES backgrounds will be assessed when the child is 18, 24, and 42 months of age.

Yet another funded project describes its method of selection as follows:

One-hundred and twenty Black third-grade boys will be recruited from 10 classrooms in the Durham, North Carolina school system. Dyad type will be assessed by pupil and teacher ratings of the extent to which pairs of boys in the classroom initiate aggression against one another.[15]

After the civil disturbances in Los Angeles triggered by the verdict handed down in the Rodney King case, James Q. Wilson (1992a) wrote an opinion piece for the *Wall Street Journal* that was widely distributed in a syndicated column. At the conclusion of this article, Wilson strongly suggested that the high rate of black crime, six to eight times higher than that of white crime, may be reduced only by profound interventions in the lives of black male infants from birth to age ten:

The best way to reduce racism real or imagined is to reduce the black crime rate to equal the white crime rate. . . . To do this may require changing, in far more profound and all-encompassing ways than anything we now contemplate, the lives of black infants, especially boys, from birth to age 8 or 10. We have not yet begun to think seriously about this, and perhaps never will. Those who must think about it the hardest are those decent black people who must accept, and ideally should develop and run, whatever is done. (Wilson 1992a)

Intervene in "profound and all-encompassing ways"? "Develop and run" a program to deal with these young black infants and children? If these same words were written by someone with a long history of emphasizing environmental explanations for criminal behavior, it would be one thing. But James Q. Wilson teamed up with Richard Herrnstein in 1985 to publish a book, *Crime and Human Nature*, that explicitly argued for American society to take a more serious look at biogenetic explanations for crime. Indeed, as recently as June 1992, Wilson published an essay in which he stated

We know now that the child brings a great deal to the parent-child relationship, that many aspects of personality have genetic origins, and that some infants experience insults and traumas. Two children in the same family often turn out very differently. This casts great doubt on the notion that the shared environment of the children is a principal—or even a very important—factor in their development. What is going on here? (Wilson 1992a, A40)

Indeed, what is going on here? Having cast doubt that environment may be given the status of "important," Wilson then goes on to offer as one of three hypotheses something that sounds very much like the Spencer of 1869 and the Jensen of 1969:

Children with low IQs find school work boring and frustrating and turn to physical activity—including rowdy, violent activity—as an alternative source of rewards. (Wilson 1992a, A40)

In the essay immediately after the Rodney King verdict was announced and urban uprisings occurred, Wilson says that a program more profoundly different "than any we can now contemplate" should "ideally" be in the hands of "decent black people." But then, since we do not live in an ideal world, the implication is that we may have to settle for someone else running "these programs."

Could raising such a concern about a program for African-American male youth be dismissed as mere paranoia? The deep and recurring concern with violent crime is still very much with us. I began this chapter by redrawing the historical link of a century ago between biological Darwinism and social Darwinism and its relevance for both the birth and direction of growth for the field of human genetics. The link is still with us, and it still fuels thought at the highest levels of government, medical, and biological research. On February 11, 1992, Frederick Goodwin, a top official in the first Bush administration, made some controversial remarks at a meeting of the National Mental Health Advisory Council. Dr. Goodwin was at the time the chief administrative officer of three federal agencies coordinated under his jurisdiction: the National Institute for Alcohol Abuse Administration, the National Institute on Drug Abuse, and the National Institute of Mental Health. The consortium is conjoined as the Alcohol, Drug Abuse, Mental Health Administration, or ADAMHA. As the chief of ADAMHA, Dr. Goodwin made remarks at that meeting that would get him "demoted" to being head of only one of the agencies, the National Institute of Mental Health.

Goodwin has said that his remarks were taken out of context. My purpose is to place Goodwin's remarks back into the proper context, the recurring interlinking of biological Darwinism and social Darwinism. He said:

We are obviously interested in the concept of conduct disorder as a common stem cell for both drug abuse and early onset alcohol abuse and violence and obviously the links between those will involve increasing work between the three Institutes. We now have conduct disorders studies going on both in NIMH and in NIDA and, by a different name, in NIAAA as well.

Somebody gave me some data recently that puts this in a perspective and I say this with the realization that it might be easily misunderstood, and that is, if you look at other primates in nature—male primates in nature—you find that even with our violent society we are doing very well.

If you look, for example, at male monkeys, especially in the wild, roughly half of them survive to adulthood. The other half die by violence. That is the natural way of it for males, to knock each other off and, in fact, there are some interesting evolutionary implications of that because the same hyper-aggressive monkeys who kill each other are also hyper-sexual, so they copulate more and therefore they reproduce more to offset the fact that half of them are dying.

Now, one could say that if some of the loss of social structure in this society, and particularly within the high impact inner city areas, has removed some of the civilizing evolutionary things that we have built up and that maybe it isn't just the careless use of the word when people call certain areas of certain cities jungles, that we may have gone back to what might be more natural, without all of the social controls that we have imposed upon ourselves as a civilization over thousands of years in our own evolution.

This just reminds us that, although we look at individual factors and we look at biological differences and we look at genetic differences, the loss of structure in society is probably why we are dealing with this issue and why we are seeing the doubling incidence of violence among the young over the last 20 years.[16]

Notice the heavy theoretical reliance upon social evolutionary theory, and the way in which Goodwin linked the concerns for biological and genetic differences to the social milieu. When reflecting upon the history of the link between human genetics and eugenics, it is tempting to suggest that only the fringes and the marginal actors were involved. That is not true. Charles Davenport was among the most influential and respected geneticists of his time, and he was an ardent eugenicist. As director of the National Institute of Mental Health, Goodwin was certainly not at the fringes of biomedical research on the causes of violence. He has been a strong advocate of a program of research to try to better explain the "violent, jungle-like" behavior of black youth he has likened to "hyper-aggressive monkeys." The fact that he invoked evolutionary theory, and that he conjectured a potential genetic link to a proneness to violence is a chilling reminder of just how much our past remains with us.

Afterword: The New and Emerging Relationship between Behavioral and Molecular Genetics

Until the middle of the 1990s, the fields of behavioral genetics and molecular genetics had very little in common. Behavioral geneticists rarely worked at the molecular level, and their methodology could be characterized as overwhelmingly committed to the use of correlations between (1) outcome data of some complex behavioral "phenotype"—such as intelligence, criminality, violence, risk-seeking, alcoholism, manic-depression, schizophrenia, or homosexuality—and (2) frequency-of-occurrence of these behaviors or attributes[1] in different populations,[2] often ethnic and racial groups.

In contrast, molecular geneticists were rarely concerned with complex behavior. During its first three decades, the field was riveted to the search for coding regions or DNA markers for such single-gene disorders as Tay–Sachs disease, hemachromatosis, cystic fibrosis, Huntington's chorea, sickle-cell anemia, and alpha-antitrypsin deficiency, to name but a few. Molecular geneticists did not concern themselves with such complex subject matter as intelligence, schizophrenia, or homosexuality.

All that has begun to change. First, there has been a sharp U-turn in the strategic orientation of the Human Genome Project. Rather than an emphasis upon our "sameness," the field of molecular genetics has now begun to emphasize the importance of looking for "differences" at the level of the DNA.[3] Second, behavioral geneticists are turning quickly to the search for genetic markers (and sometimes even coding regions) that they can associate with complex behaviors. In the last five years, we have seen claims linking DNA regions to cognitive ability in children (Chorney et al. 1998:159–66), crime (Jensen et al. 1998), violence (Caspi et al. 2002), and attention-deficit/hyperactivity disorder (Smalley et al. 2002).

The Human Genome Project and the "Turn to Difference"

In the first decade of the Human Genome Project (circa 1988 to 1998), the major focus was on how the mapping and sequencing process could be done on *any one human*, precisely because we are all so alike at the level of our DNA. Any two persons, chosen completely randomly across the globe, share 99.9 percent of the exact same sequences of nucleotides (the four famous nucleotides—Cytosine, Guanine Adenine, and Thymine—that are the building blocks of DNA) throughout the genome. That similarity was so overwhelming that it became the rationale for the conclusion that *anyone's genome would do* for generating the map. While there are approximately three billion base pairs of complete overlapping similarity (of C, G, T, A pairs), that recurring figure of 99.99 percent also means that, with only a .01 difference, there are still approximately *thirty million points of difference* in the DNA between any two people. With the use of new supercomputers, it is now possible to take a closer look at these many points of difference. Suddenly, the realization of a considerable amount of differentiation between individuals is the new perspective—and lurking in the corridors of computer-generated correlations and patterns, there will be the inevitable shift to a concern for differences between population groups. Little surprise that this turn to a concern for difference in molecular biology would capture the imaginations and the research agendas of behavioral geneticists. It was inevitable that some among them would attempt to deploy technologies to get at single nucleotides that mark DNA differences—in the hope that these might explain different behaviors.

In the late 1990s, armed with this new potential technological development, pharmaceutical companies and the biotechnology industry began to change the focus of their attention to "groups of differences" that will permit them to market drugs to select populations (whose DNA indicates a positive reaction). In March 2001, a company touted as having produced the "first ethnic drug" received a green-letter of approval from the Food and Drug Administration; this medication is purposefully aimed at a putative difference of population groups (Ron Winslow 2001). The drug, BiDil, is being developed by the pharmaceutical company Nitromed and is currently in clinical trials. The company's chief executive officer, Michael Loberg, explicitly states that the African-American population will be the marketing target for the drug, indicating that "BiDil, a heart failure product, reduced mortality in 66 percent of African Americans, but proved of very little benefit to whites" (Griffith 2001:16). This is highly contested terrain, and the fields of pharmacogenomics and pharmacotoxicology are engaged in fierce internal battles as to the appropriate role of race in diagnostics and treatment (Xie et al. 2001; Braun 2002; Frank 2001; Lee et al. 2001; Risch et al. 2002). This is not the place to address this dispute; however, it is important to address the serious implications, *for behavioral genetics*, of having race reenter the scientific and medical literature through the DNA.

The forensic applications of the molecular genetics turn to difference are now well known, converted into household conversations by sensational murder trials and the exculpation of those on death row who have been set free by evidence showing that it was not their DNA that was left at the crime scene (Dwyer et al. 2000). This renewed legitimacy of an emphasis upon both *individual* differences in the DNA and *group* differences (the Haplotype Maps) has not been lost on behavioral geneticists.

If leading figures in the field of pharmacogenomics could publish, in 1999 in the journal *Science*, the claim that "all pharmacogenetic polymorphisms studied to date differ in frequency among ethnic and racial groups" (Evans and Relling 1999:487–91), and subsequently, in the same article, that "the marked racial and ethnic diversity . . . dictates that race be considered in studies aimed at discovering whether specific genotypes or phenotypes are associated with disease risk or drug toxicity" (Evans and Relling 1999:487–91), then it was sure to be only a matter of time before behavioral geneticists would generate correlational data in the attempt to link such behaviors to violence, impulsivity, crime—and lurking in the background—race. It took less than thirty months.

The MAOA Gene and Predicting Violent Behavior

In the last half of 2002, *Science* published an article that cemented the new engagement between behavioral genetics and molecular genetics, with a promissory note of impending marriage. This was a report of research in which the authors claim that their

> findings provide initial evidence that a functional polymorphism in the MAOA gene moderates the impact of early childhood maltreatment on the development of antisocial behavior in males. (Caspi et al. 2002)

The last two sentences of this article are pregnant with policy implications that will revive a somewhat dormant social and ethical debate about the advisability of early identification of young people at risk for becoming violent and/or antisocial:

> Moreover, 85% of cohort males having a low activity MAOA genotype who were severely maltreated developed some form of antisocial behavior. Both attributable risk and predictive sensitivity indicate that these findings could inform the development of future pharmacological treatments. (Caspi et al. 2002)

The notion that one can intercept and then treat with pharmaceuticals presumes a much higher correlation than this study has reported. In particular, in that very same paragraph the authors report that those having "the combination of low-activity *MAOA* genotype and maltreatment were only 12 percent of the male birth cohort, they were 22 percent of those with multiple antisocial outcomes, yielding an attributable risk fraction (11 percent)." (Caspi et al. 2002). Isolating, identifying, and treating subjects has its own social dynamic. There is a remarkable slippage here. In this research, the concept of "antisocial" rests entirely upon measures that look only at the individual. However, both the ideas of "antisocial" and "maltreatment" are fundamentally interactional. Some substantially greater attention to the *interactional* dynamics needs to be a part of any larger framing of attempts at early identification and, even more significant, identifying the components of *antisocial*. Getting in trouble with the criminal justice system is partly about individuals, but it is also about individuals with membership in particular social groups on which the criminal justice system focuses its attention more closely. For example, the War on Drugs, which accounts for more than half of all those incarcerated in U.S. jails and prisons, has been remarkably disproportionately aimed at African Americans and Latinos (Mauer 1999; Miller 1996; Cole 1999; Reinarman and Levine 1997).

Race and DNA: Tensions and Current Tendencies Relevant to Behavioral Genetics

Miami Florida was the scene of the most notorious and widespread DNA dragnet of the last decade. Between September 1994 and January 1995, six women were killed and their bodies were left just outside the Miami city limits on a street known as the Tamiami Trail. More than 2,300 men were stopped by the police as they drove down streets in the area, and each was asked to provide saliva samples for the purposes of determining a possible DNA match (Pan 1998). The so-called Tamiami Strangler was identified through other means, but this dragnet is of particular interest because (1) almost all of the men who were asked for DNA samples were African Americans, and (2) their DNA samples were stored. These stored samples can be used in subsequent criminal investigations, of course, but they can also be used in behavioral genetics research—with its new turn to the molecular level of DNA markers associated with different behaviors.

There have been two strongly conflicting voices about the role of DNA in addressing racial taxonomies. At the White House news conference announcing the completion of the first draft of the complete human genome on June 26, 2000, Francis Collins (director of the Human Genome Project) and Craig Venter (who headed the rival private mapping and sequencing venture at Celera) agreed that human similarities at the DNA level were so dramatic that "race is of no significance" (*Human Genome News*, 2000:1–2). This statement by Collins and Venter echoed assertions in the literature of physical anthropology, the updated UNESCO statement on race, and a host of other official positions by associations of scientists.

However, on the other side, there are practitioners who make use of DNA analysis for the practical task of delivering pharmaceuticals, or who try to determine from DNA evidence at a crime scene whether there can be an estimate of the suspect's probable identification with some specific population group. As we shall see, this is often an effective proxy for race. This latter group of researchers have held to the position that race *is* a meaningful category both for delivering pharmaceuticals and for assessing risk for genetic disorders or predispositions to disorders (Risch et al. 2002; Lin and Kelsey 2000; Evans and Relling 1999). Others are pursuing work in forensic science with the hope of finding particular allelic frequencies more common in one group than another (Lowe et al. 2001). Readers interested in pursuing these arguments for the merits of the case should consult the following literature: Braun 2002; Risch et al. 2002; Rosenberg et al. 2002; Frank 2001; Lee et al. 2001; Evans and Relling 1999. Quite demonstrably, race is still very much alive, both as a concept and in use, in molecular genetics. It is therefore inevitable that this use, and this debate, would spill over into behavioral genetics which, as we have seen, now has a formidable branch of its discipline linked to molecular genetics.

We can all celebrate the use of DNA technology to free nearly one hundred wrongly convicted prisoners, some who were on death row facing execution, and others who had served decades for crimes they did not commit (Dwyer et al. 2000). Similarly, when law enforcement can score a "cold hit" and catch a rapist because his DNA was on file, there are reasons to applaud. The use of this technology in these high-profile cases has led to a full set of arguments for widening the net of the DNA database so that more and more samples can be included, ranging from convicted felons to arrestees to suspects to the whole population. What more objective way could there be of exculpating the innocent and convicting the guilty? However, this conflates three quite distinct strategies and practices of the criminal justice system, which need to be separated and analyzed for their disparate impact on different populations.

The first is the use of DNA in postconviction cases to determine whether or not there was a wrongful conviction, the kind of situation that would help to free the innocent. The second is the collection of the DNA of suspects or arrestees in pretrial circumstances to help law enforcement determine if there is a match with tissue samples left at an unsolved crime—the net to catch the guilty. The third is the advocacy of increasing the collection of DNA from a wider and wider band of felons and misdemeanants in the postconviction period, to increase the DNA database and so that there is a record on file in the event of recidivism. Much like the current situation, in which the police can stop a driver and determine whether there are outstanding warrants or traffic ticket violations that have piled up, the new technology would permit authorities to see if the DNA of the person stopped and arrested matched the DNA on file for someone at an unsolved crime scene. This is not hypothetical.

In early 2000, the New York Police Department began a pilot project experimenting with portable DNA laboratories (Flynn 2000). The police take a buccal swab—some saliva and cells from inside the cheek of the person stopped—and place it on a chip the size of a credit card. Next they put this card through a machine no larger than a hand-held compact disc player, where the DNA is read via a laser in two minutes, isolating about thirteen DNA markers to create a profile of the suspect. When this task is completed, the police can then transmit this data to a central database, where it currently requires about twelve minutes to determine if there is a match with a sample.

Who could possibly be opposed to the use of these technologies for such crime-fighting purposes? The answer is a bit complex, but it has to do with (1) some hidden social forces that create a patterned bias determining that certain populations will be more likely subjected to DNA profiling, and (2) the resuscitation of some old and dangerously regressive ideas about how to explain criminal behavior.

To provide the context for the discussion of expanding DNA databases, it is important to point out yet again the systematic bias, by race, of a full range of behaviors displayed across the criminal justice system, from the decisions by police at the point of stop, search, and arrest, through the sentencing guidelines and practices, to incarceration. I then turn to empirical evidence that documents recent developments in the literature of forensic science that claim to be able to predict ethnic affiliation from population-specific allele frequencies. It is the relationship between these two developments that is the source of easily crafted DNA-based research programs with the consequent misattribution of genetic causes of crime.

Phenotypical Expression at the Point of Arrest: The Selective Aim of the Artillery in the War on Drugs

In the last three decades, the War on Drugs has produced a remarkable transformation of the U.S. prison population. If we turn the clock back sixty years, whites constituted approximately 77 percent of all prisoners in America, while blacks were only 22 percent (Hacker 1992:197). This provides the context in which we might best review Table 1, which shows the recent historical evolution of general prison incarceration rates by race. Notice how in the last half-century, the incarceration rate of African Americans in relation to whites has gone up in such a striking manner. In 1933 blacks were incarcerated at a rate approximately three times that of whites (Graph 1). In 1950 the ratio had increased to approximately four times; in 1960; in 1970 it was six times; and in 1989 it was seven times that of whites.

Table 8.1 Incarceration Rates by Race

Year	Population[a]			Incarceration[b]			Rate (%)[c]			Approximate Ratio
	total	white	black	total	white	black	total	white	black	Black to White
1933	125,579	112,815	12,764	137,997	102,118	31,739	.11	.09	.25	2½ : 1
1950	151,684	135,814	15,870	178,065	115,742	60,542	.12	.09	.38	4 : 1
1960	180,671	160,023	19,006	226,065	138,070	83,747	.13	.09	.44	5 : 1
1970	204,879	179,491	22,787	198,831	115,322	81,520	.10	.06	.36	6 : 1
1989	248,240	208,961	30,660	712,563	343,550	334,952	.29	.16	1.09	7 : 1
1995	263,168	218,149	33,095	1,126,287	454,961	546,005	.43	.21	1.65	8 : 1

[a] Total population of the United States by ethnicity (in thousand). Source: Series A 23–28: Annual estimates of the Population, by Sex and Race: 1900–1970. In *Historical Statistics of the United States*, 1976: Department of Commerce, Bureau of the Census, 1976: Department of Commerce, Bureau of the Census, 1976, pp. 9–28. No. 19: Resident Population—Selected Characteristics: 1790–1989. *Statistical Abstract of the United States 1991*, 111th edition, Bureau of the Census, 1991, p.17. Statistical Abstract of the U.S., 1997, 117th ed., Bureau of Census, p.9, 19.

[b] Total number of prison population by ethnicity. Note: Data for incarceration reflect the estimated number of prisoners surveyed on a particular date. Source: Table 3–31 Characteristics of Persons in State and Federal Prisons. *Historical Corrections Statistics in the United States*, Bureau of Prison Statistics, 1986, p.65. Bureau of Justice Statistics, Correctional Population in the U.S., 1995, Department of Justice, 1997, p.91.

[c] Incarceration/population.

Population vs. Incarceration Rate

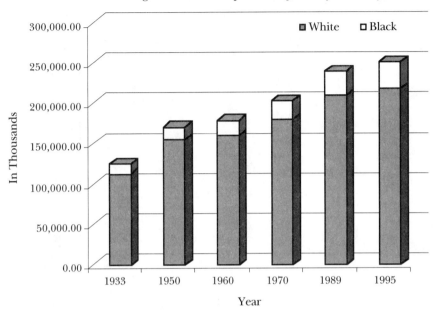

Figure 1   Total Population of U.S. by Ethnicity

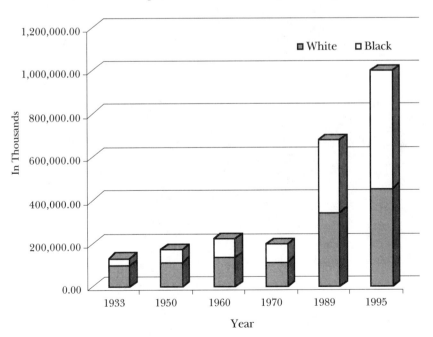

Figure 2   Incarceration Population by Race

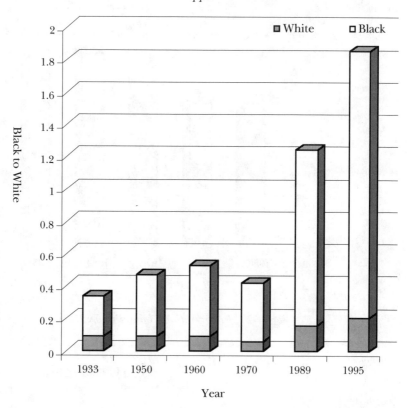

Figure 3   Incarceration Rate by Race
Approximate Ratio

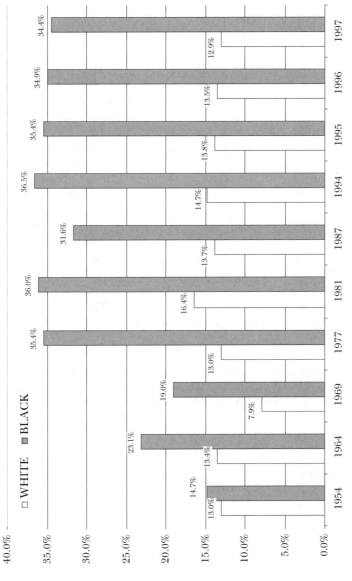

Figure 4 Male Unemployment Rates[a] by Race and Ages 18–19

□ WHITE ■ BLACK

[a]Represent number of unemployed as percentage of civilian labor force.

Source: Table A-30 Unemployment Rates, by Sex, Race, and Age: Annual Averages, 1952–81. *Employment and Training Report of the President*, 1982, pp. 195–196. Unemployment Rates of Civilian Workers by Sex, Race, Hispanic Origin, and Age, 1948–1997. *Handbook of U.S. Labor Statistics: Employment, Earnings, Prices, Productivity, and Other Labor Data*, 1998, pp. 81–83.

However dramatic these figures are, incarceration is but one end of the long process through the criminal justice system, which starts with being stopped by the police, arrested, held for trial, and convicted.

The War on Drugs plays the dominant role in this story. While racial profiling seems often to be characterized as a local police practice, the phenomenon of young minority males being "just stopped by the police" was actually a national strategy first deployed by the Reagan administration. In 1986 the Drug Enforcement Administration initiated *Operation Pipeline*, a program that ultimately trained 27,000 law enforcement officers in forty-eight participating states over the ensuing decade. The project was designed to alert police and other law enforcement officials to the likely profiles of those who should be stopped and searched for possible drug violations. High on the list were young, male African Americans and Latinos driving in cars, which signaled that something might be amiss. For example, a nineteen-year-old African American driving a new Lexus would be an obvious alert, because the assumption would be that his family could not afford such a car, and the driver must therefore be involved with drugs.

According to the government's own best statistics, during the height of the intensity of the War on Drugs, blacks constituted only 15 to 20 percent of the nation's drug users (Flanagan and Maguire 1990), but in most urban areas, they constitute approximately one-half to two-thirds of those arrested for drug offenses. Indeed, in New York City, African Americans and Latinos constituted 92 percent of all those arrested for drug offenses (Edna McConnell Clark Foundation 1992). In Florida the annual admissions rate to the state prison system nearly tripled from 1983 to 1989, from 14,301 to nearly 40,000 (Austin and McVey 1989:4). This was a direct consequence of the War on Drugs, since more than two-thirds of these felonies were drug-related. The nation gasped at the national statistics reported by the Sentencing Project in 1990, citing the figure that nearly one-fourth of all young black males twenty to twenty-nine years of age were either in prison, in jail, on probation, or on parole on a given day in the summer of 1989.[4] This figure has been recited so often and inured so many that there was (relatively) a collective yawn greeting an announcement in mid-1992 that a study of Baltimore revealed that 56 percent of that city's young black males were under some form of criminal justice sanction on any given day in 1991 (Miller 1992). Indeed, of the nearly 13,000 individuals arrested on drug charges in Baltimore during 1991, more than 11,000 were African Americans.

The War on Drugs also affected the races quite differently with regard to their respective incarceration rates. The most striking figure showing this is the shift in the racial composition of prisoners in the state of Virginia. In 1983 approximately 63 percent of the new prison commitments for drugs were white, with the rest, 37 percent, minority. Just six years later in 1989, the situation had reversed, with only 34 percent of the new drug commitments white, but 65 percent minority. It is not just the higher rate of incarceration, but the way in which the full net of the criminal justice system all the way through mandatory sentencing falls selectively on blacks. For example, powder cocaine is most likely to be sold and consumed by whites, while blacks are more likely to sell and consume crack (Flanagan and Maguire 1990; Reinarman and Levine 1997: 26–33). The sentencing guidelines for possession of crack cocaine are much more harsh than those for possesion of cocaine powder.

Background to "Ethnic-Affiliation Markers" at the DNA Level

At the level of the DNA, recall that the mappers and sequencers of the human genome assure us that humans are 99.99 percent alike. But if humans are 99.99 percent alike and "race" is purportedly a concept with no scientific utility, what are we to make of a series of articles appearing in the scientific literature over the last decade looking for genetic markers of population groups coinciding with common-sense, lay renditions of ethnic and racial phenotypes? It is the forensic applications that have generated much of this interest. Devlin and Risch (1992a) published an article on "Ethnic Differentiation at VNTR Loci, with Specific Reference to Forensic Applications," a research report that appeared prominently in the *American Journal of Human Genetics*.

> The presence of null alleles leads to a large excess of single-band phenotypes for blacks at D17S79 (Devlin and Risch 1992b), as Budowle et al. (1991b) predicted. This phenomenon is less important for the Caucasian and Hispanic populations, which have fewer alleles with a small number of repeats (figs. 2–4). (540)

> [I]t appears that the FBI's data base is representative of the Caucasian population. Results for the Hispanic ethnic groups, for the D17S79 locus, again suggest that the data bases are derived from nearly identical populations, when both similarities and expected biases are considered (for approximate biases, see fig. 9). For the allele frequency distributions derived from the black population, there may be small differences in the populations from which the data bases are derived, as the expected bias is .05. (546)

When researchers try to make probabilistic statements about which group a person belongs to, they look for variation at several different locations in the DNA, usually from three to seven loci.[5] For any particular locus, there is an examination of the frequency of that allele *at that locus, and for that population*. In other words, what is being assessed is the frequency of genetic variation at a particular spot in the DNA in each population.

The work of Devlin and Risch (1992a 1992b), Evett et al. (1993, 1996), Lowe et al. (2001), and others suggests that only about 10 percent of sites in human DNA are useful for making distinctions. This means that at the other 90 percent of the sites, the allele frequencies do not vary between such groups as Afro-Caribbean people in England and Scottish people in England. But it does not follow that because we cannot find a *single* site where allele frequency matches some phenotype we are trying to identify (for forensic purposes only, we should be reminded), that there are not *several* (four, six, or seven) that will not be effective for making highly probabilistic statements about suspects and the likely ethnic, racial, or cultural populations from which they can be identified—statistically.

So when it comes to molecular biologists asserting that race has no validity as a scientific concept, there is a contradiction with the practical applicability of forensic and medical research attempting to use allele frequencies to identify specific populations that correspond to common public uses of racial categories. It is possible to sort out and make sense of this, and even to explain and resolve the apparent contradiction, but only if we keep in mind the difference between using a taxonomic system having sharp, discrete, definitively bounded categories, and a system whose categories show patterns (with some overlap), but which may prove to be empirically or practically useful. When representative spokespersons from the biological sciences say that there is no such thing as race, they mean, correctly, that there are no discrete categories that come to a definitive beginning or end, that there is nothing mutually exclusive about our current (or past) categories of race, and that there is more genetic variation within categories of race than between. While all this is true, it is a discussion more appropriate to abstract theorizing in the logic and philosophy of science, and it bears little relevance to the practical matter of helping to solve a crime or the practical application of molecular genetics to health delivery via genetic screening. In both real-world sets and settings, messy overlapping categories are inevitably a feature of these enterprises. When Scotland Yard or the Birmingham, England, Metropolitan Police or the NYPD want to narrow the list of suspects in a crime, they are not primarily concerned with tight taxonomic systems of classification with no overlapping categories.

In other words, some African Americans *do* have cystic fibrosis, even though the likelihood is far greater among Americans of Northern European descent; and, in a parallel if not symmetrical way, some American whites *do* have sickle cell anemia, even though the likelihood is far greater among Americans of West African descent. But in the world of cost-effective decision making, genetic screening for these disorders is routinely done based on common-sense versions of the phenotype. The same is true for the quite practical matter of naming suspects.

In the July 8, 1995, issue of the *New Scientist* entitled, "Genes in Black and White," some extraordinary claims are made about what it is possible to learn about socially defined categories of race from reviewing information gathered using new molecular genetic technology. In 1993 a British forensic scientist published what is perhaps the first DNA test explicitly acknowledged to provide "intelligence information" along "ethnic" lines for "investigators of unsolved crimes." Ian Evett, of the British Home Office's forensic science laboratory in Birmingham, and his colleagues in the Metropolitan Police, claimed that their DNA test can distinguish between Caucasians and Afro-Caribbeans in nearly 85 percent of the cases.

Evett's original work (1993) was published in the *Journal of the Forensic Science Society* and drew upon apparent genetic differences in three sections of human DNA. Like most stretches of DNA used for forensic typing, each of these three regions differs widely from person to person, irrespective of race. But by looking at all three, the researchers claimed that under select circumstances it is possible to estimate the probability that someone belongs to a particular racial group. The implications of this for determining, for practical purposes, who is and who is not "officially" a member of some racial or ethnic category are profound.

The next important work on this topic appeared in the *American Journal of Human Genetics,* authored by Ian Evett and his associates (1996), and was summarized as follows:

> Before the introduction of a four-locus multiplex short-tandem-repeat (STR) system into casework, an extensive series of tests were carried out to determine robust procedures for assessing the evidential value of a match between crime and suspect samples. Twelve databases were analyzed from the three main ethnic groups encountered in casework in the United Kingdom; Caucasians, Afro-Caribbeans, and Asians from the Indian subcontinent. Independence tests resulted in a number of significant results, and the impact that these might have on forensic casework was investigated. It is demonstrated that previously published methods provide a similar procedure for correcting allele frequencies—and that this leads to conservative casework estimates of evidential value. (Evett et al. 1996:398)

In more recent years, the technology has moved along, and forensic scientists are now using VNTR loci and investigating twelve to fifteen segments of the DNA, not just the earlier three to seven. Recall that in the opening section, I referred to the pilot program of the NYPD, locating thirteen loci for identification purposes. The forensic research reported above occurred before the most recent computer chip advances, which will permit research on specific populations to achieve a Single Nucleotide Polymorphism (or SNP) profile of such a group (Hamadeh and Afshari 2000). There is a dangerous seduction when deploying the technology in this fashion. The computer will inevitably be able to find some patterns for a group of, say, three thousand burglars. But this is merely a spurious correlation of markers, and it will explain nothing, while it will have the seductive imprimatur of molecular genetic precision.

The Dangerous Intersection of Allele Frequencies in Special Populations and Police Profiling via Phenotype

The conventional wisdom is that DNA fingerprinting is just a better way of getting a fingerprint. That is wrong. The traditional physical imprint of your finger or thumb provided only that specific identifying mark, and it is attached to you and you alone.[6] Unlike an actual fingerprint, DNA contains information about many other aspects than simply a marker for identification. It contains information about potential or existing genetic diseases or genetic susceptibilities one may have, and it also contains information about one's family. This information can involve data of interest to one's employer and, of course, to insurance companies. For these reasons, law enforcement officials claim that they are only interested in that part of the DNA that will permit them to provide identifying markers that are not in coding regions. Coding regions are only 10 percent of the DNA, and it is in these regions that the nucleotides code for proteins that might relate to a full range of matters of concern to researchers: from cancer or heart disease to neuro-transmission and thus, for some, to *possible coding for impulsivity or biochemical outcomes that might relate to violence.*

While the FBI and local and state law enforcement officials tell us that they are only looking at genetic markers in the noncoding region of the DNA, twenty-nine states now require that tissue samples be retained in their DNA database after profiling is complete (Kimmelman 2000:211). Only one state, Wisconsin, requires the destruction of tissue samples once profiling is complete.

The states are the primary venues for the prosecution of violations of criminal law, and their autonomy has generated considerable variation in the use of DNA databases and storage. Even as late as the mid-1980s, most states were collecting DNA samples only on sexual offenders. The times have changed quite rapidly. All fifty states now contribute to the FBI's Combined DNA Index System (CODIS). Moreover, there has been rapid change in the interlinking of state databases. In just two years, the database went from a total of nine states cross-linking "a little over 100,000 offender profiles and 5,000 forensic profiles" to thirty-two states, the FBI, and the U.S. Army now linking "nearly 400,000 offender profiles, and close to 20,000 forensic profiles" (Gavel 2000). States are now uploading an average of three thousand offender profiles every month. If this sounds daunting, computer technology is increasingly efficient and extraordinarily fast. It takes only half a second to search a database of one hundred thousand profiles.

As we increase the number of profiles in the databases, there will be researchers proposing to provide SNP profiles of specific offender populations. Twenty states authorize the use of databases for research on forensic techniques. Based on the statutory language in several of those states, this could easily mean assaying genes or loci that contain predictive information. Tom Callaghan, program manager of the FBI's Federal Convicted Offender Program, refused to rule out such possible uses by behavioral geneticists seeking a possible profile for a particular allele among specific offender populations, including especially violent offenders and sexual offenders (Kimmelman 2000). It is useful to note here that this is the thin end of the wedge that inevitably widens to include other crimes and even misdemeanors. Indeed, in 1999 Louisiana was the first state to pass a law permitting the taking of a DNA sample for all those merely arrested for a felony, but it has now been followed by four other states.

Seven states now require keeping a DNA database on *all* felons, including white-collar felonies. In the fall of 1998, Governor George Pataki proposed that New York state include white-collar convicts in the DNA database, but the state legislative assembly balked and forced him to jettison the idea. Perhaps they were concerned that some saliva might be left on the cigars in those back rooms where price-fixing and security-exchange fraud occur. Today, nearly half the states include some misdemeanors in the DNA database. So we can now see that what started as sex offenders has now graduated to misdemeanants and arrestees. While thirty-nine states permit samples to be expunged if charges are dropped, almost all of those states place the burden on the individual to initiate the process.

Population-Wide DNA Database

It is now relatively common for scholars to acknowledge the considerable and documented racial and ethnic bias in police procedures, prosecutorial discretion, jury selection, and sentencing practices—of which racial profiling is but the tip of an iceberg (Mauer 1999). Indeed, racial disparities penetrate the whole system and are suffused throughout it, all the way up to and through racial disparities in seeking the death penalty for the same crime. If the DNA database is primarily composed of those who have been touched by the criminal justice system, and that system has provided practices that routinely select more from one group than another, there will be an obvious skew or bias toward this group. Some have argued that the way to handle the racial bias in the DNA database is to include everyone. But this does not address the far more fundamental problem of the bias that generates the configuration and content of the criminal (or suspect) database. If the attention of the criminal justice system is focused almost entirely on one part of the population for a certain kind of activity (drug-related offenses, street crime), and ignores a parallel kind of crime (fraternity cocaine sales a few miles away), then even if the fraternity members' DNA records are in the database, they will not be subject to the same level of matching or of subsequent allele frequency profiling research to help explain their behavior. *That behavior will not have been recorded.* That is, if the police are not stopping to arrest the fraternity members, it does not matter whether their DNA is in a national database or not, because they are not criminalized by the selective actions of the criminal justice system.

Thus, it is imperative that we separate two things: Arguments about bias in the criminal justice system at the point of contact with select parts of the population are distinct from the problems of bias in "cold hits." It is certainly true that if a member of that fraternity committed a rape, left tissue samples at the scene, and—because he was in a national DNA database— the police could nab him with a cold hit, that would be a source of the justifiable applause with which I opened this chapter. But my point here is that by ignoring powder cocaine and emphasizing street sales of crack cocaine in the African-American community, the mark of criminality is thereby generated, and this is not altered by having a population-wide DNA database. However, the surface fiction of objectivity will lead to a research agenda on the DNA database about which I would now like to issue a warning.

There is a serious threat of how these new technologies are about to be deployed that is masked by the apparent global objectivity of a population-wide DNA database. I am referring to the prospects for SNP profiling of offenders. As noted, even if everyone were in the national database, this would not deter the impulse to do specific and focused research on the select population that has already been convicted.

An article appeared in the *American Journal of Human Genetics* in 1997 that made the following claim:

> [W]e have identified a panel of population-specific genetic markers that enable robust ethnic-affiliation estimation for major U.S. resident populations. In this report, we identify these loci and present their levels of allele-frequency differential between ethnically defined samples, and we demonstrate, using log-likelihood analysis, that this panel of markers provides significant statistical power for ethnic-affiliation estimation. (Shriver et al. 1997:957)

As in the earlier work by Devlin and Risch (1992a), one of the express purposes of this research is its "use in forensic ethnic affiliation estimation" (Shriver et al. 1997:957). While Devlin and Risch were quite circumspect, even skeptical about the ultimately utility of such attempts, later claims by Shriver et al. (1997) and Lowe et al. (2001) claim the viability of this methodology. This research agenda is likely to produce a significant challenge to the communitarian claim of a shared public safety interest.

The right of the individual to remain in a community while she or he has a contagious disease such as smallpox or tuberculosis is trumped by the state's right to protect the general public health of the citizenry. But molecular biology has played a powerful role in fracturing the public health consensus. While we could all agree that it is in our common interest to rid ourselves of cholera, yellow fever, tuberculosis, infectious meningitis, and smallpox, this communitarian consensus has been dramatically undermined as we have learned that some groups are at higher risk for a genetic disorder than others. Cystic fibrosis is a genetic disorder that affects the respiratory system in a life-threatening manner, but only those from Northern European ancestry are at significant risk. Beta-thalassemia is a blood disorder primarily associated with those having ancestors from the southern Mediterranean region. Sickle cell anemia is primarily associated, in the United States, with Americans of West African descent. And so it goes. In the 1970s, the public health consensus about general health screening was disrupted by this development, as group interests began to emerge to demand more funding for research and genetic testing of the gene disorder most associated with "their group" (Duster 1990).

If molecular genetics and the emergence of group-based research agendas fractured the public health consensus, we can expect an even more dramatic parallel development when it comes to discussions of public safety. It is almost inevitable that a research agenda will surface to try to find patterns of allele frequencies and then SNP profiles of different types of criminals. One could do an SNP profile of rapists and sex offenders and find some markers that they share. As I have noted above, "ethnic-affiliation estimations of allele-frequencies" is high on the research agenda in forensic science. But correlation is not causation, and like the phrenology of the nineteenth century, these markers will be precisely that: markers, not explanatory of the causes of violent crime. Even if the many causes of criminal violence (or any human behavior) are embedded in the full panoply of forces that begin with protein coding, there is interaction with the environment at every level. This interaction affects all outcomes, from the cellular environment all the way up through embryological development, even to the ways in which the criminal justice system focuses on one part of town and not another when making drug busts. We are bemused today about tales of nineteenth-century scientists who sought answers to criminal behavior by measuring the sizes and shapes of the heads of convicted felons, but we, too, can be seduced. The new IBM computers can make 7.5 trillion calculations per second for biological chip analysis. These are sirens beckoning researchers who wish to do parallel correlational studies of population-based allele frequencies with ethnic estimations and groupings of felons—a recurring seduction to false precision.

Why Search for the Genetic Basis of Any Given Behavior?

Of the hundreds of thousands, even millions of different kinds of behaviors that humans engage in across time and space, why are some of those behaviors selected as the subject of a genetic explanation? For the lay person, the first answer that usually comes to mind is that some behaviors seem to run in families. But lots of behaviors that run in families (working on the railroad versus on the police force, styles of humor, political persuasion) are not conceived as explainable by the genotype. Conversely, some behaviors that do not seem to run in families do get subjected to a genetic analysis.

If we leave the laity and move to the scientific literature, the primary, first order question remains, even if stated in different terms: What is the *theoretical* warrant for designating certain behaviors the subject of behavioral genetics while ignoring or dismissing other behavioral manifestations as unlikely to be caused by a genetic condition? Indeed, the mere suggestion of designating an occupational choice such as seafaring as best explained by genetics would *now* be dismissed as ludicrous, a blind alley, a waste of time and effort, a fruitless and unproductive pursuit. However, ninety years ago, it was commonly proposed in both scientific and lay circles that there was a genetic explanation for seafaring (Kevles 1985). The reason for exploring this idea was simple and straightforward, namely, that of all the men going out to sea as sailors, a very high proportion had fathers and grandfathers who went out to sea. That is hardly a theoretical warrant. Rather, it is an observation of an empirical regularity, followed by the search backward from the behavioral manifestation, or phenotype (seafaring) to the envisioned explanatory gene, the genotype. Contemporary scientists are not searching for a seafaring gene, but some are searching for a genetic explanation for violence and for antisocial and criminal behavior. The reason resides as much in the zeitgeist as in the state of scientific knowledge.

Within the boundaries of scientific inquiry, there is a second common answer to the question of why certain substantive arenas are subjected to a genetic prism: There exists body of literature on the topic, a body of empirical research.[7] But this is an empirical context, not a theoretical warrant. This is about tradition and careers and habits of the mind, not conceptually driven theorems, axioms, and interlinked hypotheses guided by a general theory of why some behaviors are more likely than others to be genetically explicable. Furthermore, this is a second-order frame to the answer, because it does not address the prior question of why that body of empirical work on a specific behavior was generated as a first-order question.

While there is no single or simple answer to the question of why certain behaviors are subjected to a genetic explanation and others are not, there is a major avenue that is both undertheorized, unexplored, and less appreciated for the rich potential for getting at the answer(s). There is an impressive array of different kinds of data strongly suggesting that the answer lies in the zeitgeist, the spirit of the times. If this calls for an answer to the question of why in *these* times, then that is precisely the point of entry for an explanation of what it is about these times that makes for the selection of particular behaviors as genetically explorable and explicable.

Criminal behavior can be a one-time phenomenon (impulsive homicide after discovery of adultery), or it can be a profession (the cat burglar, the professional thief, or the hit-man for organized crime). The theoretical warrant for examining the impulsive homicide as having a completely different etiology from the professional thief is well developed (Wolfgang 1958; Polk 1994). In the case of the latter, the empirical literature on both the professions and professional thievery is predictive of the manners and patterns of *routinized* behavior (Black 1988; Friedson 1970). That is in sharp contrast to the literature and conceptual framework with which one approaches an understanding of most homicides (Polk 1994), where—even if impulsivity sometimes gives way to planning—patterns of jealousy, shame, and rage predominate.

Conclusion: Searching for Correlations with Variable Etiologies

Crime can be an occasional diversion from one's ordinary life, such as depicted in Cameron's (1964) classic study of shoplifting, or it can be a compulsive-neurotic habituation (sexual abuse of the young by adults); alternatively, crime can be a rational, calculated decision (stealing a loaf of bread to feed one's family), or a routine occupational imperative, as in the case of the price-fixing scandal among the largest electrical companies in the United States (Geis 1982).

Crime can be a bureaucratic response to turf invasion, such as with organized crime during Prohibition (Tyler 1962), or a violation of existing social stratifying practices, such as teaching a slave to read, or, certainly, assisting a slave to run away (Harding 1983). In short, what is criminal is as variable, and as variably explained, as what is legal. To place in the same taxonomic system the theft of bread, exposing oneself in public, cat burglary, and euthanasia, as a single examinable phenotype is to engage in a breathtaking mystification of the classification of crime.

The theoretical warrant in each of these instances is both well articulated and highly differentiated in the best empirical work in criminology. As noted above, Cameron's (1964) research on shoplifting remains the standard and the classic, distinguishing and documenting how and why this form of crime is primarily (more than 90 percent) performed by amateurs. In so doing, Cameron explained why shoplifting has the lowest rate of recidivism when the perpetrator is confronted. At the other end of the continuum is the pickpocket, almost always a professional who works with groups of other professionals, where the rate of recidivism is, by contrast, extraordinarily high. The pickpocket regards arrest as an occupational hazard and has strategies for minimizing its effect on his usual behavior.

In chapter six, it was noted that the English used the death penalty as punishment for breaking into a linen factory to steal linen.

We now see this more clearly as a narrow, politically and economically motivated definition of a serious crime, but that is because we have a few centuries of hindsight. Today, we place in the same category (crime) someone who releases lethal nerve gas in a subway station (anonymous killing) with someone who shoots an abortion provider in the back. Fifty years from now, if some researcher went through the police records to show whether adoptees had a similar inclination to commit crime as did those in their biological families, someone might point out that the system of classification was constructed in such a way as to make any claims about a genetic basis for these crimes something beyond the benign phrase, highly problematic. The search for a genetic explanation for such a demonstrably variegated phenotype (criminal) requires a theoretical warrant that has never been delivered. The closest that one can come is in the abstracted notion of an antisocial personality, but even for this abstracted version, the conceptual flaw in this arena for an attempt to link phenotype to genotype is substantial. That is, given the demonstrably high empirical variability in what constitutes a crime, and also given the even more demonstrably high empirical variability in what constitutes antisocial behavior across time and space, how is it possible to search for a genotype? The answer, and the conclusion, provide strong reasons for deep concern.

The high variability of rates of crime for any one group, and the high variability for what constitutes antisocial behavior across time and space leaves the field of behavioral genetics with a limited methodological strategy for linking these behaviors to genes. Until quite recently, this was not a matter of concern, because behavioral genetics rarely worked at the molecular level. However, with the increasing use of high-speed computers to analyze DNA samples, and the turn of human molecular genetics to a focus upon difference, the most popular strategy will be to search for correlations between genetic markers (not in coding regions) of those already caught in the web of the criminal justice system. Because that system, in the United States, has become increasingly focused upon African Americans and Latinos in the last half-century, the collection of stored tissue samples will be remarkably skewed toward this segment of the population.

In the last quarter of the nineteenth century, the search for correlations between the behavior of criminals and the shapes of their heads generated highly respected scientific work. Within a few decades, however, that work fell into disrepute. Indeed, the sciences of phrenology and craniometry are now routinely ridiculed as pseudoscience. In the first quarter of the twenty-first century, we can expect to see publications in scientific journals that report a *somewhat successful* search for correlations between the behavior of criminals and DNA markers. High-speed computers analyzing 30 million points of difference (single nucleotide polymorphisms) will generate correlations with selected behaviors. As noted, every era is certain of its facts, and its leading proponents often ridicule earlier eras as pseudoscientific. Sometimes, they are correct. But close scrutiny and skepticism should be the posture toward behavioral research where the search warrant involves correlations between unexamined outcome data (trouble with the authorities) and noncoding regions of the DNA. This could easily become the phrenology of the twenty-first century.

APPENDIX A
Intermediate Steps Between Micro and Macro Integration: The Case of Screening for Inherited Disorders

Introduction

Every generation of social scientists has its own set of injunctions about the importance of connecting theories to observations.[1] Sometimes the swing of the pendulum to one end is so dramatic as to produce a powerful reaction. At the turn of the last century, an early generation, led by Franz Boas, reacted against the grand theoretical systems of evolutionism with an emphatic swing to lengthy, comprehensive field observations and detailed taxonomy. At mid-century, Merton led a balanced attack against both grand theory and low-level empiricism with a plea for "middle-range" coverage of the empirical world.

But it is late in the twentieth century and the age of specialization is well upon us. We are presently confronted with a situation of thousands of workers in apparently unrelated vineyards, the proliferation of theoretical and methodological camps, and a wide split between those who work on what have come to be called "micro" studies of specific scenes and those who attempt "macro" studies of gross national, international, and comparatively informed historical trends in the polity and the economy. Accordingly, the sages of this period calling for the integration of theory and observation enjoin us to draw relationships between macro analysis of social structures and micro studies of local scenes. The obstacles to accomplishing this, however, are paradoxically "spacy" and intangible. A close-up study of farmworkers in the Central Valley of California may produce an elegant leap to world-systems theory, but no matter how graceful it is, unless the warrant is established with intermediate connectors, the critic has an easy mark. Likewise, when grand functionalists and grand Marxists alike see evidence of "the system" in every setting, both are open to effective broadsides that range from reification to tautologizing.

The direction one moves from microscopic to macroscopic work may well be a matter of taste or style. But for either, it is a precipitous fall or a wondrous catapult if no rungs are available on the notches in between the base and the top. If we follow the metaphor of the ladder a bit further, we see some of the problems to be encountered when trying to place intermediate rungs. A major obstacle is that each of the rungs is often associated with a different kind of methodology. The bottom rung, direct empirical observation, requires ability to engage in either partici- pant observation, the use of sympathetic informants, or experimental manipulation in a laboratory setting.

Depending upon the problem studied, the next rung might be "formed" by utilizing local and regional demographic analysis of patterns of migration; employment, age, and sex pyramids; review of racial and ethnic composition of the workforce; and a review of the educational and welfare system. The context can be forged by the ferreting and interpretation of historical materials that draw the prospective reader, where relevant, to a comparative treatment of the relative credibility of documents and the accounts of old-timers. Excellent histories themselves contain many tiers of analysis, observation, and interpretation, and a model for this kind of work is Fernand Braudel's monumental *Civilisation materielle, economie, et capitalisme.*[2] Braudel is a historian whose earlier work on Spain achieved a notable integration of both detailed portraits of daily peasant and village life and heavy attention to patterns of gross mercantile trade. While his students and followers frequently went off in the direction of local and limited descriptions of daily life, Braudel himself reasserts in his most recent work the primary importance of framing these local scenes with the larger economic and political landscape.

For a study of the contemporary world, however, another rung can be crafted from analysis of the structure or organization, both with regard to the nature of accountability to the relevant overarching organization in a highly bureaucratized world, and also with respect to the nature of the network of linkages between relevant organizations.[3]

When we finally reach the highest levels, however, we are left more with "indicators," less with the direct observation of behavior. Economies and polities cannot be seen as units in motion. Rather, what we observe are national rates of employment, gross rates of growth, surveys of attitu- dinal change along the political spectrum, summaries of voting trends, or, in wartime, body counts of the enemy killed. From these indicators, we try to weave a picture of national and international complexity and scope.

A measure of success is the degree to which the audience determines the weave between levels, observations, theorizing, and indicators to be compelling. It is the kind of enterprise attempted by William Shawcross (1979) in his account of the destruction of Cambodia. Shawcross's analysis takes him from the organization level at the State and Defense departments, through the analysis of documents of committee meetings and memos from key figures, through direct interviews with embassy personnel in Saigon and Phnom Penh. Shawcross is not an academic trying to generalize about the use of theory and methods. He is a journalist giving an account of a particular historical development in two countries. However, the methods that he employs and the case that he presents are both excellent models for the integration of levels in inquiry.

As a journalist, Shawcross was not limited by the "trained incapacity" of the academic specialist who uses only a limited arsenal of methods. Academics in the social sciences go through a training in which there is a subtle process of differentiation and stratification that accompanies the learned use of a specific method. We may be told by the writers of methods textbooks, and by graduate instructors, that a method is only as good as its applicability to the specific question it is designed to help answer. However, the structure of the disciplines, the weighing of graduate curricula in methods at the "better" departments, and the path to publication in the "better" journals quickly give graduate students the message. Methods are stratified!

There are exceptions, but the pattern is irrefutable, and few object to graduate methods courses being taught overwhelmingly by specialists in surveys, factor and network analysis, and model building. Status positions in the professional hierarchy produce an entrenchment to the use of preferred methods. Method A gets professionally treated as superior to method B quite independent of the problem addressed. While methods are stratified, it does not end there. No less than theories, methods carry with them ideologies. The qualitative camp fights back with their own journals, increasing the specialization. Feeling embattled, the survey researchers counter with ideological formulations about "field methods" as being prior to the *real* testing of hypotheses. Direct observation is characterized as hypothesis-generating, little more.

This career preference for certain methods is one reason why, on any given research problem, it is difficult to connect the micro studies to macroscopic analysis. The intermediate steps (links, rungs, or connectors) often call for the use of different methods.

Before I turn to an illustration of this, it will be useful to specify what is meant here by this notion of intermediate steps, and why this may be theoretically as well as empirically useful. A "ladder of abstraction" carries the implicit notion that direct observation of a local setting (especially in contemporary, urban, bureaucratized, technologically advanced countries) is insufficient to understand the social forces that help to explain the social behavior observed.

While one kind of explanation can be taken from the people in the scene (their stated motives and interests), actors themselves are often unaware of historical, demographic, and other factors that can better account for what occurs than the stated motives.

Interposed between the individual in the local scene and the gross explanations of social, economic, and political patterns, we have strong theoretical grounds for assuming that an intermediary interpolation exists—an institution, organization, or bureaucratic structure. Grounds for this assumption can be located in every forum, from classical theory (Weber) to a wide spectrum of empirical studies of formal organizations to contemporary prognosticians and observations about the "bureaucratization" of the world.

If much of the world is broken down into intermediate organizations that mediate much of social life between grand cultural ethos or federal law or international cartel, then a strategy for apprehending that world must include a concern for this level.

The choice of levels of analysis is generated from our broadest understandings of the relevant points of reference and sources of decisions, policy, action, and behavior in Western cultures. As we have just noted, almost all behavior in these cultures can be located in an institutional or bureaucratic context. Whether it is the practice of medicine, the marketing of a product, a small local business enterprise, or the education of the young, most of human social life that we would like to study can be situated in an organizational or institutional context that approximates the old sociological notion of "formal organizations."

In a study of a particular empirical or theoretical problem, the choice of the specific organizational level should be dictated by the theoretical question posed. For example, in studying local policy in an elementary school, one could choose variably between the local school board, the office of regional superintendent, or the state department of public education. While ideally one might wish to deal with all three levels of organizational context, practical limitations might necessitate a theoretically dictated selection. In any event, the organizational frame is one of the "rungs" that we can reasonably conceptually interpose between the micro level of individual, situated, local action, and grand federal, or national, policy in education.

Technically, the demographic, epidemiological, or historical analyses of a particular local scene are, of course, not so much different levels (with respect to abstraction) as they are ways of placing context around the scene and providing grounding. Before we move to different levels of abstraction, we need to take an early step of mapping the larger terrain. Again, choice of *how* one enlarges the scope is determined by the theoretical bent of the researcher and the empirical problem under investigation. If we return to the example of a study of a school, if it is a new experimental school, we won't have as much history as a study of a school steeped in tradition. However, the former might better choose to emphasize more changing migration and birth patterns that generated the constituency for a new school.

All social action can be conceived as local in the sense that it must occur in settings bounded by local time and local space and the local constitutive expectancies of social exchange. It may ramify and serve as a future point of reference for many other local scenes, both temporally and spatially. Great moments in history and great centers of power share this character-istic, and in this sense there could be resistance to the characterization of these situations as "local." But the question of whether the local scene has some future historic import is a problematic matter for empirical assessment. That it is local is the empirical given, and provides justifica-tion for taking the natural setting as a central point of origin of social research.

The choice of a local scene is determined by some practical or theoreti-cal concern. The specific empirical problem of gene screening illustrates possible ways to achieve the integration between the micro observations of the local scene and the gross general patterns and understandings of larger social and political forces. The following remarks address the focus for the approach that I have taken.

The "Natural Setting" as the Starting Point

Ethology emerged from the naturalist critique of the zoological method.[4] The latter took highly controlled surroundings, the zoo, as an adequate setting for the close and systematic observation of animal life. The ethological critique stressed the inviolate character of the natural habitat as the starting point of observation, despite the obstacles to direct observation in natural settings.

If one were searching for an analog to zoology in human life, it would be penology. Clearly, certain important things can be learned about humans from studying them in prisons. It is equally clear that the prison has features that prohibit one from learning about other important as-pects of human social life. Two basic considerations are the variable transmutations of sexual energy by locking out the opposite sex, and the powerful constraints on exchange/market relations. Would we not be grossly misled about key elements of Italian, French, or American life if we were restricted to the study of Italian, French, and American prisons?

For humans, the "natural setting" means something quite different than what it means for animals. The corporation, the law office, the factory are not in the same way naturalistic as the forest, riverbanks, and wild habitats. For humans, "natural settings" in this usage means simply the places where people would ordinarily or routinely be doing what they are doing as they live out their lives. If one is to study or measure "intelligence" among humans, then, even if one assumes capacity for abstract reasoning to be central, the best place to do it would be in the natural setting in which intelligence is called forth as a feature of living. With both parties using abstract reasoning powers, a factory worker might be measured as far more intelligent on the shop floor than the corporate lawyer. If we take them both out of their "natural settings" and put them in the "neutral" setting of an IQ test, it may be more like studying animals in zoos and people in prisons, in that it so removes the participants from the natural setting that it distorts the meaning of intelligence.

With such "neutral" IQ testing, the lawyer might do better precisely because this test setting more closely approximates his or her natural setting (routine way of living) than that of the factory worker. Such tests are zoological. Likewise, a two-hour interview, a mailed questionnaire, a laboratory experiment, while useful techniques for certain purposes, are all analogous to the zoological study of animals. To repeat, important things can be learned from prison studies or zoological studies. However, such research needs to be complemented by other kinds and levels of research if we are to have confidence that the findings apply to human social behavior in the setting in which it ordinarily occurs.

If we combine observation in the natural setting with these other methods, we may be able to supplement our knowledge in the same way that zoologists and ethologists can complement one anothers' work.

To return to the notion of the ladder, I noted earlier that in attempting to move from local empirical detail and grounded observation (micro studies) to a highly generalized understanding and explanation of gross economic, social, or political trends, if we are to avoid a gigantic "leap" to the highest rung, we have to place more rungs on the ladder.

Levels and Methods of Inquiry

In order to carry out research in this area and to integrate the "micro" empirical scenes, ultimately, with a "macro" analysis, a research plan is imperative. Below is the outline to incorporate four distinct, complementary levels of inquiry into the problem of genetic screening is outlined. The goal is to draw the interrelationships between these levels, partly by tracing problems through them to illustrate the nature of the connections, or lack of connection. The four levels are:

1. *The Step to Macro-Analysis*
   Law and lobbying: vertical integration of federal and state, with intersection of lobbying interests that are potentially international.

2. *Intermediate Steps to Vertical Integration*
   Administration and organization: vertical integration of federal (Public Health Service), state (state Department of Public Health), and local (clinic or hospital) levels.

3. *Two Micro-Observational Levels*
   a) Physician and client: vertical integration of physician as professional (thus, connection to organizational base, with ideology and interests) with client or patient (lodged in particular community or cultural base).
   b) Family and community: loop back integration to lobbying federal and state; tie-in to clinics with communal sanctions, positive and negative, for participation in screening programs.

4. *History and Context as Grounding Step*
   Discussion of the history of mass health screening, and the technological changes that have permitted new forms of screening for inherited disorders.

APPENDIX B
Screening Issues in Counseling

A research team from a well-used amniocentesis center in northern California at the end of the seventies reported the following patterns it had uncovered from an analysis of more than three thousand amniocenteses. The excerpt which follows refers to a one-year period of the study, and data presented in chapter 4 support these findings:

> A survey of the patients seen from July, 1976, through June, 1977, reveals that 56.2 per cent of the mothers and 78.6 per cent of their mates had some college education, including 25.9 per cent and 35.5. per cent, respectively, who had done graduate work. The average gross annual income for all families was $25,271. These statistics suggest that the lower socioeconomic groups have yet to use prenatal diagnosis facilities as fully as those in the higher socioeconomic groups. (Golbus et al., 1979:158)

There are no quick and easy socio-linguistic devices for the summary analysis of the several score lengthy interviews and genetic counseling sessions collected and recorded in this project. Given the time and space constraints of a manuscript (and the taxation of the reader's interest beyond reasonable limits), it is neither possible nor desirable to include all the transcriptions of interviews and counseling sessions. One strategy is to present select material, with analysis running alongside, afterwards or intermittently. But this raises the insoluble problem of a convincing justification for the selection of case materials. A sampling and coding solution fail for two reasons: if the data were "quantified" in some manner, then the selection of every nth entry or every nth case would provide us with the notion that randomization assures representation. But every nth sentence makes no sense with these interview data, *for only the context* of the nth sentence can provide us with its probable meaning for the relevant actors.

The second reason is related. The coding of these data could not get at the issue central to this section of our work: namely, what clients take from the presentation of genetic information that informs their further action (outside the session) in sustaining or terminating a pregnancy after the information about the fetus is obtained.

From the work of Sorenson and his associates (1981, 1980, 1977, 1975), we already know a great deal about what clients of genetic counseling remember and forget, how they evaluate the counselors, and the likely imputation of neutrality and bias. Our concern is located at a different level. On the one hand, each counseling session is a unique configuration of personal experience, of familial and peer pressures (or lack of them), of religious and spiritual beliefs (or lack of them), of connections of specific histories to the genetic disease (or lack of them), and, of course, the social and cultural meanings attached to each.

But while there are necessarily uniquely important variables in each case, there are some invariant features to each session. Indeed, this is one of the most striking and theoretically critical observations that will occupy our attention. While well aware of the high variability and idiosyncracy of each case, the counselor tries to communicate very similar content across cases, as if this variability and uniqueness were momentarily suspended or "bracketed." This is a feature of the bureaucratic organization of the counseling task, the essence of the professionalization of genetic counseling discussed in chapter 5.

The strategy chosen here, and the rationale for it, are tied directly to these theoretical and methological considerations. I have chosen to focus on two sessions in which there is a sharp contrast between clients, but where the counselor tries to communicate the same kind of information.

The second strategy of presentation is related to these concerns. In addition to the analysis of the actual counseling session, we report on interviews completed with the couple independently. These interviews were conducted (a) in the privacy of the respondent's home, where the genetic counselor was not present; (b) with the male and female separately, before the diagnostic test; and (c) with the male and female separately, after the diagnostic test had been reported to the couple. In the presentation and the analysis, we will see how significant set and setting can be for making sense of what does and does not occur in the counseling session.

In sum, the following kinds of socio-linguistic assumptions have been made:

1. That the counselor uses the same linguistic register and repertoire in a bureaucratic setting. We have an abundance of evidence that these discourse strategies tend to be invariant (Gumperz, 1982).

2. That the knowledge base of the client had extraordinary variability, and this variability, coupled with the invariant features of the counselor's

discourse, produces a tension with direct implications for social policy and social theory. (Again, our concern is not with sampling a population screened genetically, but with the framing of choice.)

3. That the "register" of the counselor presupposes that the clients understand and know what is important, even when the counselor and the counseled have quite different reference points for what is "important." The short time period of the counseling session insures this, and the counselor literally cannot afford to spend time going through "the basics" with respect to the "important" genetic knowledge base.

Risk Taking versus Risk Aversion

While the genetic counselor tries to convey some notion of the reduction of risk (through testing, counseling, etc.), the counselee is likely to see an important measure of risk whatever avenue chosen. This is explained by two factors. Those who are counseled about the level of risk for a genetic disorder in their prospective offspring hear numbers and probabilities. These "hearers" tend to convert probabilities into an either/or risk, and decide in a corresponding binary mode. In the work of Lippman-Hand and Fraser (1979), and Beeson and Golbus (1984), those who make decisions after a genetic counseling session typically reconceptualize their prospective situation in terms of "What would I do if?" versus "What would I do if not?"

This combined with the tendency of the counselor to converge the *logic* of risk reduction with the *sense* of risk aversion. We come to this conclusion on grounds that are partly theoretical, partly empirical. For the latter, although no claim is made about the representativeness of the two cases to be presented in terms of the counselees, the counselor's remarks are typical of the kinds of remarks made throughout the more than forty cases that provide the basic data for this study. But more significant is the theoretical case. The content of the genetic counseling is heavily loaded, while what the genetic counselor delivers is muted by the professionalism of the bureaucratic style of communication. Tversky and Kahneman (1981, 1978) and Cicourel (1982) have data to show that in situations of uncertainty, people are likely to let a "hunch" override the risk figures presented to them.[1]

The formal situation, then, is that individual actors are asked to make a decision under conditions of both stress and uncertainty. The professional counselor is trying to relieve that sense of uncertainty by providing in a calm and rational tone, and in a linear style, what is known, including risk figures for this *particular* individual case (based upon available family history, national reports, etc.),[2] providing factual information that makes things appear clear and straightforward. But uncertainty dominates the scene, nonetheless. Let us say that the counselor provides the risk figure of 1 in 600; or 1 in 350. What do these figures represent, phenomenologically, for the person listening? As these risk figures move up or down, what does and what should this mean for decision-making? The common-sense notion is simple enough: that as the risk figure goes up, the chances are fewer, and one should act accordingly. But we shall see in one of our cases (a typical one) how the report of a risk figure of 1 in 200 is converted, comparatively, to a much higher risk figure.

Data Collection and the Selection of the Two Cases

The following section contains data collected in genetic counseling and interview sessions, conducted from early 1976 through the middle of 1978. The women were between thirteen and eighteen weeks pregnant, and had either been referred by their own physicians, or had sought the appointment at the amniocentesis clinics themselves. The genetic counseling sessions average approximately fifteen minutes in length and, in every instance reported here, preceded the amniocentesis.

Before the session, the woman (or, when the husband or prospective father was present, both parties) signed a consent form, after being told about the sociological aspects of the study. The sociologist was present in the room for the genetic counseling session, and took notes and obtained permission to tape record the session. In both clinics, the genetic counselor was a white woman in her middle to late thirties.

Two cases were selected for detailed reports and analysis. These cases are presented to show the invariances in the counselor's communication style and strategy, all the while remaining within the limits of the normal range of variability of the knowledge base of the clients. To emphasize and clarify this point, I did not choose a couple with a professional health science background and contrast them with a couple who are functionally illiterate, and whose class and economic backgrounds would put them at the extreme ends of a continuum. Instead, in the first instance, I chose a professional couple with moderate knowledge of the genetic disorder, and in the second instance, a young Chicano couple with some knowledge of Down syndrome from a family history.

We will analyze two transcripts. However, in the interests of space and time, narrative summaries are provided in sections where what transpired does not require the full transcription.

The following exchange is a session of genetic counseling prior to the administration of the test. Following Kessler (1981), the purpose of this presentation is not to evaluate the counselor, but to illustrate a number of social issues. I have chosen this case because it typifies some of the common questions, problems, and issues that come up in such a session.

The only editing that has been done entails an occasional summary of a section of the transcript. The purpose of these summaries is to provide relief from some tedious repetitions or tangential remarks, while maintaining continuity for the reader about what materials were covered in the section not reported verbatim. The reader will note by the numbers on the left side of the page when there is a direct quotation from the session. All numbered lines are direct quotations, a system that facilitates referral back to the text during analysis and summaries. The husband is a lawyer, forty years of age. The woman about to undergo amniocentesis is thirty-six. Both are white. In the second column, C is for counselor, M is for male, and F is for female:

1. C: All right, have a seat. Robert, do you like to be called Robert or Bob?
2 M: Bob.
3 C: OK. I understand you've agreed to participate in the social research
4   study?
5 F: Yes.
6 C: Well, let's begin with your age. How old are you Bob?
7 M: Me? Forty.
8 C: I already have M's age. That's why I didn't need to ask. Now I need
9   to know about pregnancies that the two of you have had together, including
10   miscarriages and abortions and live-born children.
11 F: None.
12 C: None. OK. Do you have children by a previous mate?
13 F: No.
14 C: You've never been pregnant?
15 F: No.
16 C: OK, how about you? Do you have children?
17 M: No, we've been married for thirteen years.
18 C: Oh, was this a plan? A surprise?
19 F: A plan.
20 C: OK, that's all I need to know. Essentially you are here because at the
21   age of thirty-five there is an increased incidence of a chromosomal disorder
22   known as the Down syndrome. Many people call it mongolism, but they
23   are the same thing. What it is is an extra chromosome. All of us have
24   forty-six chromosomes. This is how many we are supposed to have. That's
25   how many there are supposed to be. Occasionally, there is an accident of
26   cell division and a fetus will end up with forty-seven. Then it has the Down syn-
27   drome or mongolism. It's an accidental happening. No one has any con-
28   trol over it and there is no way to know that is has happened unless you
29   do this test. This test takes fluid out of the amniotic sac. Not for the

30   fluid, but for the cells that are shed into the fluid from the fetus. We can
31   grow these cells and at some point look into the nucleus and see the
32   chromosomes and count them. The doctor will take out eighteen cubic centi-
33   meters of fluid. That is this tubeful. (She shows the tube.) Your body
34   will make the eighteen back in a few hours, so it's just like nothing has been
35   done. You read the letter describing in some detail what the test will be
36   like. The discomfort associated with it is about the same as when you
37   get a shot because you do get a shot of zylocaine, a local anesthetic and
38   that stings, and however much you react to a shot, you will no doubt
39   react to that. But you will be lying down.

In the introductory exchange, the counselor's questions were perfunc-
tory. However, after only a few of these questions, we note a shift in the
counselor's presumption about her clients. We see evidence that she
assumes that she is dealing with a couple possessing technical knowledge
based upon their educational backgrounds; she uses without explanation
the terms "amniotic sac," "18 cubic centimeters," and "zylocaine, a local
anesthetic." But more significantly, notice that when she explains that the
"cells . . . are shed into the fluid from the fetus" (line 30), she comfortably
presumes that her audience receives the information with a nodding
acquaintance.

As we will see in our next session where the clients are working-class
Latino, the case before us presents an extraordinarily sharp contrast in
the presumption of understanding. Keep in mind that these sessions
average only fifteen minutes in length.[3]

41 F: I would think that if women are going to have a baby, they ought to be
42   able to take a shot.

43 C: [Laughs] Well, people often don't think in those terms. But you are

44   right, it's a fairly minor outpatient procedure. The only risk that we
45   know can happen is that about 1 woman in 200 will have a miscarriage.
46   The danger of miscarriage is over in four to six days. We don't think it
47   is elevated over what the danger is just by being pregnant at this stage,
48   but since you have had the test, we can't say that it would have happened
49   anyway, because we don't know what would have happened. That's
50   what you trade for the information that we can give you. At your age
51   there is a 1-in-100 chance of having a child with the Down syndrome. I
52   don't know if you think that is big or little.

53 M: The odds of having a Down's child is 100-to-1 and the odds of miscarrying
54   200-to-1?

55 C: Yes.

56 F: It sounds like a very small chance to me, 1 in 100.

57 C: When you were in your 20s, it was 1 in 1,200.

58   F: Yet, it's much more likely than I would care to risk.

59   C: OK, then, that's why you have chosen to have the test.

60   F: Yet, that's why I did it.

In this exchange, the counselor provides the risk figure of 1 in 100 chances for the child to have Down syndrome. She then asks what appears to be a substantive question, namely, whether this risk is "big or little" (line 52). The husband makes one of many possible reasonable juxtapositions of risks. He contrasts the 100-to-1 risk of Down's with the 200-to-1 risk of miscarriage brought about by amniocentesis. When the wife counters with her commonsense observation that the 1-in-100 risk figure for Down's sounds like a very small risk to her, the counselor shifts the comparative frame for her.

Here we have the portrait of figure and ground, the choice of which relief to provide by the counselor. How does she choose to place these comparative figures—in what context—for a decision? The counselor might have chosen a "nondirective" path and said nothing, exacting instead more from the couple about their feelings about the risks, letting them air possible alternative fears and hopes about how great a risk would be involved. Or, she could provide data indicating that the figure of 1 in 100 is either high or low.

The counselor's response (line 57) is clear and decisive. In response to the woman client's rumination that the 100-to-1 chance of Down's as a low risk, the counselor says, "When you were in your 20s, it was 1 in 1,200."

Notice the changing response of the pregnant woman. She perceives that the new "relevant" contrast is no longer the 200-to-1 risk (amniocentesis and onset of a miscarriage risk) versus 100-to-1 (Down syndrome child), but the 200-to-1 risk versus the 1,200-to-1 risk of having a child with Down's when she was younger. But where is the choice for her? She cannot return to her twenties. The woman then says that "it is much more likely than I would care to risk." But what is more likely? Is it not the relief provided by the counselor that shapes the new response? The counselor then "explains" to the woman that this is why she (the pregnant woman) has chosen to have the amniocentesis (lines 59–60). The woman replies, "Yes, that's why I did it."

There is subtlety in this exchange that demands closer scrutiny and analysis. In particular, note the continuing theme in the counselor's remarks that these are "medical" problems, and her reminder to her clients that they are not "here" for sex determination. The phrasing is noteworthy:

62   C: Because the test can tell you if that's happened and if the fetus is male or

63   female. I don't know whether you want that information. You don't
64   have to have it if you don't want it. It's all your choice, whatever you
65   want to do.

66 F: Sure.

67 C: The hard part of this test, the hardest part, is going to be waiting to get
68   the results. It takes about four weeks, sometimes as long as five or six
69   weeks.

70 F: Oh, really.

71 C: We wish it would be a month and very rarely it is. But it almost always
72   takes five weeks and it can be six. And that is because cell growth is slow
73   and it is variable. Different cells grow at different rates, from different
74   people, at different times and in different atmospheric conditions. It's a
75   very complex kind of involved process, and if we tell you it takes less
76   time, it really makes it hard for you.

(At this point, the counselor takes a few minutes to review phone numbers where
the couple can be reached in order that they can be informed of the results of
the test.)

78   Let me see, is there anything I have not covered that you need to know?

79 M: Yes, I want to go in with her when she has the test.

80 F: You want to go in—that's fine.

81 C: No reason why you can't. Now, I'll just tell you what will happen. The
82   doctor will do a sonogram. What he'll do is give you a pelvic examina-
83   tion just like Dr. X does. He is an obstetrician. He is an expert in
84   high-risk pregnancy and in genetics, so if you have any questions on your
85   mind that you want to ask, you've got an expert captive for a while, so
86   feel free to ask him. After the sonogram you will just lie back and relax.
87   He'll clean your tummy off real clean and he'll give you a shot of zylo-
88   caine way down here. That will sting. Then he'll put the amniocentesis
89   needle in, which is just the same gauge. It's a very narrow needle. And
90   he'll draw out the fluid. He'll put on a bandaid and tell you to go home.
91   There is nothing you have to do today or tonight that is any different
92   than what you did last week, OK?

93 F: Are they any after-effects?

94 C: Well, we have some women reporting cramps, which we think has a lot to
95   do with how tense you get, because if you tense up your stomach muscles,
96   you tend to get cramps. This is sort of involuntary. There isn't much
97   you can do about it. Sometimes breathing through your mouth helps and
98   sometimes it doesn't. All you have to do now before the test is go to the
99   ladies' room and empty your bladder. Whatever you did last night you
100   can do tonight.

(The counselor has an exchange here about the other uses of the
diagnostic test, then hands the couple a pamphlet summarizing results

of the tests for the previous decade. The counselor says that the test has been performed for a dozen years, and the woman responds that she recently read about it in a magazine.)

There is a deep assumption in the session on the part of all three parties, but especially on the part of the counselor, that the woman (F) is going through with the amniocentesis. At several points, there is an exchange in which thoughtful reconsideration of the odds and benefits might have produced some doubt. At each of those points, the counselor provides both emotional and empirical support for continuation, even anticipating the couple's anxiety level on these matters, assuaging that anxiety even before it might be uttered. For example, from lines 62 to 100, the counselor is gracious, empathetic, emotionally supportive, and comforting on the matter of a lengthy delay in obtaining the results. She *anticipates* the anxiety they might experience from not knowing the outcome of the test for five weeks or more. As she sets the stage for this delay, she shapes the concern around the timing of the communication from the laboratory. With consideration for the possible anxiety of the couple, she appropriately wants to err on the side of overestimating the delay of that communication.

The concern is focused upon a specific anxiety and, of course, a legitimate and important issue. But in terms of the physiological changes in the body, the psychological connections to it, and the medical and health concerns, a wait of five weeks could just as easily have produced an analysis by the counselor about the difficulties of such a delay, on these other grounds. That is, a counseling session of such short duration needs to be analyzed as much for what is not said, as for what is said. A second-trimester abortion could have been accurately characterized as much more difficult to handle emotionally, psychologically, and physiologically. I do not mean to imply that the counselor is therefore selectively and consciously using only information to weight a decision in favor of the test. Rather, the main issue here at which to take a closer look is the implicit set of assumptions that are likely to guide a counseling session on imparting information about the uses of the new genetics technology. It should be kept in mind that the couple counseled above are both college educated, well into their adult lives, and are sufficiently sophisticated about new developments to ask about the uses of this test.

A number of researchers and commentators have noted that the notion of unbiased, nondirective genetic counseling is a fiction. Hsia (1979) takes the position that by raising the option of prenatal diagnosis, counsel is implicit endorsement not only of procedures for detection of inherited disorders, but of the termination of pregnancy if the test is possible. Kessler (1981) emphasizes what he calls the "meta-message" of genetic counseling. Kessler presents a transcript of a counseling session for content analysis, but he is careful to note than an examination of the content of such a session may miss the larger message that is conveyed to the clients. The state endorses genetic counseling by funding the training of genetic counselors. In this context, the genetic counselor's neutral information-provider presentation, with state sanction, is a meta-message that any of the choices offered is acceptable, including inaction.

Let us contrast this with a hypothetical state medical facility offering "counseling" for back ailments, referring patients alternately to options including orthopedic surgery, chiropractry, and osteopathy. To present a potential client with alternatives is to give implicit sanction to each. In our hypothetical case, the state would find itself on a collision course with the medical establishment, since chiropractry and osteopathy fall outside of the traditionally sanctioned medical practices. Hsia is correct in noting that the mere existence of prenatal diagnosis as a part of the package of alternatives provides a new kind of legitimacy. And Kessler's character-ization of a meta-message is possibly the implicit message that informs much of what is not said in the session recorded above.

In the next session, we have material from an exchange between the genetic counselor and a Chicano couple. He is a carpenter, aged twenty-seven. The wife does not work outside the home. Their first daughter, Juanita, has Down syndrome. Thus, they have come in for amniocentesis because the view is that the fetus may also be at risk. We pick up the session when the counselor is out of the room; the female turns to the social researcher (E) and asks a question:

1 F: I'm kind of scared it might hurt the baby.

2 E: Talk to C about that when she comes back. She'll tell you why you don't
3   need to worry about that.

4 F: If it hurts me, it doesn't matter as much as the baby.

5 M: Do they do it here?

6 E: No, they do it next door in a room just like this.

7 M: What's going to happen here?

8 E: She's just going to tell you about it and ask you some questions.

9 F: Do they take the blood out of the baby or out of me?

10 E: They don't take blood from the baby, they take some fluid from around
11   it.

12 F: Oh, not the baby, just the fetus.

13 E: Well, the fetus is the baby before it is big enough to live on its own.
      [Enter C]

14 C: Why don't you ask me some of your questions?

15 F: Well, what I'm really concerned about is if it's going to hurt the baby. It

16   pokes the bag, right? Can it leak?

17   C: Leakage is very, very rare. It seals right away.

18   F: What they take out is the fluid that's in the bag, right?

19   C: They take out some of the fluid that's in the bag. They only take out a
20   little bit of what's in the bag. What they take out is made back by your
21   body in just a couple of hours.

22   F: Because I thought this test would poke the baby.

23   C: Oh no, definitely not. It just gets some of the fluid. And the reason we
24   want to get some of that fluid is that in the fluid cells that have shed
25   off the body of the fetus. It's those cells that can tell us whether this
26   fetus has the Down syndrome. The way they told that Juanita had that
27   problem is they took cells from her blood, but we don't need to do that
28   because we can get cells from the fluid that have washed off the fetus.

29   F: And how long does it take to grow?

30   C: It takes a month. You won't know for about four weeks.

31. M: Do you know how many months she is pregnant?

32   C: I know, I checked it out with the doctor and that's fine.

33   F: If my baby's got Down syndrome, it's not going to hurt me, it's going to
34   hurt her. It's going to hurt the baby, that's why.

35. C: Therapeutic abortion can be done here at that point if you and your hus-
36.   band agree and want that done. It's safer for your health than full-term
37   delivery. It would be done in a hospital and done properly so there
38   wouldn't be a danger to you.

39   F: One more thing. Do you know a lot about Down syndrome?

40. C: I know something about it. You probably know a lot about it yourself.

41   F: Not really. Just what the doctors have said. They've told me usually if
42   it comes from inheritance it's from the mother, right? The mother's the
43   one and the father didn't have anything to do with it?

44   C: We don't know that. We don't know that for sure. We don't know if
45   it's the mother or the father, or both of you. We don't know. We are
46   doing research all the time to try to find out. And the kind of Down syn-
47   drome that Juanita has is what is called the accidental kind. That means
48   it does not run in your family. It means that it was an accident at the
49   time of conception or just before in which just one extra chromosome got
50   put into all the cells in Juanita's body. None of us have any way of con-
51   trolling how our cells divide. None of us have any choice in the matter.
52.   We just have to accept what happens.

53. M: Excuse me, could you explain that again? How does that work?

54   C: I have a book for you. I'd like you to come to my office and get this
55   book. I will give you instructions for when you leave here where to go
56   and pick up this book. Because it's very important that you read this
57   book, the two of you. And after I'm done talking to you, I want you to

58   go out in the waiting room and watch the slide show. The very first part
59   of that slide show explains some of this to you. I don't really have
60   enough time to explain everything to you. But I want you to know that
61   there is no way that either of you did anything that made Juanita
62   have the Down syndrome.

Culpability, Knowledge, and Expertise in Counseling

One of the recurrent themes in the counseling sessions we monitored, and which reappeared in interviews with those who later went through genetic screening, is the location of blame. Contrary to the conventional wisdom and popular belief, the amount of formal education or class position has no bearing upon the tendency to find culpability. For some, the blame may lie in human agency. For others, it may be the fates. But the college-educated and the postgraduate professionals were just as likely to blame external forces beyond their control for their "victimization" as were the high school dropouts.

In the exchange reported above, the counselor is careful to reassure the couple that neither is to be blamed for their first child having a chromosomal abnormality that resulted in Down syndrome. The counselor emphasizes the accidental nature of the occurrence, and draws the relevance for how the couple can think about the birth of their next child. But we should note here an interesting contradiction. The counselor correctly contradicts the medical doctor who reportedly informed the woman that inheritance from the mother's side "causes" Down syndrome. As she says, "We just don't know." But if we reread lines 44 to 62 carefully, we see an important strategy of support by the counselor. After appropriately assessing the state of current scientific and medical knowledge about the causes of Down syndrome, she asserts that it does not run in the family.

Recall that there are two primary grounds for referring a pregnant woman to a clinic for prenatal diagnosis by amniocentesis: (a) the woman is over thirty-five or (b) there is a family history of an inherited disorder. In the case before us, the woman is twenty-one years old. She was referred because her first child had Down syndrome. The counselor is in a "counseling bind." For dealing with the emotional support issue of blame and culpability, there will be an insistence that "this is the accidental kind that does not run in families." Yet, the very reason for referring this very young ·mother for amniocentesis is that she has had one child with an inherited disorder, and "we just don't know" about lineage and causation. A woman who has had a child with Down syndrome, is for some unknown reason, at a greater risk for having another child with this chromosomal abnormality than women in the greater population. If the increased probability does not "reside" in the family, does it "inhere" in the individual? Yet, the counselor is also concerned with the psychological state of the couple. The avoidance of any grounds for assigning culpability is an important goal. The counselor says little about the clear *location* of increased risk, except in a general diffusion of the issue of blame. As we return to the current session, notice the use of risk figures, by age:

64 F: It can happen to anyone.

65. F: How many people have they found that the babies have Down syndrome?

66 C: One to two percent of the time. You are only twenty-one. We think your chance
67   is about 1 percent. If you were thirty-five or thirty-six, we'd tell you around 1 per-
68   cent. This is what we know happens to families who have already had
69   one child like that. And again, we know that there is absolutely nothing
70   that you did or didn't do to cause it. There is no way to make sure that
71   that hasn't happened to you except by taking this test.

72 M: I see my daughter and to me she is—I mean compared to other children
73   I've seen around, she's as normal as anyone. She's a mongoloid, but she
74   brings us joy, she's beginning to speak already.

75 C: She's about a year and a half?

76 F: She's twenty months.

77 C: I would like very much to give you the name of someone here in our
78   genetics clinic that would be able to sit down and talk with the two of
79   you at great length about what kinds of things are the same about chil-
80   dren with mongolism, and what kinds of things are different. What you
81   might be able to expect. Does Juanita have any heart problems?

82 F: No, just a heart murmur.

83 C: She doesn't have any medicine she takes?

84 F: No.

85 C: What we know about these children is that many of them start out pretty
86   much like children who don't have the Down syndrome, and as they get
87   older and older they start to slow down, not quite keeping up. It usually
88   takes a longer time for them to talk. It usually takes longer to learn to
89   walk, and they don't keep developing as long. But you know, all chil-
90   dren are different. There are lots of things you can do with Juanita to
91   make the most of the potential that she has. And she has potential, you
92.   know that. Are you with a regional center? Who's your social worker
93   at the regional center?

94 F: Oh no. We don't have one.

95 C: I think it would be very much worth your while to see this lady at our
96   genetics clinic, because she can put you in touch with the appropriate
97   regional center and see that you can get Juanita into early-stimulation
98   programs. She can also give you the benefit of all the things she knows
99   about children with Down syndrome, because they are all different, OK?

100   I think you will really find it a big benefit. She's the lady I want you to
101   go across and see when you are done here. If you see her while you are
102   here, you won't have to make another trip.

Here, the counselor skillfully communicates basic information about Down syndrome that is apparently news, and potentially upsetting, to the mother. The latter is oblivious to the problems she will face if she anticipates the "normal" progression of her child. This exchange (immediately above) between counselor and client provides a critical bit of data for the counselor. She is almost bound to conclude that she is dealing with a client who, although the mother of a Down syndrome child, has little understanding of the problem. The effect upon the session is profound, providing coloration and suffusion for the remainder of the session. If the client doesn't comprehend the reasons for the genetic screen, a fifteen-minute session will hardly be sufficient to communicate all that is even minimally required for an informed decision, much less for informed consent. It is certainly appropriate and commendable that the counselor refers the client to a regional center and other health professionals for more information and support. However, it is equally clear that subsequent referrals to obtain information reflect upon the limits of a genetic counseling session as a vehicle for imparting information. Only when counselor and client share many assumptions about a disease and some of its implications will a basic new set of data be passed in these sessions.

104   F: With the test, what do they do, do they numb the stomach first?

105   C: Oh, yes, you get a local anesthetic which is like—have you ever been to
106   the dentist and had novocain?

107   F: In the face, not in the stomach. [*Laughs*]

108   C: It's no different.

109   F: It isn't?

110   C: No, it's the same thing. They'll just give you a little shot right here.

111   F: Does my husband get to come with me?

112   C: If he wants to, he is certainly welcome. You are not troubled by needles
113   or watching medical procedures, are you, M?

114   M: I don't like to see big needles.

115   C: This needle is called a 22-gauge needle. It's a very narrow needle. The
116   same as used to take your blood. The only reason it's any longer is
117   because your tummy has muscle and fat and we have to get through that.
118   It's not how long a needle is that you feel, it's how fat it is. I don't want
119   to encourage you to go in if you are nervous around needles, because
120   that's not a good thing, but I don't want you to have the impression that

121   it's a big one.

122 F: I'm scared.

123 C: Of course you are scared. Every woman you see out in that waiting room
124   is having this test and they are all scared.

125 F: I'm really nervous.

126 C: Sure you are. I'm writing you a note. The lady I want you to see is
127   Joyce. I think maybe Elizabeth can walk you over there. She will give
128   you a book about Down's and you can get an appointment and the name
129   of the person to see at the regional center. You'll be feeling OK after
130   the test.

131 F: Could they tell if it's a boy or a girl?

132 C: Yes, we can tell.

133 F: By the cells, too?

134 C: Your chromosomes have two that are called XX, and his chromosomes
135   have two that are called XY, and that's how we tell.

136 F: [*To M*] You want to know?

137 M: I don't want to know.

138 C: You have a month to decide. I will ask you again when I call you with
139   the results. Now the only risk of this test is a slight risk of miscarriage.
140   About one-half of 1 percent of women who have had this test have miscarried
141   within two to five days. There is nothing that you need to do. Just go about your
142   normal life. And it will take about four weeks to get the results.

143 F: OK, so if I have this done, I have the right to an abortion, right?

144 C: If the test shows a chromosome abnormality and that's what you want to
145   do, yes.

146 F: Is this the only place that does this?

147 C: Yes.

148 C: Now, I have a whole bunch of questions I have to ask you. It's for the
149   state, and it doesn't have your name on it.

    M—Age 27

    Both Catholic

    F—Born in Mexico

    M—Born here, parents Mexican

    M—Carpenter, unemployed

    F—High school

    M—One year college

    F—Second pregnancy

    F—Found out about amnio from Dr. Bramston?

    F—Will deliver at General Hospital

M—Income 10–12,000

150 F: How come when they found out my baby had the Down syndrome they
151   didn't want to test him (M), they only tested me?

152 C: I don't know. Usually they test both. I don't know.

153 F: But they didn't test me because they found out the baby was the acciden-
154   tal kind.

155 C: That's right. And when we find the baby is not the accidental kind, we
156   always test the mother and the father. So I don't know why they did it
157   that way, that's not the way we do. This is the medical-legal release
158   form. I want you to both read and sign this.

In the session just reported, the sociologist-observer at the genetic counseling session was aware that a twenty-minute counseling session cannot answer the many questions the couple would have pursued under other circumstances. But even more important for this work, we were concerned with finding out much more about the social and cultural circumstances that give such variable meaning to those questions. Thus, we chose to interview each member of the couple separately. More than twenty such interviews were conducted. In the one that follows, the respondent is the male from the genetic counseling session reported above. The interview was conducted several weeks after the session.

1 E: Can you give me some background?

2 M: I was born June 10, 1950. I'm twenty-seven. I was the oldest of five, four boys
3   and one girl. Mother was nineteen when the first was born, twenty-nine when the last
4   was born. My father worked for a paint company in the East Bay.
5   Mother never worked. Both my parents are Catholic. We went to
6   church every Sunday.

7 E: Have your religious attitudes changed?

8 M: No, they haven't. I still am Catholic and I go to church just about every
9   Sunday.

10 E: Are all your friends Catholic?

11 M: No.
12   I am a carpenter, but right now I'm looking for work. I was twenty-four when I
13   got married. Juanita is my first child (she has Down's).
14   My father was born in this country. My mother was born in Mexico. I
15   was born here and I was raised here until I was about eleven years old and
16   then I went to Mexico to live. I was down there until I was about twenty
17   and then I came back. My brother introduced me to my wife. He was
18   taking out her sister. We met a week later, but then we got married first,
19   and they got married last year in December.

20 E: Did you have hopes or plans for children?

21 M: Well, my wife wanted a lot, four I guess, and I said OK, if I do good, if
22   I make enough money in my work, if I get a good job. Then I was
23   working in a factory. So later we had Juanita and since then I've
24   changed. I don't feel like I want to have a lot of children, just two or
25   three.

26 E: What changed?

27 M: Well, living is hard and you got to have a lot of money to support your
28   family.

29 E: How did you find out about your daughter's condition?

30 M: Well, I was here when she was born, in the hospital, but the doctor
31   didn't talk to me right away, until afterwards, I guess about a week, a
32   week or two weeks, that's when I found out about it.

33 E: Who told you then?

34 M: My wife did. She said that she was sick, you know—at first I didn't
35   understand what the sickness was. Later I understood it and they had a
36   couple of tests done at Children's Hospital and they came out positive
37   that she was sick.

38 E: What did they say about that kind of sickness?

39 M: I can't remember the exact words now, but she told me.

40 E: What did you understand was the problem?

41 M: Oh, Down's syndrome.

42 E: Did you know what that was?

43 M: Yes, one of my relatives has a child with Down's syndrome. Twenty-six
44   or twenty-seven years old.

45 E: So when she mentioned it to you, did you think of that person?

46 M: Yes.

47 E: What did that mean to you?

48 M: That's a tough one. I thought she would never be able to support herself,
49   you know. You hope to see your child grow up and get married and
50   become something, you know. Probably she won't have a chance to do
51   that. Have a normal life, you know, like any other child. I just
52   hoped that she would have a better future, you know, than she's probably
53   going to get. I'm trying to do everything I can to help her.

54 E: What did it mean to this other family that they had a child with Down's,
55   do you think?

56 M: Impression was that the child would have to depend on the parents for
57   the rest of its life.

58 E: Has having a child with Down's changed your life, or plans?

59 M: No, not really, it's just—well, there's nothing you can do about it, you
60   know, it's just—you already had the child, you can't take them back
61   where you got them from. You gotta keep it.

62 E: Any benefits?

63 M: Benefits?

64 E: Well, some people think of it as a blessing in disguise in some ways.

65 M: No, it's not a benefit, it's just that, well, it's harder for her. I think it
66   would be harder for her to go through life, something like that. I
67   wouldn't say it would be a benefit.

68 E: What are the hard parts?

69 M: Well, I think it will be harder when she grows up, you know. And for
70   her to keep up with the other children. They will do things she can't do.

For the first time, we learn here that the husband is quite familiar with Down syndrome, and has relatively close-up experience with someone in his family. He speaks knowledgeably about the effects of Down's and expresses some deep concerns about the problem of dependency which mental retardation brings. Note that he did not mention this in the session with the genetic counselor. Moreover, the response of his wife in this session would lead one to conclude that he has not fully discussed this matter with her. We will see in the very next session a plausible explanation for his unwillingness to be straightforward. There are strong bases for speculation that the issue comes down to locating blame. As we return to the interview, the disclaimer about knowledge of Down's takes a different turn:

72 E: Have you read anything about Down's?

73 M: No. F read a little to me in this one book, and she tells me what she
74   reads. If I have a question, I ask her. She seems to know more about it.

75 E: Did you ever wonder about the cause?

76 M: Well, I was wondering who was at fault. We had these tests at Children's
77   Hospital on the—what is it, chromosomes?—and they didn't say nothing
78   like that, but a doctor told me that that stuff is inherited, mostly from the
79   mother's side, so I was wondering. But I didn't blame my wife. I felt
80   sad for my daughter when I found out. And I was kind of disappointed,
81   but to me she is the best thing that ever came into my life and that's it.

82 E: Ever blame yourself?

83 M: Never thought of it that way.

84 E: What was the reaction of your family?

85 M: Well, at first we didn't want to tell them anything, you know. We tried to
86   keep it to ourselves.

(F brings tea in from kitchen and says "He blamed it on me. He said that it was inherited and it came from the mother's side. And you know that really got me upset. Because that's not what C told me and the doctor told me the same thing she did. That's why I want his parents to read this book they gave me at U.C. He told us people used to hide their child like this when people would come around. He was trying to get across that we could help her a lot if we didn't try to hide it." F leaves the room.)

87 E: Was the pregnancy planned?

88 M: At the beginning it wasn't. No, it wasn't. We were planning to wait
89   about three years. So we thought at first maybe an abortion, I did. But
90   my wife was against that. Later on we accepted it, that it was our fault.

91 E: When did you hear about the test?

92 M: I think when Juanita was born somebody mentioned it. Then when she was
93   pregnant, Kaiser told her about it.

When the wife brought in the tea, she told a side of the story that brought much of the discussion into greater focus. Not only did she reveal that the assignment of blame to her was an issue for the two of them, but that it extended to the husband's family. The books that she was given at the clinic became a weapon in this battle. The husband later recants, and goes so far as to say that he will now do whatever his wife wants with respect to the consumption of the new technology.

Within a week of this interview with the husband, the following interview was conducted with the wife. The results of the amniocentesis were not yet known. The husband was not present.

1. E: What is your father's occupation?

2   F: He worked in a cannery. My mom was working, but she's not working
3   anymore. She was working most of the time that I was growing up.

4   E: How old was she when she had her first child?

5   F: She was twenty-four and I don't know how old she was when the last one was
6   born. We were nine in the family and—she was supposed to have nine
7   but there were three miscarriages and one was born suffocated. Oldest one
8   was twenty-three and the youngest is fifteen. The last baby died; she was ok except
9   my mom was anemic. I guess the baby came out anemic too and she
10   died. She must have been about thirty-four then.

11. E: Are your parents religious?

12. F: Both are Catholic. They never really talked to me about religion and stuff
13   like that. We went every Sunday to church, and I guess I am pretty
14   religious. I don't really practice my religion or anything, I just go to
15   church every Sunday, and that's all. And pray, you know.

16 E: How did you find out about Down's?

17 F: Well, it was in the hospital and the doctor told me that she had the
18   Down's, and, you know, I couldn't believe it.

19 E: Did you know what that was?

20 F: Yeah, because my aunt had a baby with Down's syndrome too. And then
21   I felt really bad and I started thinking how come two in our family. And I
22   thought they were probably because of my family that they, you know,
23   when I had the tests, I didn't have the tests but when they tested her
24   somebody told me I would have to be tested. But you know, it's kind of
25   hard going through that. But, you know, I guess I wouldn't trade her for
26   anything right now. She's really something else.

Here we learn that Down syndrome is also on the young mother's side of the family (lines 16 to 26). And more important, because of this fact, the mother both knows more about Down than the genetic counseling session revealed, and absorbed more initial guilt and blame because she thought it "ran in her side of the family." As for the importance of locating blame in the dyadic relationship of the couple, take special note of the fact that the wife says that the way her husband knew about Down syndrome was only through observation of the wife's four-year-old cousin. She makes no mention of the fully adult Down syndrome member of her husband's side of the family that we discovered in the earlier interview with the husband alone. For our discussion of the "effective location of blame," it does not matter whether the husband deliberately concealed this from his wife, or whether he told her and she "forgot." Either way, we can discern where culpability was placed, until the clinical session with the genetic counselor and, of course, the book.

28 E: Was it hard to tell your family?

29 F: No, I told my mom right away because you see we're really close. I told
30   my mom right away. And she says, oh don't believe that, the baby's
31   all right. But then after a while, you know, my mom did feel bad, she did
32   feel bad, because you know I'm her daughter and we're really close. So
33   is M's mother, and they really love her, because they've mostly given her
34   everything; they brought the bed for her from Mexico. They brought her
35   earrings, and my mom too, so she's the only granddaughter for both fami-
36   lies now. Whenever I don't take her down there they always ask for her,
37   or my mom does too.

38 E: What's the biggest problem as a result of Down's?

39 F: I started thinking, well, she won't be able to get married and lead a normal
40   life like other kids do, but you know it was mostly her and like thinking a
41   lot about her. She's the only child and I really love her. We've got pic-
42   tures of her and everything.

43 E: Any benefits from her having Down's?

44 F: No, I don't think so. I guess everything's the same.

45   E: Did you blame yourself?

46   F: Yeah, in a way, I did. 'Cause I thought I didn't take care of myself well
47   enough.

48   E: Like what?

49   F: Like, I guess I could have eaten more. And, you know, I'm the go, go,
50   go type and I like to get everything fast and I like to do my housework
51   and stuff like that. And then I like to dance. I went to dances and stuff
52   like that. But the doctors told me nothing like that did it.

53   E: Did M ever blame you?

54   F: No. His family, though, it's like my family—my family was saying it's
55   because of them and his family said it was because of me. But me and
56   him, we just don't mind them because we don't think so.

At this point in the interview, the wife chooses to mute the difference between herself and her husband on where blame was originally placed. But we have already seen three points that reveal how deep was the concern for locating blame. First, in the interview with the husband, he wondered out loud if the wife's side of the family was "at fault." Second, when the wife brings in the tea near the end of the interview with the husband, she notes how he originally blamed her. Third, earlier in this very interview with the wife, she recounts how she wondered whether her side of the family "was the problem." Now, in the next exchange, we will see just how important it was to all sides to find a culprit in the lineage of the other's side of the family. Keep in mind that the husband's side of the family also had an experience with Down syndrome. This fact never surfaces in all the dialogue with the wife, even in the exchange which follows:

58.   E: Do they still say that? [That is, does the family still blame you?]

59   F: Well, his mother's always saying it. She says that Juanita looks a lot like
60   his father, everybody said that. And afterwards, when they found out there
61   was something wrong with her, they said she looked like my family. It
62   kind of got me upset because of that, because before they said, oh, she
63   looks a lot like our family and now you know, when they found that she
64   was kind of sick, oh, she's got her mom's nose and her mom's eyes, she's
65   got everything from me.

66   E: When did you first hear about the test?

67   F: Well, I went to have the pregnancy test done over at a clinic in Fairmont
68   and they told me that I was pregnant and I told them that I had a child
69   with Down's syndrome. They told me that there was a test—but I guess
70   the people there didn't really know when the test was going to be made,
71   how far along the mother had to be.

72 E: Did you know about the test before getting pregnant this time?

73 F: No, I found that out too through the TV. I was watching a program and
74   they said that, like the alcoholism one, they said that they found out that
75   women that drink a lot have a lot of babies with this. Well, then they
76   showed the test being done. What happened in that program, they didn't
77   say how old the woman had to be or how far along. I didn't hear.

The significance of the mass media cannot be overestimated in providing information that is taken as authoritative in this area of high technology and genetics. Recall that earlier the wife has expressed considerable
anxiety and guilt about how her "fast living" and consumption of alcohol
and cigarettes might have had an influence on her first child's having a
chromosomal abnormality. The television broadcast to which she refers
undoubtedly made some mention of the connection between alcohol
consumption and birth defects. However, there is also a very highly
probability that the language used to make this association was appropriately hedged. The response above shows how this was interpreted to
mean "that women that drink a lot have a lot of babies with this."

79 E: Has anybody been negative or unsupportive about the test?

80 F: No. Oh, my mother was the one who didn't want me to have the test
81   because she was scared that the baby was going to get hurt. But she
82   didn't know that much about it. I thought that they, you know, when they
83   made the test, stuck the needle into the baby and took blood out of the
84   baby. You know, I didn't know it was only the fluid. And she was
85   scared.

86 E: You told her that they were going to take blood out of the baby?

87 F: I didn't know. That's what I told her, that I thought they were going to
88   take fluid out of the baby. And she told me not to have it done because it
89   was going to hurt me and the baby.

90 E: Did you think you should follow her advice?

91 F: No, because I wanted to know. Right after I was going to have the test
92   done, I went over to her and I told her that I was going to have the test
93   done and she got upset and she told me, I don't want you to go. You
94   know, kind of like ordering me because she was scared and didn't want
95   me to go. And I said, I already made the appointment, I'm going. So I
96   left, and she worried afterwards and after I came out of the clinic I went
97   straight to her house. And I told her it was nothing big and it was all right
98   and she felt better then.

99 E: Who have you talked to most about the test?

100 F: Well, I've talked to my aunt, you know the one with the little girl who has
101   Down's syndrome. Well, I just told her that the test isn't that bad and
102   that they could tell if it was a boy or a girl. And she told me, 'cause I

103   told her that I might have, 'cause I wanted to know if it was going to be,
104   if it was going to have Down's syndrome, and she told me she was
105   satisfied with her baby and that she wouldn't trade her for anything. And
106   that she really loved her and that she doesn't want, she's not, she doesn't
107   want like abortion. Like I told her, yeah, but the one that's going to
108   suffer is the baby and she agreed with me on that.

APPENDIX C
The Ethnic Distribution of Disease

Ethnic Group	High-Frequency Diseases	Low-Frequency Diseases
Africans	Hemoglobin S (14190)* Hemoglobin C (14190) Alpha-thalassemia (14180) Beta-thalassemia (14190) Hemoglobin F (14190) G6PD deficiency (30590) Disaccharide intolerance III (22310)	Cystic fibrosis (21970) Hemophilia (30670) Phenylketonuria (26160) Wilson disease (27790) Pseudocholinesterase type E(1) (17740) Antitrypsin PI (10740)
American Indian	Albinism (tyrosinase negative) (20310)	
Armenians	Familial Mediterranean fever (24910) Familial paroxysmal polyserositis (12820)	G6PD deficiency (30590)
Burmese	Hemoglobin E (14210)	
Chinese	Alpha-thalassemia (14180) G6PD deficiency (30590) Disaccharide intolerance III (22310)	
Costa Rican	Osteopetrosis, malignant (25970)	
Druze	Alkaptonuria (20350)	
English	Cystic fibrosis (21970) Amyloidosis III (10500)	
Eskimos	Pseudocholinesterase type E (17740) Adrenal hyperplasia III (20191) Kuskokwin disease (20820) Methemoglobinemia (25080)	
French Canadians	Corpus callosum, agenesis of, with neuronopathy (21800) Morquio syndrome A (25300) Tyrosinemia type I (27670)	
Gypsies (Czech)	Glaucoma, cogenital (23130)	
Icelanders	Phenylketonuria (26160)	
Irish	Phenylketonuria (26160)	

Ethnic Group	High-Frequency Diseases	Low-Frequency Diseases
Japanese	Axatalasia (20020) Oguchi disease (25810) Dyschromatosis universalis hereditaria (12750)	
Jews Ashkenazi	Abetalipoproteinemia (20010) Bloom syndrome (21090) Brachydactyly type D (11320) Colorblindness, partial, Deutan series (30380) Disaccharide intolerance III (22310) Factor XI(PTA) deficiency (26490) Familial dysautonomia (22390) Gaucher disease, adult noncerebral type (23080) Gilles de la Tourette disease (13758) Mucolipidosis type IV (25265) Niemann-Pick disease, infantile type (25720) Pentosuria (26080) Spongy degeneration of CNS (27190) Tay-Sachs disease (27280) Torison dystonia (22450)	
Oriental	Aldosterone deficiency due to defect in 18-hydroxylase (20340) Alpha-thalassemia (14180) Beta-thalassemia (14190) Familial neutropenia (16270) G6PD deficiency (30590) Hematuria, benign familial (14120) Hexokinase deficiency hemolytic anemia (23570) Ichthyosis vulgaris, X-linked (30810) Ichthyosis vulgaris, simplex (14670) Metachromatic leukodystrophy (Habbanite Jews from S. Arabia) (25020) Phenylketonuria (26160) Pituitary dwarfism II, Laron type (26250) Thrombasthenia of Glanzmann and Naegeli (27380) Werdnig-Hoffman disease (25330)	
Sephardi	Adrenal hyperplasia III (20191) Adrenal hyperplasia IV (20201) Ataxia-telangiectasia (20890) Brachydactyly type D (11320) Cogenital deafness I (22070) Cystinosis (21980) Cystinuria types II and III (22010) Disaccharide intolerance III (22310)	

Ethnic Group	High-Frequency Diseases	Low-Frequency Diseases
	Familial Mediterranean fever (24910) Glycogen storage disease III (23240) Pernicious anemia, juvenile, due to selective intestinal malabsorption of vitamin B12 with proteinuria (26110) Peroxidase and phospholipid deficiency in eosinophils (26150) Phenylalaninemia (26158)	
Lapps	Hip, dislocation of, cogenital (14270)	
Lebanese	Dyggve-Melchior-Clausen syndrome (30495) Juvenile Tay-Sachs disease (27277)	
Mediterranean Peoples (Italians, Greeks)	Beta-thalassemia (14190) G6PD deficiency (30590) Familial Mediterranean fever (24910)	Cystic fibrosis (21970) PKU1, southern Italians (26160)
Norwegians	Cholestasis-lymphedema (21490)	
Nova Scotia Acadians	Niemann-Pick disease type D (25720)	
Polish	Phenylketonuria (26160)	
Portuguese	Azorean neuologic disease (Joseph disease 10915)	
Scots	Phenylketonuria (26160) Cystic fibrosis (21970) Amyloidosis type III (10500)	
Swedes	Sjogren-Larsson syndrome (27020)	
Thai	Disaccharide intolerance III (22300)	

*Five-digit numbers reflect catalog number in *Mendelian Inheritance in Man* by Victor A. McKusick, MD. The entry numbers are used in the catalog as follows: autosomal dominant phenotypes (10010–19447); autosomal recessive phenotypes (20005–27890); X-linked phenotypes (30010–31500).

Sources: Cohen, Felissa L., *Clinical Genetics in Nursing Practice* (Philadelphia: Lippincott, 1984); Damon, A., "Race, Ethnic Group, and Disease," *Soc. Biol.* 16:69–80, 1969; McKusick, V. A., "The Ethnic Distribution of Disease in the United States," *J. Chronic Dis.* 20 (1967):115–118; McKusick, V. A., "Ethnic Distribution of Disease in Non-Jews," *Israel J. Med. Sci.* 1973:1,375–1,382; McKusick, V. A., *Mendelian Inheritance in Man*, 6th ed. (Baltimore: Johns Hopkins University Press, 1983); Goodman. R. M., *Genetic Disorders among the Jewish People* (Baltimore: Johns Hopkins University Press, 1979).

Notes

Prologue

1. See chap. 7.

2. While I occasionally must turn my attention in that direction, I should say at the outset that this book is not about biology as practiced by molecular biologists, nor is it about genetics. I approach the subject as a social analyst, and will emphasize the social organization of knowledge discoveries and structures.

3. This was Charles B. Davenport (Ludmerer, 1972:48).

4. The sterilization of hundreds of thousands of women in America, a topic that is addressed in the second chapter, can certainly also be seen as a circuitous route to eugenics. Indeed, in its heyday several decades back, it was termed "negative eugenics." But I will argue that there is a great difference in the quality, nature, and character of the contemporary "halo effect" obtained from today's new technology.

5. These populations have different access to the levers of power that link back to the effectiveness of lobbying in different nations, and within nations, as they comprise either political minorities or dominant power groups.

6. Theologians, ethicists, and legal scholars debate these matters with the experts in the sciences and medicine, but this has not been a public debate that reaches the informed laity.

7. Today, about as much as we get in the public sphere is a Nobel laureate in molecular genetics debating on public television (or some other ten- to fifteen-minute forum) a "critic" who wants to shut down the machinery of the new science technology. The debate is cast in terms of potential medical, health, and scientific benefits versus some unknown consequence of creating a health hazard or a Frankenstein. This skews the grounds upon which an informed debate about other social, cultural, and political questions can arise.

8. In looking at particular aspects of this subject, one tends to get caught in the positions and points of view that necessarily characterize ongoing work in different fields of study. It is natural, then, to take one's eyes away from the larger mosaic and fail to make the explicit linkages and characterize the moods that influence patterns of discourse in each field.

9. See the work of Sorenson and his colleagues, and several others cited in the book, especially in chapters 5 and 6.

Chapter 1

1. The well-to-do circumnavigated the problem by paying handsome fees for sometimes imaginatively constructed but "authenticated" genealogies (Davies, 1969).

2. By "prism of heritability," I mean a way of perceiving traits and behaviors that attributes the major explanatory power to biological inheritance.

3. I refer here to the public expression of racial explanations and racial beliefs. In a society with racial diversity and stratification, it is probably inevitable that privately held views about racial explanations widely persist.

4. The social scientists were not alone. Immunology and protein chemistry have helped geneticists identify large numbers of human genes that code for specific enzymes. Scores of thousands of individuals from around the world have been tested to determine their genetic makeup with respect to these enzymes, and the results indicate remarkable similarities across "racial" groups, and far more variability within groups than among them. "The genetic variation between one Spaniard and another, or between one Masai and another, is 85 per cent of all human genetic variation, while only 15 per cent is accounted for by breaking people into groups" (Lewontin et al., 1984:121–126).

5. That of course, coincided with ethnicity and race.

6. For an excellent and measured analysis of these debates and the many issues raised by these developments, see the report of the President's Commission for the Study of Ethical Problems in Medicine and Biomedical and Behavioral Research, especially the monograph *Splicing Life*, published in Nov. 1982 by the U.S. Government Printing Office.

7. Among the important exceptions: Kaye (1986), Yoxen (1983), Holmes et al. (1981), and Goodfield (1977).

8. The Human Genome Project, a national program to map every human gene, is projected to cost several billion dollars.

9. More than 90 percent of American blacks were in the agrarian South even as late as 1905, a period of industrial growth in the North and the Midwest. Mexican-Americans were in the Southwest during this era, and exclusionary laws severely restricted the immigration of Asians.

10. In both Europe and the United States, social class as much as race and ethnicity was an important element of social stratification. Accordingly, the "genetic interpretations" of the lower strata addressed the "lower intelligence" of those at the base, regardless of color.

11. This includes residential segregation in urban areas. The new domination of people of color in major American cities has been paralleled by an increase in their occupational segregation, with higher rates of unemployment, consignment to the secondary labor market, strikingly higher rates of rates of incarceration, and strikingly higher rates of rates of infant mortality and deaths from cancer, heart, and lung diseases.

12. See chaptets 2 and 3.

13. See Nichols (1988).

14. See chapter 3.

15. For example, sickle-cell anemia can be a life-threatening disorder, or simply a painful disease that requires special medical treatment; but one may live a productive life

well into one's sixties. This obviously complicates the matter of screening for the disorder as if it were a single phenomenon. See chapter 3 for a further development of this point, and a fuller characterization of the complex clinical expression of sickle-cell anemia.

16. For a more extensive table, see Appendix C.

17. Incidence refers to the number of cases occurring among live-born babies. The term *genetic disorders* corresponds to typical usage, even though, as I have pointed out, many of these disorders are really multifactorial and have some unknown genetic component. Finally, these figures refer to the U.S. population, except where noted otherwise.

18. The full table on the ethnic distribution of disease (Appendix C) provides more information on the relative frequency of the appearance of a genetic disorder. One of the striking things about this table is how much is known about some groups, and how little is known about others. Second, note that the category "African" as an ethnic group lumps together sub-Saharan blacks with North Africans, and fails to distinguish even between major categories of East and West, whether Ethiopian and Egyptian or Kenyan on the one hand, or Tunisian, Moroccan, or Ghanian on the other. This list reflects current knowledge of the ethnic distribution of what are described as genetic disorders in major texts on the topic. Until there is further research, the question remains as to what extent the table represents more the actual distribution, or rather, that the reported distribution represents more the knowledge base.

19. Indeed, the field of statistics was born from such a concern in the late nineteenth century (Haller, 1963:13).

20. Called biometrics.

21. An allele is one member of a gene pair occupying a particular site on a homologous choromosome. ABO blood groups are so indicated.

22. Karl Pearson was a late nineteenth-century English zoologist who later in his career became a statistician.

23. This was also the era of measurements of human head shapes; the scientific practices of this period have been well analyzed by Gould (1981).

24. After World War I, a partial reconciliation and convergence developed between population geneticists, who relied heavily on quantitative measures of frequencies, and Mendelian geneticists. Today, for example, estimates of carriers for genes that might produce a genetic disorder come from such a merger.

25. This is not to suggest that all or even most geneticists were eugenicists (advocates of breeding "good" human stock, or discouragers of "bad breeding"). For a lengthy discussion of the differences and the overlap, see Ludmerer (1972) and Kevles (1985).

26. There is a tendency for people to respond to this finding by concluding that the test must have been linguistically and culturally biased.

27. From Bingham's 1923 monograph, quoted by Gould (1986:226).

28. For a detailed critique of the Army IQ test, see Gould (1981:192–233).

29. For a detailed and scholarly account of the history and politics of IQ testing and how and why the link between intelligence and heredity was forged during this era, see Leon Kamin (1974). A more recent work by Schiff and Lewontin (1986) elaborates this analysis.

30. See the discussion regarding the escalation of "genetic explanations" of a variety of social issues in the first part of chap. 6.

31. Jensen used statistical analyses of aggregate data, invoking probability arguments from population genetics, but he also made inferential reference to Mendelian principles through the use of adoption and twin studies. As noted earlier, the same techniques with gentiles as a target population compared to the high IQ scores of Jews in this era would have produced startlingly different results than those obtained by Goddard in 1917.

32. This story has often been told elsewhere, most recently and effectively by Schiff and Lewontin (1986).

33. It was later learned that high levels of phenylalanine are caused by other factors than the presence of phenylketonuria. Indeed, there are real and important dangers to PKU screening, when an infant who is tested positive, but who does not have PKU, is put on a low phenylalanine diet. A normal child needs a daily requirement of phenylalanine to build body protein. Some who have been deprived of this requirement have died, and several critics of PKU screening have documented these dangers (Bessman and Swazey, 1971; Nitowsky, 1973; Buist and Jhaveri, 1973).

34. Most significantly, with PKU legislation on the books, states would later add on other provisions for other kinds of genetic screening, more controversial because it was prenatal screening (See chap. 4).

35. These developments include the production of human growth hormones, the manufacture of insulin, and DNA analysis of saliva for prenatal diagnosis. See chaps. 3–6.

36. This is taken up in chap. 2.

37. Despite the prevailing belief that this new technology will bring greater health benefits to various "target" populations, I will present evidence in chaps. 4 and 7 indicating that, given the current state of knowledge, the genetic prism is not the most public-health-effective way to perceive the problem, nor even the most cost-effective way to proceed.

Chapter 2

1. It is also true that the most ardent advocates of racial purity in the eugenics movement were wealthy white Anglo-Saxons of the "old stock" (Ludmerer, 1972:25–30).

2. Stark (1958), Curtis and Petras (1970), Simonds (1978), Barnes (1974, 1977), H. Collins (1981), Knorr-Cetina and Mulkay (1983).

3. The development of AIDS in the 1980s is the exception, but it can be argued that this is more of a health and mortality issue than the hereditary concern for "bloodline." The offspring of those who have the AIDS virus may contract the disease and die.

4. This has not always been so, as students of criminology know well. Nineteenth-century studies of criminals emphasized head shape and physiognomy as predictive of criminal behavior.

5. The influence of social concerns on scientific research is hardly a one-way proposition, even in this arena. It was the work of the researchers on the Army's data bank during World War I that originally did so much to influence social opinion about the role of environment versus heredity (in this case, race). Northern black recruits scored

higher on IQ tests than Southern whites, and this finding was one of many that influenced the Supreme Court in its 1954 ruling on school desegregation.

6. It was the social vulnerability of the "witches" in the earliest stages that explained the patterns of who were named and hung.

7. Over the last three decades, billions of dollars have been spent searching for a cancer cure. Despite bimonthly claims of these cures being "around the corner" since 1965, a cure for cancer(s) has always eluded researchers. But this has hardly occasioned an epistemological crisis for the cancer research establishment (MacIntyre, 1980). For an excellent summary of the highly variable successes and failures of cancer treatments and cures for highly variable cancers, see John Cairns, "The Treatment of Diseases and the War Against Cancer," *Scientific American* 253, no. 5 (November 1985); also Stephen Hilgartner, "Telescoping Policy-Relevant Science: 'Summaries' of the Evidence on Dietary Fibre and Colon Cancer," paper presented at the 1986 annual meetings of the Society for Social Studies of Science.

8. The peers, after all, are those called to Washington, to the National Institutes of Health, and the National Science Foundation to review requests for funding of research programs. These tend, of course, to be those who have established reputations by publishing good works in peer-refereed journals. If these journals are in turn controlled by a particular paradigmatic emphasis, the circle is hard to break. Many other commentators have noted that the peer review process is therefore both a floor (setting a standard below which work cannot be done) and a ceiling.

9. Which is, after all, the major banner of both high-tech medicine and the new genetics claims.

10. See chapter 7 for a fuller discussion.

11. This is not to suggest that subsequent twin research is suspect. The fact that later researchers consistently could not find the high degree of similarities in IQ scores for identical twins is both evidence that Burt fabricated the data, along with the fact that he kept the exact same correlations even though he kept adding new twin data sets. In chapter 6, I review and contrast twin study findings on the relatively high rates of similarity for identical twins with autism concordance, and contrast that with the much lower rates for schizophrenia.

12. For a discussion of the sickling process, see p. 45.

13. National Academy of Sciences–National Research Council.

14. *New York Times,* Jan. 13, 1981.

15. Indeed, to this day, in spite of being told the contrary by the experimenters, one of the subjects believes that the experimenters projected images on the wall, or into the translucent goggles he was wearing.

16. The discussion in this section on Supreme Court decisions on sterilization laws is indebted to Philip Reilly's *Genetics, Law and Social Policy* (Cambridge, Mass.: Harvard University Press, 1977), 121–148. For a fuller discussion of these cases and issues, the reader is referred to this excellent source.

17. In the United States, members of certain racial and ethnic minorities comprise a category that has sometimes been called "people of color." They total approximately 20 percent of the population of the United States. However, they comprise more than 60 percent of the people imprisoned (Irwin, 1980; Kassebaum et al., 1971). Moreover, the rate of incarceration for blacks is nine times that for whites (Dunbaugh, 1979).

18. For a more detailed discussion of the problematics of criminological studies of prisoners and genetic interpretations of crime, see chapter 6.

19. For a further development of why prison studies of criminal populations are fundamentally flawed in their abilities to generalize to the "genetic explanation of criminal behavior," see chapter 6.

20. Initially, there was a health and medical cast to the development of prenatal genetic decoding. In particular, the discovery of potential birth defects was the primary justification of this work. The detection of the sex of the fetus in such x-linked disorders as hemophilia is partly a medical issue. The determination of the sex of the fetus as a sole matter of investigation is clearly *not* a health issue. However, it has been, and will continue to be, done.

21. The cost for an amniocentesis in India varies from seventy to six hundred rupees (about eight to sixty-five dollars), and the cost for an abortion is about the same (Rao, 1988).

22. Why should the Indian Council of Medical Research be the final arbiter on such a matter? Is it a medical matter? Should the American Medical Association play a major role in this, and if so, why, etc.? For a discussion of the controversy over whether these are primarily medical issues, see Daniel Wikler and Norma J. Wikler, "Turkey-Baster Babies: the De-Medicalization of Artificial Insemination," (forthcoming) Millbank Quarterly, Spring, 1990.

Chapter 3

1. The annual costs have been estimated at nearly one and a half billion dollars. Blank (1981:39) estimated the number of infants born with congenital malformations, single-gene hereditary disorders, or chromosome abnormalities at between 100,000 and 200,000.

2. These factors include genetic transmission (20 percent), chromosomal abnormalities (5 percent), maternal metabolic imbalance (3 to 5 percent), infection (2 to 3 percent), and therapeutic radiation (1 percent) (Flynt et al., 1987:1).

3. Three reasons are a history of a genetic disorder in the family, high levels of a substance in the blood that point to the need for more precise testing, or the woman being over age 35 (at greater risk for a chromosome abnormality).

4. By 1988, more than 5,000 "genetic disorders" had been catalogued, but only 380 could be detected prenatally.

5. The issue is no longer the control of an epidemic, such as smallpox; and groups may jealously guard control over "their inherited disorder," lobby in "their interest" as opposed to other groups with "their own disorders," etc. Each of these matters is taken up later in this chapter.

6. The fact that the Scots and Danes already do this for their native-born populations is noteworthy, and relates to a point that will be made later in this chapter about racial and ethnic variation in state populations in the United States. That is, Wyoming, with less than 1 percent blacks in the population, has mandatory sickle-cell screening, but the District of Columbia, with more than 50 percent blacks, has a voluntary program.

7. For a full discussion of the three forms of genetic screening and the attendant increasing political controversy around each form, see pp. 51–56 of this chapter.

8. This sometimes produced unanticipated outcomes. Blacks are at so much lower risk for PKU than whites that in some jurisdictions that were predominantly black, no cases turned up for several years (e.g., the District of Columbia), and health officials began to question the wisdom of continuation.

9. Phenylketonuria (PKU) is an "inborn error of metabolism" associated with mental retardation. If the newborn child is given a special diet, there is evidence that this will ameliorate the retardation. Almost all newborn in the United States are now screened for phenylketonuria.

10. Massachusetts has been a front-runner in the creation of screening programs for inherited disorders (Stine, 1977:507–508; Powledge, 1974; Lappé, 1979; Bessman and Swazey, 1971:55–57).

11. These programs generated considerable controversy, and added fuel to the recombinant DNA controversy, which also flared early in Cambridge (Jackson and Stitch, 1979). This particular law is no longer in effect.

12. This discussion is indebted to Marc Lappé, *Genetic Politics*, (New York: Simon and Schuster, 1979) 21–29.

13. I shall return to this controversy.

14. Some estimates have been as high as 1 in 9.

15. Carrier screening for Tay-Sachs is a different matter than prenatal diagnosis. Even for couples where both members are carriers, the chances are that in three of every four pregnancies, the fetus will be normal. Thus, prenatal detection offers the opportunity of selective abortion of that one in four instance of the disorder.

16. Those of child-bearing age, 18–43 (Stine, 1977:465).

17. A cooperative project included the United States, Canada, Great Britain, Israel, and South Africa (Goodman and Goodman, 1982:20).

18. New York, Illinois, Massachusetts, Virginia, Mississippi, and Georgia.

19. To demonstrate how deeply this notion goes, a prepublication reviewer of this manuscript after having read my account of a visit to Orchomenos, Greece (see chapter 5), commented as follows "The 'sickle-cell' that Duster describes in Greece is actually beta thalassemia, which is far more severe and less variable in expression than sickle cell. Children require regular transfusions and rarely live beyond their teens, even today. The response of the Greek communities both in Greece and abroad, differs from the response of the Black communities in part because the disorder is so much more severe." The belief that sickle hemoglobin could not be found in Greece was so strong that the author of these remarks did not even bother to check the literature (see, for example, Stamatoyannopoulos, 1974: Powledge, 1974; Kenen and Schmidt, 1978; Bowman, 1977; Hollerbach, 1979).

20. They also participated in alarmist exaggerations and excesses by "informing" those screened that they would die before their twentieth birthday, because the screeners did not distinguish between sickle-cell anemia and sickle-cell trait. However, it was not only the Panthers and community groups that failed to make this important distinction. The airlines and the Air Force Academy, as noted in chapter 2, made the same mistake. The Panthers and community groups are discussed later in this chapter.

21. Bowman, a physician and expert who attended the meeting where these figures were disclosed, was appalled at the level of misinformation distributed by these community groups (Bowman, 1977:123–126).

22. It may be recalled that this was the period of the FBI Cointel program designed to smear and discredit, and ultimately crush, the Panthers.

23. See chapter 5 for an elaboration of the Tuskegee syphilis case.

24. While we have no direct report on income level, in a study of over a thousand voluntary Jewish screenees for a Tay-Sachs detection program, Kaback et al. (1974) report that over 70 percent were college graduates. Even more striking, 43 percent had engaged in postgraduate study. The median income of this group is substantially higher than that of the general population.

25. As noted earlier, this is the reason why phenylketonuria screening, which is neonatal, was the wedge opening the door to other forms of screening legislation.

26. This is not to say that such screening does not have problems that are worthy of serious discussion and consideration. Bessman and Swazey (1971:49–76) pointed out serious problems with screening for phenylketonuria. Early assumptions that every newborn with high blood levels of phenylalanine must have phenylketonuria turned out not only to be false, but damaging. Babies so diagnosed were given a special diet low in phenylalanine, but since some did not have PKU, this treatment was seriously injurious. Partly as a result of this research, corrective steps were taken. It is now clear that many other genetic disorders will follow a similar path to mass neonatal screening noted for PKU. Galactosemia was screened in only six states in 1974. By the end of 1976, Reilly (1977:107) found that seventeen states were screening for this disorder. In the same time period, twelve states began neonatal screening for congenital hypothyroidism.

27. In most cases, this is usually because interaction with the environment is also necessary for the disorder to become manifest.

28. By political, I mean here only that different interests are vying for the same sets of resources in attempting to obtain research funding to support "their explanations."

29. There are related alternatives. The first alternative is to terminate a pregnancy if conception has occurred and there is prenatal detection in time for abortion. The second is to set up screening programs to alert potential couples, the purpose of which is to inform them of the risk of conceiving a child with a genetic disorder. I go into more detail on this matter of the three forms of genetic screening in chapter 2.

30. Three levels of entry are: (1) direct observation of behavior in the local setting in which it routinely occurs, the grounding for the "micro" base of the study; (2) observation and analysis of the administrative, bureaucratic, or organizational unit(s) that are interposed between the local scenes; and (3) the "macro" trends, rates, or perhaps law or federal policy developments.

31. The evidence for this is addressed in chapter 7.

Chapter 4

1. Sometimes insurance companies don't even wait for a genetic disorder if they can find out anything that might justify raising rates. We have noted several times already that being a carrier of the sickle-cell gene does not place one at greater health risk. However, a survey of the forty major insurance companies in the mid-1970s revealed that over half had raised their premiums for persons with sickle-cell trait (Bowman, 1977:128).

2. It is certainly true that the federal government enters into the health picture with great effect with the power to tax.

3. Colorado, Georgia, Louisiana, New Mexico, New York, Texas, and, Wyoming.

4. In contrast, the way in which Tay-Sachs and sickle-cell centers got established and funded reveal how the variable social status of the consumers of the new technology played vastly different roles in how state health policy got translated into funding decisions.

5. In June 1988, a California court ruled in favor of Charlie Krueger's case against the San Francisco 49ers. Rather than an extended appeal procedure, there was an out of court settlement for over one million dollars (*San Francisco Examiner*, Jan. 22, 1989; p. 47, *Image Magazine*).

6. *New York Times*, Feb. 3, 1980.

7. No one argues that nuclear power is safer than solar power. They argue that it is more immediately available, and point out that solar energy utilization is at least thirty years away even if research and development began today. This is as much a function of the machinery set in motion for the last two decades as any intrinsic feature of the two contrasting sources of energy.

8. See Appendix A for an elaboration of the rationale for an attempt at the vertical integration of differing levels of study and analysis.

9. Recall that a study of the forty major life insurance companies revealed that half had raised the rates for sickle-cell carriers. What of confidentiality, much less an erroneous assessment of health risks (Bowman, 1977:128)?

Chapter 5

1. That is, all the Latino, Asian-American, and black genetic counselors together make up less than 5 percent of the total of the profession.

2. Screens are set up to keep things out, including weapons on airlines, insects, ne'er-do-wells, bums, and babies who will have chronic health problems.

3. Chapter 7 contains a fuller discussion of the considerable variability of clients of genetic counseling.

4. For two years, I was a member of this advisory board.

5. While it was a distortion of what routinely occurs in human society, genocide did occur. In contrast, complete neutrality in a racially and ethnically diverse and stratified society may be even more rare.

6. Whether the screening is "objectively" a positive or negative outcome for the community, or for its individuals, is yet another matter, as the Goodmans (1981) point out.

Chapter 6

1. More than twice the number that appeared in the previous decade.

2. Crime, mental illness, intelligence and alcoholism.

3. To characterize these as "behaviors" is a short-hand, since mental illness and intelligence are arguably not "human behaviors." However, the only way that one makes an assessment of either is with some behavioral manifestation, then observation and,

ostensibly, measurement. It is the behavioral component that is usually the source of disagreement as to its root causes.

4. It does not follow that highly esteemed scientists in biological research then come forward with jewels of social and political wisdom. In the first chapter, a quote from Linus Pauling on genetic screening, a quote from Jonas Salk in this chapter on the stratification of the sciences, and Stern's comment (also in this chapter) on "controls" in social science research all reveal how modesty is the best strategy as one steps into social analysis.

5. The *New York Times* editorial of April 4, 1981, captured the image well. The *Times* was sympathetic to social research, but tried to explain why Reagan's budget cutters at the Office of Management and Budget had targeted the social sciences for specific surgery, while leaving the natural sciences intact. The editorial speculated that the image of the social sciences is that they are imprecise, common-sensical, and not of particular or practical use.

6. *San Francisco Chronicle*, Nov. 26, 1981.

7. The evidence that a few individuals are committing many of the reported crimes is based upon the self-reports of criminals, who in turn "confess" to a number of reported crimes that have not been "cleared by arrest." The police have a strong interest in a favorable ratio of "cleared by arrest" statistics. While some of these self-reports may be accurate, in the aggregate they hardly constitute data hard enough to justify "genetic" correlations and explanations.

8. Rowe (1986) does use a self-report mailed questionnaire for data for a twin study. In this article, his focus is upon "anti-social" behavior."

9. An excellent example is Paul Bohannan's (1960) classical work on the extraordinary low rates of homicide in sub-Sahara Africa. No empirical research before or since has thrown into better relief how ludicrous is the argument (pre-Bohannan) that the higher rate of homicide among American blacks is genetic.

10. Those who would suggest that rape during slavery is a political concept are on a slippery slope of logic that leads not only to joining with an old Eldridge Cleaver formulation about rape during rebellious periods as politics, but even more radically, to then have to address a rhetorical question from the Marxists: When is crime not political?

11. It has been estimated that Americans steal $38,000,000 per day in shoplifting alone. The President's Crime Commission's survey of 10,000 households concluded that "91 percent of all Americans have violated laws that could have subjected them to a term of imprisonment at one time in their lives" (Reiman, 1984:81).

12. Nicolas said that sociologists should rearrange their priorities, and put their "hands down, and their eyes up." In the last two decades, things have improved somewhat, as indicated by the references provided in the discussion at a later point in this chapter.

13. To the social analyst of crime, Al Capone's organizational skills meant that he had more in common with the meticulous chief executive officer of a large corporation than with a spontaneous and passionate perpetrator of a single "crime of passion."

14. See, Jane Doe et al. v. The State of Louisiana, no. 78-9513, in which Louisiana's registrar of vital statistics in the Department of Health and Human Resources was taken to court in 1982 for insisting on maintaining records that a citizen of the state was black even if "31/32" of the traceable ancestry was white.

15. American blacks are at greater risk for the genetic disorder sickle-cell anemia, but

this is no more the defining feature of the racial category than beta-thalassemia is the defining category for Mediterranean peoples, who are at greater risk for this disorder.

16. Hoffman's critique is based upon personality issues and not mental illness per se, but the criticism is applicable.

17. Adoptive parents have higher socioeconomic status, are older, and are carefully screened on scores of variables that make them systematically different from the rest of the population of parents.

18. In November 1988, two studies were published claiming that researchers had found the "neighborhood" of the exact chromosome, but these were two separate spots for two different families.

19. Garmezy's (1974) review demonstrated that the genetic model dominates the debate on the etiology of schizophrenia. Kahn's (1980) summary discussion of the literature further describes Kety and his colleagues' research on the Danish registry as the most sophisticated.

20. The numbers are not always so small. Kendler and Robinette (1983) have summarized the data from the U.S. National Academic of Sciences–National Research Council Twin Registry. Of the 31,848 twins in the registry, schizophrenia was equally common in identical and fraternal twins. Concordance for schizophrenia was significantly greater in monozygotic (30 of 164, or about 18 percent) than in dizygotic twins (9 of 268, or about 3 percent). While one can certainly see the logic of concluding that there may therefore be a genetic component, more could certainly be made of the finding that over 80 percent of identical twins were discordant.

21. Moreover, while institutional records provided the baseline, these researchers were quite thorough in going beyond the records, and conducted hundreds of psychiatric interviews with relatives.

22. When "personal investigation" was used, 21 of the 55 pairs, or 38 percent, were both diagnosed as having a serious mental problem such as schizophrenia, reactive psychosis, or manic depression.

23. In a more recent summary, Kety (1976) has concluded that the evidence from different sets of twin studies is sufficiently consistent and compelling to warrant a genetic interpretation of schizophrenia. However, each of the studies cited has the same methodological problem of the small numbers of pairs and problematic controls cited here. All of these studies are correlational.

24. Dworkin and Lenzenweger (1984) note in their introduction that identical twins are "often discordant" for schizophrenia and conclude that this must mean that environmental forces are important. In fact, identical twins are usually discordant, and one could use this bit of data to conclude that the environment was dominant.

25. This is actually a reanalysis of the Kety et al. data from the Danish registry.

26. Winston Churchill is reported to have written a note to himself in the margins of one of his prepared speeches: "Weak point: Shout!" In 1978, I served as a member of the Research Task Panel of the President's Commission on Mental Health. One of our assignments was to give suggestions and guidelines to the federal government on where funds should be allocated during the next decade, to meet the nation's sizeable mental health problems. At several meetings, I was astonished to learn how passionately several of my colleagues were committed to a biological or genetic interpretation of the causes of mental illness. During one session, a psychiatrist with this orientation went so far as to state that the National Institute of Mental Health's

mission had been perverted during the previous two decades, by funding studies that sought to explain mental illness problems by reference to poverty and its attendant stresses. The real problem, he asserted, had been ignored: a focus upon the genetic or biological underpinnings of mental illness.

27. These are real crimes by the same definition of index crimes, namely, acts committed against the criminal statutes.

Chapter 7

1. The genocidal program carried out on gypsies and Jews is the most famous of the eugenic strategies, but the Lebensborn project was the opposite strategy: recruitment and selection of "fine Aryan stock" for the purposes of selective breeding, for leadership qualities of the next generation.

2. Most could be counted as hard-nosed secular pragmatists who hardly wished to submit to the constraints of the clergy.

3. Bentham is the father of utilitarian theory, an eighteenth-century doctrine that posited that humans seek to maximize pleasures and minimize pain, and assumed a rational-decision model of behavior.

4. In the mid-1980's, black males reduced their cigarette smoking slightly, but still have much higher rates than whites.

5. *Washington Monthly,* June 1987:41.

6. Age-adjusted death rates for heart disease for persons under 45, 1979–1981. Report from the National Center for Health Statistics, Bureau of the Census, Task Force on Black and Minority Health.

7. A poverty area was defined as one with a high proportion of families with low income, a high proportion of substandard housing, low educational attainment, and high unemployment.

8. This group is at higher risk for low-birthweight babies.

9. But choice and options for clients of the new technology in genetics are always framed by such factors as (a) the existing social distribution of knowledge and (b) the ways in which information about the new technology is presented to an uninformed audience.

10. New York was a distant second, with seventeen million.

11. From the "Review of Current Programs" of the Genetic Disease Branch, California Department of Public Health Services, January 1987.

12. If a Nobel laureate in molecular genetics would come forward to make the case for an environmental intervention, his/her "hidden arguments" of the politics that underpin that position would more likely surface, since that is not the arena of established expertise.

13. Two and a half years later, *Science* would publish a research report on this topic (Mednick and Gabrielli, 1984), and the researchers would conclude that there is a "biological predisposition" for some forms of criminal behavior.

14. For an account of how the press routinely covers announcements of scientific claims of advances and breakthroughs, without critical review, see Dorothy Nelkin (1987).

15. Alexis de Tocqueville noted that while the tyranny of monarchs can be starkly visible

and cruel, this very starkness means that it can be overthrown by the masses. In contrast, the tyranny of the mass is harder to dislodge from the backs of a minority.

16. Theologians, ethicists, and legal scholars debate these matters with the experts in the sciences and medicine, but this has not been a "public debate" that reaches the informed laity.

Chapter 8

1. There are some missing links, and there are some leaps of faith; and indeed, as unreconstructed creationists (and not a few hard-nosed empiricists) are happy to point out, some faith.

2. Spencer actually sold 300,000 copies of his books in the United States alone (Haller, 1971:128.).

3. Objecting to an opinion from the majority, Holmes' dissent included the statement "The Fourteenth Amendment does not enact Mr. Herbert Spencer's Social Statistics." (Seagle, 1946:417n)

4. This was from a letter written December 10, 1866, to Joseph Hooker (Darwin, 1959). Four years later, Darwin would write in another letter to E. Lankester that "I suspect that hereafter he (Spencer) will be looked at as by far the greater living philosopher in England; perhaps equal to any that have lived." (Darwin, 1959,2:301).

5. Not aware of this history, current common sense and conventional wisdom unreflexively attributes this notion to Darwin, since it is now also vital to Biological Darwinian theory of the evolutionary tree in the animal kingdom.

6. It is true that Spencer and Edward B. Tylor (1871), the author of a similar treatise about the evolution of cultures each claimed priority and accused the other of plagiarism. Nonetheless, it is without challenge that Spencer was the most influential social thinker of his era.

7. Frazer did not posit a lock-step evolution. He acknowledged a zig-zag path to "progress" and liked the metaphor of waves sweeping up the shore line, ever constantly progressing even as there is receding at times.

8. Even into the 1920s with the famous Darrow trial; and even into the early 21st century, there are still strong holdouts on evolutionary theory.

9. In the middle of the nineteenth century, the theory had prominent proponents who lectured at Oxford and other major universities in the West.

10. Karl Pearson was a late nineteenth century English zoologist who later in his career became a statistician.

11. Pearson had a special strategy: After getting school teachers to rank students for such traits as vivacity, introspection, popularity, and handwriting, he found correlations between siblings for these traits to range between .43 and .63. Since these correlations were about the same as those between siblings for physical traits, he assumed they were hereditary. Thus, "Pearson concluded that personality and intelligence too were predestined in the germ plasm before birth." (Haller, 1963:13)

12. In the later years after World War I, a partial reconciliation and convergence would develop between population geneticists and the heavy reliance on quantitative measures of frequencies, and the Mendelian geneticists. Today, for example, estimates of carriers for genes that might produce a genetic disorder come from such a merger.

13. I have argued this position elsewhere, and only summarize the key issue here (see Duster and Garrett, 1984:1–37).

14. Current work in anthropology attacks this particular example as factual, but it lives in the popular imagination as good an illustration of the point as we have. And the point is, at least, as valid a formulation that what is important to a group can take on a varied and texture character which to outsiders is seen only as one-dimensional and simple. For aficionados of the problematics of the example, see Laura Martin, "Eskimo Words for Snow: A Case Study in the Genesis and Decay of an Anthropological Example," *American Anthropologist*, June, 1986, 418–423.

15. Grant Number R29 MH46925 R01 MH38765

16. Transcript of February 11, 1992 meeting of the National Mental Health Advisory-Council,

Afterword

1. Some empirical work continued to look at family data, and to pursue the quest for Mendelian inheritance patterns, but as the summary of empirical work reported later in this paper reveals, this method of investigation is done by a small minority of behavioral genetics researchers. Twin studies are actually a variant of correlational studies of two populations, since the dominant method is to compare (concordance rates) monozygotic and dizygotic twins. A related method compares twins adopted in different environments, but once again, none of these methodologies, historically, have deployed molecular genetics.

2. As with all such outcome data analyses dependent upon correlations, the Achilles heel of such research has always been that scores of other factors (that can not be controlled for) could easily explain more of the underlying source of variance than the surface simple correlations.

3. The next stage of the project, the Haplotype Map, is being designed to look at sections of the DNA to find markers with the purpose of making differentiations.

4. Reported in the New York Times, February 27, 1990.

5. Each location is called a locus, and the plural, or several in combination are called "loci."

6. Simon Cole (2001) has just published a book challenging some of the long-held beliefs about the infallibility of the physical fingerprint, but that is another story.

7. When I raised this question at a conference on behavioral genetics at Cold Spring Harbor in the winter of 1995 (Banbury Conference, March 5–8), the responses ranged from focusing on human suffering to the existence of a body of literature already in place on a topic. While the grounds may be noble, humanistic, or practical – none really addressed the theoretical warrant. As I pointed out, there are many forms of human suffering that are not presumed to have a genetic base – and the existence of a body of literature on a topic is a matter of traditional and career ladder, not a conceptual frame.

Appendix A

1. Portions of this appendix appeared under this title in K. Knorr-Cetina and A. V. Cicourel, Advances in Social Theory and Methodology: Toward an Integration of Micro- and Macro-Sociologies, Boston: Routledge & Kegan Paul, 1981:109–35.

2. See especially: The Wheels of Commerce, New York: Harper and Row, 1982.

3. One may certainly study organizations through direct observation, but the concern for

formal as well as informal structural arrangements alters the research strategy, in that a key question for all parties becomes the tension or degree of fit between the formal and informal.

4. This discussion is indebted to David Matza.

Appendix B

1. This brings us full circle to where we began in Chapter 2 with Malinowski's observation that magical thinking emerges where uncertainty is the dominant feature of a situation.

2. But there is so much that is unknown. Why do 198 of the 200 cases not get Down syndrome?

3. In our next session, the Latino couple will confront the counseling setting with a lack of information about a matter that the counselor regards as basic, yet requiring more time to elucidate than available for a genetic counseling session. I point this our here because it is critical to an analysis of how the social frame of knowledge transmission is so deeply related to implicit common assumptions of class and ethnicity, to education and educability.

References

Abrams, Charles. 1966. "The Housing Problem and the Negro" in T. Parsons and K. Clark, eds. *The Negro American*. Boston: Houghton Mifflin, 512–524.

Abrams, R., and M. A. Taylor. 1983. "The Genetics of Schizophrenia: A Reassessment Using Modern Criteria." *American Journal of Psychiatry* 140:171–175.

Apgar, Virginia and John Beck. 1974. *Is My Baby Alright?* New York: Pocket Books.

Arney, William Ray, and Bernard J. Bergen. 1984. *Medicine and the Management of Living*. Chicago: University of Chicago Press.

Ashby, Eric. 1966. *Universities: British, Indian, African*. Cambridge, Mass.: Harvard University Press.

Austin, James S. and Aaron David McVey, "The Impact of the War on Drugs," *Focus*, San Francisco, CA: The 1989 National Council of Crime and Delinquency Prison Population Forecast, 39 (December, 1989:1–7).

Ball, Susie. 1988. *Strategies in Genetic Counseling: The Challenge of the Future*. New York: Human Sciences Press.

Barnes, B. 1977. *Interests and the Growth of Knowledge*. London: Routledge & Kegan Paul.

———. 1974. *Scientific Knowledge and Sociological Theory*. London: Routledge & Kegan Paul.

Baron, Miron, et al. 1985a. "A Family Study of Schizophrenic and Normal Control Probands: Implications for the Spectrum Concept of Schizophrenia." *American Journal of Psychiatry* 142 (April):447–455.

———. 1985b. "Familial Transmission of Schizotypal and Borderline Personality Disorders." *American Journal of Psychiatry* 142:927–934.

Becker, Howard S. 1963. *Outsiders*. New York: Free Press.

Beeson, Diane, and Mitchell S. Goldbus. 1984. "Patient Decision-Making: Whether or Not to Have Pre-natal Diagnosis and Abortion for X-linked Conditions." *American Journal of Medical Genetics*.

———, and Rita Douglas. 1983. "Prenatal Diagnosis of Fetal Disorders." *Birth* 10, no. 4 (Winter): 227–241.

Behrman, Richard E. 1985. "Prenatal Care and Low Birthweight: Effects on Health Care Expenditures." *Preventing Low Birthweight*. Committee to Study the Prevention of Low Birthweight, Institute of Medicine, Washington, D.C.: National Academy Press, 212–237.

Belth, N. C., ed., 1958. *Patterns of Discrimination against Jews*. New York: Anti-Defamation League.

Bennett, A. M. Hastin. 1961. "Sensory Deprivation in Aviation." In P. Solomon et al., *Sensory Deprivation*. Cambridge, Mass.: Harvard University Press, 161–173.

Bergsma, Daniel, et al. 1974. *Ethical Social and Legal Dimensions of Screening for Human Genetic Disease*. New York: Stratton.

Bessman, Samuel P., and Judith P. Swazey. 1971. "PKU: A Study of Biomedical Legislation." In E. Mendelsohn, J. P. Swazey and I. Traviss, eds. *Human Aspects of Biomedical Innovations*. Cambridge, Mass.: Harvard University Press, 49–76.

Biersecker, B., P. A. Magyari, and N. W. Paul. 1987. *Strategies in Genetic Counseling II: Religious, Cultural and Ethnic Influences on the Counseling Process*. White Plains, N.Y.: March of Dimes Birth Defects Foundation (November), 23, no. 6.

Bishop, Jerry E. and Michael Waldholz, *Genome*, New York: Simon and Schuster, 1990.

Black, Jack, *You Can't Win: The Autobiography of Jack Black, Professional Thief*, New York: Amok, 1988 (originally published by Macmillan, 1926).

Blank, Robert H. 1981. *The Political Implications of Human Genetic Technology*. Boulder, Colo.: Westview Press.

Bluestone, B., and B. Harrison. 1982. *The Deindustrialization of America*. New York: Basic Books.

Bock, Kenneth. 1980. *Human Nature and History: A Response to Sociobiology*. New York: Columbia University Press.

Bohannan, Paul. 1960. *African Homicide and Suicide*. Princeton, N.J.: Princeton University Press.

Bowman, James E. 1977. "Genetic Screening Programs and Public Policy." *Phylon* 38:117–142.

Boyer, Paul, and Stephen Nissenbaum. 1974. *Salem Possessed: The Social Origins of Witchcraft*. Cambridge, Mass.: Harvard University Press.

Braithwaite, John. 1984. *Corporate Crime in the Pharmaceutical Industry*. London: Routledge & Kegan Paul.

Brandt, Allan M. 1981. "Racism and Research: The Case of the Tuskegee Syphilis Study." In Ian Robertson, *The Social World*. New York: Worth, 186–195.

Braudel, Fernand. 1971. *Civilisation materielle, économie et capitalisme*. Paris: Armand Colin.

Braun, Lundy, "Race, Ethnicity, and Health: Can Genetics Explain Disparities?" *Perspectives in Biology and Medicine*, 45, No. 2 (Spring, 2002): 159–174.

Braverman, Harold. 1958. "Medical School Quotas," in N. C. Belth, ed. *Barriers: Patterns of Discrimination Against Jews*. New York: Anti-Defamation League. 74–77.

Brenner, M. Harvey. 1973. *Mental Illness and the Economy*. Cambridge, Mass.: Harvard University Press.

Brodeur, Paul. 1985. *Outrageous Misconduct: The Asbestos Industry on Trial*. New York: Pantheon.

Brown, G. W., and T. Harris. 1978. *Social Origins of Depression: Study of Psychiatric Disorder in Women*. London: Tavistock.

Buist, N. R., and B. M. Jhaveri. 1973. "A Guide to Screening Newborn Infants for Inborn Errors of Metabolism." *Journal of Pediatrics* 82, no. 3:511–522.

Burchard, W. W. 1954. "Role Conflicts of Military Chaplains." *American Sociological Review* 19:528–535.

Burhansstipanov, L., et al. 1987. *Prevention of Genetic and Birth Disorders*, Sacramento: California State Department of Education.

Burman, Sandra B., and Barbara E. Harrell-Bond. 1979. *The Imposition of Law*. New York: Academic Press.

Burney, L. R., et al. 1987. "The Southeast Asian Refugee: The Impact of Cultural Variation on the Genetic Counseling Process." In B. Biesecker, P. A. Magyari, and N. W. Paul, eds., *Strategies in Genetic Counseling II: Religious, Cultural and Ethnic Influences on the Counseling Process*. White Plains, N.Y.: March of Dimes Birth Defects Foundation (November), 239–244.

Cairns, John. 1985. "The Treatment of Diseases and the War Against Cancer," *Scientific American*, November, 253, No. 5.

Cameron, Mary Owen, *The Booster and the Snitch*, New York: Free Press, 1964.

Capron, Alex M. 1973. "Legal Rights and Moral Rights." In B. Hilton et al., eds., *Ethical Issues in Human Genetics: Genetic Counseling and the Use of Genetic Knowledge*. New York: Plenum, 221–244.

———. 1973. "Informed Decision-Making in Genetic Counseling: A Dissent to the 'Wrongful Life' Debate." *Indiana Law Journal* 48.

———. "Tort Liability in Genetic Counseling." *Columbia Law Review* 79 (1979).

Carneiro, Robert L., *The evolution of society; Selections from Herbert Spencer's Principles of Sociology*, edited and with an introduction by Robert Carneiro, Chicago: University of Chicago Press 1967, xxix.

Caspi, Avshalom, Joseph McClay, Terrie E. Moffitt, Jonathan Mill, Judy Martin, Ian W. Craig, Alan Taylor, and Richie Poulton, (2002) "Role of Genotype in the Cycle of Violence in Maltreated Children," *Science*, 2002 Aug 2;297(5582):851–4.

Chambliss, William J., and Robert B. Seidman. 1971. *Law, Order and Power*. Reading, Mass.: Addison-Wesley.

Chang, Hsiao-Chen, and Oliver Jones. 1988. "*In Vitro* Characteristics of Human Fetal Cells Obtained from Chorionic Villus Sampling and Amniocentesis." *Prenatal Diagnosis* 8:367–378.

Chase, Allan. 1977. *The Legacy of Malthus: The Social Costs of the New Scientific Racism*. New York: Alfred A. Knopf.

Chavez, G. F., J. F. Cordero, and J. E. Beccera. 1988. "Leading Major Congenital Malformations among Minority Groups in the United States, 1981–1986." *Morbidity and Mortality Weekly Report, Centers for Disease Control*, Surveillance Summaries, 37, no. 3:17–24 (July).

Cherfas, Jeremy. 1982. *Man-Made Life: An Overview of the Science, Technology, and Commerce of Genetic Engineering*. New York: Random House.

Childs, Barton. 1979. "Genetics and Preventive Medicine." In T. L. Sadick and S. M. Pueschel, eds., *Genetic Diseases and Developmental Disabilities: Aspects of Detection and Prevention*. Boulder, Colo.: Westview Press.

Chorney, MJ, K Chorney, N Seese, MJ Owen, J Daniels, P McGuffin, LA Thompson, DK Det-
terman, C. Benbow, D Lubinski, T Eley, and R Plomin, (1998) "A Quantitative Trait
Locus Associated with Cognitive Ability in Childen," *Psychological Science*, 9, 3 (May)
159–66.

Cicourel, Aaron V. 1982. "Language and Belief in a Medical Setting." In *Contemporary Percep-
tions of Language: Interdisciplinary Dimensions*, ed. Heidi Byrnes. Washington, D.C.:
Georgetown Univ. Press.

Clark, B., and A. Graybiel. 1957. "The Break-Off Phenomenon: A Feeling of Separation
from the Earth Experienced by Pilots at High Altitudes." *Journal of Aviation Medicine*
28:121.

Clark, Edna McConnell Foundation, *Americans Behind Bars*, New York, May, 1992.

Clark, Kenneth. 1965. *Dark Ghetto*. New York: Harper and Row.

Clinard, M. B., and P. C. Yeager. 1980. *Corporate Crime*. New York: Free Press.

Clipper, Stephanie E. 1998. *Huntington's Disease: Hope through Research*, Bethesda, MD:
Office of Scientific and Health Reports, National Institute of Neurological Disorders
and Stroke, National Institutes of Health.

Cohen, Felissa L. 1984. *Clinical Genetics in Nursing Practice*. Philadelphia: Lippincott.

Cole, David, *No equal justice: race and class in the American criminal justice system*, New York:
New Press: Distributed by W. W. Norton, 1999.

Cole, Simon A., *Suspect Identities: A History of Fingerprinting and Criminal Identification*, Cambridge, MA: Harvard University Press, 2001.

Collins, H. 1983. "An Empirical Relativist Programme in the Sociology of Scientific Knowledge." In K. Knorr-Cetina and M. Mulkay, *Science Observed: Perspectives on the Social
Study of Science*, 85–113.

———, ed. 1981. "Knowledge and Controversy: Studies of Modern Natural Science." *Social
Studies of Science* 11, no. 1 (special issue).

"A Commentary on Sickle-Cell Disease." 1971. *Journal Amer. Med. Assoc.* (January).

Conrad, Peter, and Joseph W. Schneider. 1980. *Deviance and Medicalization: From Badness to
Sickness*. St. Louis: C. V. Mosby Co.

Cooke, R. E. 1974. "Societal Mechanisms to Cope With the Application of Advances in the
New Biology." In M. Lipkin and P. Rowley, eds., *Genetic Responsibility: On Choosing Our
Children's Genes*, N.Y.: Plenum Press.

Cooper, Richard, and Brian E. Simmons. 1985. *The New York State Journal of Medicine*
(August).

Corea, Gena. 1985. *The Mother Machine: Reproductive Technologies from Artificial Insemination
to Artificial Wombs*. New York: Harper and Row.

Coulton, G. G. 1938. *Inquisition and Liberty*. London: Heinemann.

Crane, James P., Heidi A. Beaver, and Sau Wai Cheung. 1988. "First Trimester Chorionic
Villus Sampling versus Mid-Trimester Genetic Amniocentesis—Preliminary Results of
a Controlled Prospective Trial." *Prenatal Diagnosis* 8:355–366.

Crawfurd, M. 1988. "Prenatal Diagnosis of Common Genetic Disorders." *British Medical
Journal* 297 (August):502–506.

Currie, Elliot. 1985. *Confronting Crime: An American Challenge*. New York: Pantheon.

Curtis, James E., and John W. Petras. 1970. *The Sociology of Knowledge*. New York: Praeger.

Damon, A. 1969. "Race, Ethnic Group, and Disease," *Social Biology*. 16:69–80.

Darwin, Francis, ed., *The Life and Letters of Charles Darwin*, in two volumes, New York: Basic Books, 1959.

Davenport, Charles B., "The Eugenics Programme and Progress in its Achievement," Eugenics: Twelve University Lectures, New York: Dodd, Mead and Co., 1914.

Davies, R. Trevard. 1969. "Golden Century of Spain: 1501–1621." In Paul J. Hauben, ed. *The Spanish Inquisition*. New York: Wiley.

Dawkins, Richard. 1976. "Karyotype, Predictability and Culpability." In A. Milunsky and G. J. Annas, eds. *Genetics and the Law*. New York: Plenum Press, 63–71.

Dershowitz, A. M. 1976. "Karyotype, Predictability, and Culpability." In A. Milunsky, ed., *Genetics and the Law*. N.Y.: Plenum Press.

Devlin, B., and Neil Risch, "Ethnic Differentiation at VNTR Loci, with Specific Reference to Forensic Applications," *American Journal of Human Genetics*, 51:534–548, 1992a.

———, "A Note on the Hardy-Weinberg equilibrium of VNTR data by using the Federal Bureau of Investigation's fixed-bin method, *American Journal of Human Genetics*, 51:549–553, 1992b.

Dodge, J. A. 1988. "Implications of the New Genetics for Screening for Cystic Fibrosis." *Lancet* ii (September): 672–673.

Dollard, John. 1957. *Caste and Class in a Southern Town*. Garden City, N.Y.: Doubleday.

Donovan, Jenny L. 1984. "Ethnicity and Health: A Research Review." *Social Science and Medicine*. 19, no. 7:663–670.

Draper, Elaine. 1990. *Risky Business: Genetic Testing and Exclusionary Practics in the Hazardous Workplace*. New York: Cambridge University Press.

———. 1986. "High Risk Workers or High Risk Work? Genetic Susceptibility Policies in the Hazardous Workplace," *International Journal of Sociology and Social Policy* (Fall).

Dunbaugh, Frank M. 1979. "Racially Disproportionate Rates of Incarceration in the United States." *Prison Law Monitor* 1:9.

Dunn, L.C., "Cross Currents in the History of Human Genetics," *American Journal of Human Genetics*, 14:1–13, 1962.

Dunstan, G. R. 1988. "Screening for Fetal and Genetic Abnormality: Social and Ethical Issues." *Journal of Medical Genetics* 25:290–293.

Durkheim, Emile, Elementary Forms of the Religious Life, London: Allen & Unwin, 1957

Duster, Troy, *Backdoor to Eugenics*, New York: Routledge, 1990.

Duster, Troy, "A Social Frame for Biological Knowledge," in Troy Duster and Karen Garrett, *Cultural Perspectives on Biological Knowledge*, Norwood, NJ: Ablex, 1984, 1–37.

Dworkin, Robert H., and Mark F. Lenzenweger. 1984. "Symptoms and the Genetics of Schizophrenia: Implications for Diagnosis." *American Journal of Psychiatry* 141 (December):12.

Dwyer, Jim, Peter Neufeld and Barry Scheck, *Actual innocence: Five Days to Execution and Other Dispatches from the Wrongly Convicted*, New York: Doubleday, 2000.

Edelstein, Stuart J. 1986. *The Sickled Cell: From Myths to Molecules*. Cambridge, Mass.: Harvard University Press.

Edgerton, Robert B. 1976. *Deviance: A Cross-Cultural Perspective*. Reading, Mass.: Cummings.

Edlin, Gordon J. 1987. "Inappropriate Use of Genetic Terminology in Medical Research: A Public Health Issue." *Perspectives in Biology and Medicine* 31, no. 1:47–56.

Emery, A. E. H. 1976. "A Computerized 'At Risk' Register for Genetic Disease." In *Prevention of Handicap through Antenatal Care, Review of research and Practice*. No. 18 of the Institute for Research into Mental and Multiple Handicap. Edinburgh, Scotland.

Etzioni, Amatai. 1973. *Genetic Fix*. New York: Macmillan.

Eugenical News, 1, 11, (November) 1916:79.

Evans, William and Mary Relling, "Pharmacogenomics: Translating Functional Genomics into Rational Therapeutics," *Science*, Oct. 1999 286, 487–91.

Everes-Kiebooms, G., and H. van den Berghe. 1979. "Impact of Genetic Counseling: A Review of Published Follow-up Studies." *Clinical Genetics* 15:465–474.

Evett, I.W., I.S. Buckleton, A. Raymond, and H. Roberts. "The Evidential Value of DNA Profiles," *Journal of the Forensic Science Society*, 33 (4):243–244, 1993.

———, P.D. Gill, J.K. Scranage, and B.S. Wier, "Establishing the Robustness of Short-Tandem-Repeat Statistics for Forensic Application," *American Journal of Human Genetics*, 58:398–407, 1996.

———, "Criminalistics: The Future of Expertise," *Journal of the Forensic Science Society*, 33 (3):173–178, 1993.

Eysenck, H. J. 1975. *The Inequality of Man*. London: Temple Smith.

———. 1971. *The IQ Argument: Race, Intelligence, and Education*. London: Library Press.

———. 1971. *The Structure and Measurement of Intelligence*. Berlin: Springer-Verlag.

———, and Eysenck, S. B. G. 1978. "Psychopathy, Personality, and Genetics." In R. D. Hare and D. Schallings, eds., *Psychopathic Behavior: Approaches to Research*. Chichester: Wiley.

Farag, Talaat I., and Sadika A. Al Awadi. 1988. "Community Genetics and Counseling in Arab Countries." In S. Bell, *Strategies in Genetic Counseling: The Challenge of the Future*. New York: Human Sciences Press, 241–243.

Federal Bureau of Investigation. 1988. *Crime in the United States* Supplement. *Age-Specific Arrest Rates and Race-Specific Arrest Rates for Selected Offenses, 1965–86*. United States Department of Justice (June).

Field, Mark G. 1953. "Structured Strain in the Role of the Soviet Physician," *American Journal of Sociology*, 58, no. 5, 493–502 (March).

Fingarette, Herbert. 1988. *Heavy Drinking: The Myth of Alcoholism as a Disease*. Berkeley, Calif.: University of California Press.

Fischer, Margit. 1971. "Psychosis in the Offspring of Schizophrenic Monozygotic Twins and Their Normal Co-Twins." *British Journal of Psychiatry* 118:43–52.

Fisher, R. A., *The Genetical Theory of Natural Selection*, Oxford, England: Clarendon Press, 1930.

Fisse, Brent, and John Braithwaite. 1983. *The Impact of Publicity on Corporate Offenders*. Albany: State University of New York Press.

Flanagan, Timothy J., and Kathleen Maguire, eds., *Sourcebook of Criminal Justice Statistics 1989*. U.S. Department of Justice Statistics, Washington, D.C: USGPO, 1990.

Fleck, Ludwik. 1979. *Genesis and Development of a Scientific Fact*. Chicago: University of Chicago Press.

Fletcher, Joseph. 1974. *The Ethics of Genetic Control*. New York: Doubleday.

Fletcher, John C. 1983. "Ethics and Public Policy: Should Sex Choice Be Discouraged?" In Neil G. Bennett, ed., *Sex Selection of Children*. New York: Academic Press, 213–252.

Flynn, Kevin, "Police Gadgets Aim to Fight Crime with 007-Style Ingenuity," *New York Times*, March 7, 2000. (A21).

Flynt, J. W., et al. 1987. "State Surveillance of Birth Defects and Other Adverse Reproductive Outcomes." Center for Environmental Health, Center for Disease Control, DHHS (April).

Frank, Reanne, "A Reconceptualization of the Role of Biology in Contributing to Race/Ethnic Disparities in Health Outcomes, *Population Research and Policy Review*, 20:441–455, 2001.

Fraser, Robert, *The Making of the Golden Bough: The Origins and Growth of an Argument*, New York: St. Martin's Press, 1990.

Frazer, James George, *The Golden Bough: A Study in Magic and Religion*, New York: Macmillan, 1951, six volumes.

Freeman, R. B., and H. J. Holzer. 1986. *The Black Youth Unemployment Crisis*. Chicago: University of Chicago Press.

Fujimura, Joan. 1988. "The Molecular Biological Bandwagon in Cancer Research: Where Social Worlds Meet." *Social Problems* 35, no. 3, (June). 261–283.

Gardner, Stuart W. 1975. "Ethnicity and Work: Occupational Distribution in an Urban Multi-Ethnic Setting, Georgetown, Penang, West Malaysia. Ph.D. diss., University of California, Berkeley.

Garmezy, Norman. 1974. "Children at Risk: The Search for the Antecedents of Schizophrenia. Part I. Conceptual Models and Research Methods." *Schizophrenia Bulletin* 8:14–90.

Gault, Robert H. 1932. *Criminology*. New York: Heath.

Gavel, Doug "Fight Crime Through Science," *Harvard Gazette*, November 30, 2000.

Geis, Gilbert, *On White Collar Crime*, Lexington, Mass.: Lexington Books, 1982.

Goddard, Henry H. 1917. "Mental Tests and the Immigrant." *Journal of Delinquency* 2, 243–277.

Golbus, M. S., et al. 1979. "Prenatal Genetic Diagnosis in 3000 Amniocenteses." *New England Journal of Medicine* 300:157–163.

Goldsby, Richard A. 1955. "Race and Mental Ability." In Adela S. Baer, ed., *Heredity and Society: Readings in Social Genetics*. 2nd ed. New York: Macmillan, 406–408.

Goodfield, June. 1977. *Playing God: Genetic Engineering and the Manipulation of Life*. New York: Harper.

Goodman, Madeleine J., and Lenn E. Goodman. 1982. "The Overselling of Genetic Anxiety: The Jews as a Target Population." *The Hastings Center Report*, 20–26.

Goodwin, Frederick, transcript of February 11, 1992 meeting of the National Mental Health Advisory Council.

Gordon, Robert A. 1987. "SES versus IQ in the Race-IQ-Delinquency Model." *International Journal of Sociology and Social Policy* 7, no. 3:30⁻92.

Gore, Albert, Jr. 1983. *Human Genetic Engineering*. Hearings of the Subcommittee on Investigations and Oversight of the Committee on Science and Technology, United States House of Representatives, November 16⁻18. Washington, D.C.: U.S. Government Printing Office.

Gortmaker, S. L. 1979. "The Effects of Prenatal Care on the Health of the Newborn." *American Journal of Public Health* 69:653⁻660.

Gottesman, H., and J. Shields. 1982. *Schizophrenia: The Epigenetic Puzzle*. Cambridge: Cambridge University Press.

Gould, Stephen Jay. 1985. *The Flamingo's Smile: Reflections in Natural History*. New York: W. W. Norton, 319⁻332.

———. 1981. *The Mismeasure of Man*. New York: W. W. Norton.

Griffin, Margeret L., Carole M. Kavanagh, and James R. Sorenson. 1976. "Genetic Knowledge, Client Perspectives and Genetic Counseling." *Social Work in Health Care*, 171⁻179.

Griffiths, P. D., et al. 1988. "Evaluation of Eight-and-a-half years of Neonatal Screening for Haemoglobinopathies in Birmingham." *British Medical Journal* 296 (June): 1,583⁻1,585.

Grover, Ranjeet, et al. 1983. "Current Sickle Cell Screening Program for Newborns in New York City, 1979⁻1980." *American Journal of Public Health* 73:249⁻252.

Grover, Ranjeet, Syed Shahidi, Bernice Fisher, Doris Goldberg, and Doris Wethers. 1983. "Current Sickle Cell Screening Program for Newborns in New York City, 1979⁻1980." *American Journal of Public Health* 73, no. 3.

Gumperz, John J. 1982. *Discourse Strategies*. New York: Cambridge Univ. Press.

Gusfield, Joseph. 1963. *Symbolic Crusade*. Urbana, Ill.: University of Illinois Press.

Guttentag, Marcia, and Paul F. Secord. 1983. *Too Many Women? The Sex Ratio Question*. Beverly Hills, Calif.: Sage Publications.

Gutting, Gary ed., *Paradigms and Revolutions*, Notre Dame, Ind.: Notre Dame U. Press, 1980.

Haan, Mary, George A. Kaplan, and Terry Camacho. 1987. "Poverty and Health: Prospective Evidence from the Alameda County Study." *Amer. Journal of Epidemiology* 125:6.

Hacker, Andrew, *Two Nations: Black and White, Separate, Hostile, Unequal*, New York: Scribner's, 1992.

Haller, John S. Jr., *Outcasts from Evolution: Scientific Attitudes of Racial Inferiority, 1859⁻1900*, Urbana, Ill.: University of Illinois Press, 1971.

Haller, Mark H. 1963. *Eugenics: Hereditarian Attitudes in American Thought*. New Brunswick, N.J.: Rutgers University Press.

Hamadeh, Hisham, and Cynthia A. Afshari, "Gene Chips and Functional Genomics," *American Scientist*, 88, 508⁻515, November-December, 2000.

Harding, Sandra. 1986. *The Science Question in Feminism*. Ithaca, N.Y.: Cornell University Press.

Harding, Vincent, *There is a River: The Black Struggle for Freedom in America*, New York: Vintage, 1983.

Harsanyi, Zsolt, and Richard Hutton. 1981. *Genetic Prophecy: Beyond the Double Helix.* New York: Rawson, Wade.

Hay, Douglas, et al. 1975. *Albion's Fatal Tree: Crime and Society in Eighteenth Century England.* New York: Pantheon.

Heilbron, J. L., and Daniel J. Kevles. 1988. "Finding a Policy for Mapping and Sequencing the Human Genome: Lessons from the History of Particle Physics," *Minerva*, 26, no. 3:299–314 (Autumn).

Heron, W. 1961. "Cognitive and Physiological Effects of Perceptual Isolation." in P. Solomon, et al., (eds.), *Sensory Deprivation.* Cambridge: Harvard University Press.

Herrick, James B. 1910. "Peculiar Elongated and Sickle Shaped Red Corpuscles in a Case of Severe Anemia." *Archives of Internal Medicine* (November).

Herrnstein, Richard J. 1971. "I.Q." *The Atlantic* (September):63–64.

———. 1989. "IQ and Falling Birth Rates." *The Atlantic Monthly* (May):73–79.

Hibbard, B. M., et al., 1985. "Can We Afford Screening for Neural Tube Defects? The New South Wales Experience." *British Medical Journal* 290:293–295.

Hilgartner, Stephen. 1986. "Telescoping Policy-Relevant Science: 'Summaries' of the Evidence on Dietary Fibre and Colon Cancer." Paper presented at the *Annual Meetings of the Society for Social Studies of Science.*

Hilton, B., et al. 1973. *Ethical Issues in Human Genetics: Genetic Counseling and the Use of Genetic Knowledge.* New York: Plenum.

Hobsbawm, E. J. 1965. *Primitive Rebels.* New York: W. W. Norton.

Hochstedler, Ellen, ed. 1984. *Corporations as Criminals.* Beverly Hills, Calif.: Sage Publications.

Hoffman, John C. 1979. *Ethical Confrontation in Counseling.* Chicago: University of Chicago Press.

Hoffman, Lois Waldis. 1985. "The Changing Genetics/Socialization Balance." *Journal of Social Issues* 41, no. 1:127–148.

Hofstadter, Richard, *Social Darwinism in American Thought*, Boston: Beacon, 1955.

Hollerbach, Paula E. 1979. "Reproductive Attitudes and the Genetic Counselee." In Y. Edward Hsia et al., eds., *Counseling in Genetics.* New York: Liss, 155–187.

Hollingshead, A. B., and F. Redlich. 1958. *Social Class and Mental Illness.* New York: Wiley.

Holmes, Helen, Betty Hoskins, and Michael Gross. 1981. *The Custom-Made Child.* Clifton, N.J.: Humana Press.

Hsia, Y. E. 1973. "Choosing My Children's Genes: Genetic Counseling." In *Genetic Responsibility*, ed. R. T. Rowley, New York: Plenum Press.

Hsia, Y. Edward, et al. 1979. *Counseling in Genetics.* New York: Liss.

Hubbard, Ruth. 1986. "Eugenics and Prenatal Testing." *International Journal of Health Services* 16, no. 2:227–242.

Hultjen, M., and P. Needham. 1987. "Preventing Feticide." *Nature* 325, no. 6101:190.

Human Genome News, Human Genome Program, U.S. Department of Energy, (v1ln1–2).

Ingle, D. W. 1973. *Who Should Have Children: An Environmental and Genetic Approach.* New York: Bobbs-Merrill.

Irwin, John. 1970. *The Felon.* Englewood Cliffs, N.J.: Prentice-Hall.

———. 1980. *Prisons in Turmoil.* Boston: Little, Brown.

Jablonski, N. and G. Chaplain, "The Evolution of Skin Color" *Scientific American*, October, 2002, 75–82.

Jackall, Robert. 1988. *Moral Mazes: The World of Corporate Managers.* New York: Oxford University Press.

Jackson, David A., and Stephan P. Stitch, eds. 1979. *The Recombinant DNA Debate.* Englewood Cliffs, N.J.: Prentice-Hall.

Jacobs, P., et al. 1965. "Aggressive Behavior, Mental Subnormality, and the XYY Male." *Nature* 208:1351–1352.

Jacoby, Henry. 1973. *The Bureaucratization of the World*, translated from the German by Eveline L. Kanes. Berkeley: University of California Press.

Jensen, Arthur R. 1969. "How Much Can We Boost IQ and Scholastic Achievement?" *Harvard Educational Review* (Winter; 1–123).

———. 1977. "Race and the Genetics of Intelligence: A Reply to Lewontin." In Adela S. Baer, ed. *Heredity and Society: Readings in Social Genetics.* 2d ed. New York: Macmillan, 395–405.

Jensen, Per, Kirsten Fenger, Tom G. Bolwig, and Sven Asger Sorensen. "Crime in Huntington's Disease: A Study of Registered Offences Among Patients, Relatives, and Controls" *Journal of Neurology, Neurosurgery, and Psychiatry*, (1998) 65:467–471.

Johnston, Kathy. 1987. "Sex of New Embryos Known." *Nature* 327, no. 6123:547.

Jones, James H. 1981. *Bad Blood: The Tuskegee Syphilis Experiment.* New York: Free Press.

Jones, S. R., R. A. Binder, and E. M. Donowho, Jr. 1970. "Sudden Death and Sickle-Cell Trait." *New England Journal of Medicine* 282:323.

Kaback, M. M., M. H. Becker and M. V. Ruth. 1974. "Sociologic Studies in Human Genetics: I. Compliance Factors in a Voluntary Heterozygote Screening Program." In D. Bergsma, ed., *Ethical, Social and Legal Dimensions of Screening for Human Genetic Disease.* N.Y.: Stratton.

———, M. H. Becker, and M. V. Ruth. 1974. "Sociologic Studies in Human Genetics: I. Compliance Factors in a Voluntary Heterozygote Screening Program." In D. Bergsma, et al., *Ethical, Social and Legal Dimensions of Screening for Human Genetic Disease.* New York: Stratton.

———, S. Greenwald, and R. Brossman. 1981. "Carrier Detection and Prenatal Diagnosis in Tay-Sachs Disease (TSD): Summary Experience of the First Decade." *Pediatric Research* 15, no. 632:1,138.

Kahn, Eva. 1980. "Genetics and Schizophrenic Behavior." *Psychiatric Quarterly* 52, no. 4 (Winter):251–269.

Kamin, Leon J. 1974. *The Science and Politics of I.Q.* New York: Humanities Press.

Karabel, Jerome. 1984. "Status Group Struggle, Organizational Interests, and the Limits of Autonomy: The Transformation of Harvard, Yale, and Princeton, 1918–1940." *Theory and Society* 18:1–40.

Kasarda, J. D. 1983. "Caught in the Web of Change." *Society* (November):41–47.

Kass, Miriam, and Margery W. Shaw. 1976. "The Risk of Birth Defects: Jacobs v. Thiemer and Parents' Right to Know." *American Journ. Law and Medicine* 2, no. 2:213–243.

Kassebaum, Gene, David A. Ward, and Daniel M. Wilner. 1971. *Prison Treatment and Parole Survival*. New York: Wiley.

Katz, Solomon H., "Is Race a Legitimate Concept for Science?" *The AAPA Revised Statement on Race: A Brief Analysis and Commentary*, University of Pennsylvania, February, 1995.

Kaye, Howard L. 1986. *The Social Meaning of Modern Biology*. New Haven: Yale University Press.

Keena, B. A., M. Jawanda, and J. G. Hall. 1987. "Cultural Influences and Neural Tube Defects in the East Indian Sikh Population of British Columbia." In B. Biesecker, P. A. Magyari, and N. W. Paul, eds., *Strategies in Genetic Counseling II: Religious, Cultural and Ethnic Influences on the Counseling Process*. White Plains, N.Y.: March of Dimes Birth Defects Foundation (November), 245–248.

Keller, Evelyn Fox. 1984. *Reflections on Gender and Science*. New Haven: Yale University Press.

———. 1982. "Feminism and Science." *Signs* 7:589–602.

Kelly, Patricia T. 1977. *Dealing with Dilemma: A Manual for Genetic. Counselors*. New York: Springer-Verlag.

Kendler, K. S., and A. M. Gruenberg. 1984. "An Independent Analysis of the Danish Adoption Study of Schizophrenia. VI: The Relationship between Psychiatric Disorders as Disorders as Defined by the DSM-III in the Relatives of Adoptees." *Archives of General Psychiatry* 41:555–564.

———, and C. Dennis Robinette. 1983. "Schizophrenia in the National Academy of Sciences-National Research Council Twin Registry: A 16-Year Update." *American Journal of Psychiatry* 140, no. 12 (December):1,551–1,563.

Kenen, R. H., and R. M. Schmidt. 1978. "Stigmatization of Carrier Status: Social Implications of Heterozygote Genetic Screening Programs." *American Journal of Public Health* 68:1,116–1,120.

Kenen, Regina H. 1988. "What Next for Genetic Counseling?" In S. Bell, *Strategies in Genetic Counseling: The Challenge of the Future*. New York: Human Sciences Press, 21–38.

Kessler, Seymour. 1980. "Genetic Services/Counselors in Genetic Services." *American Journal of Medical Genetics* 7:323–334.

———. "Psychological Aspects of Genetic Counseling: Analysis of a Transcript." *American Journ. Medical Genetics* 8 (1981):137–153.

Kety, S., D. Rosenthal, P. Wender, and F. Schulsinger. 1968. "An Epidemiological-Clinical Twin Study on Schizophrenia." In D. Rosenthal and S. Kety, eds., *The Transmission of Schizophrenia*. Oxford: Pergamon, 49–63.

———. 1976. "Genetic Aspects of Schizophrenia." *Psychiatric Annals* 6:6–15.

Kevles, Daniel J. 1985. *In the Name of Eugenics: Genetics and the Uses of Human Heredity*. New York: Alfred A. Knopf.

Kevles, Daniel J. and Leroy Hood, *The Code of Codes: Scientific and Social Issues in the Human Genome Project*, Cambridge, Mass.: Harvard University Press, 1992.

Kevles, Daniel J., "Controlling the Genetic Arsenal," *Wilson Quarterly*, Spring, 1992.

Kilbrandon, Lord. 1973. "The Comparative Law of Genetic Counseling." In B. Hilton et al., *Ethical Issues in Human Genetics: Genetic Counseling and the Use of Genetic Knowledge.* New York: Plenum, 245–260.

Kimmelman, Jonathan, "Risking Ethical Insolvency: A Survey of Trends in Criminal DNA Databanking," *Journal of Law, Medicine and Ethics*, vol 28:209–221, 2000.

Kitsuse, John I., and Aaron V. Cicourel. 1963. "A Note on the Use of Official Statistics." *Social Problems* 2:131–139.

Knorr-Cetina, Karin D. 1981. *The Manufacture of Knowledge.* Oxford: Pergamon.

———, and A. Cicourel. 1981. *Advances in Theory and Methodology: Toward an Integration of Micro- and Macrosociologies,* London: Routledge and Kegan Paul.

———. 1983. "The Ethnographic Study of Scientific Work: Towards a Constructivist Interpretation of Scientific Work." In Karin Knorr-Cetina and Michael Mulkay, eds. *Science Observed: Perspectives on the Social Study of Science.* Beverly Hills, Calif.: Sage Publications.

———, and Michael Mulkay, eds. 1983. *Science Observed: Perspectives on the Social Study of Science.* Beverly Hills, Calif.: Sage Publications.

Kogan, S., M. Doherty and J. Gitschier. 1987. "An Improved Method for Prenatal Diagnosis of Genetic Diseases by Analysis of Amplified DNA Sequences." *New England Journal of Medicine* 316, 16:985–90.

Kolata, Gina. 1980. "Prenatal Diagnosis of Neural Tube Defects." *Science* 209:1,216–1,218.

Korenbrot, Carol C. 1984. "Risk Reduction in Pregnancies of Low-Income Women." *Mobius* 4, no. 3:34–43.

Krimsky, Sheldon. 1983. *Genetic Alchemy: The Social History of the Recombinant DNA Controversy.* Cambridge, Mass.: MIT Press.

Kringlen, Einar. 1968. "An Epidemiological Twin Study on Schizophrenia," in D. Rosenthal and S. Kety, eds., *The Transmission of Schizophrenia.* Oxford: Pergamon Press. 49–63.

Kuhn, Thomas S., *The Structure of Scientific Revolutions.* 2d ed., enl., Chicago: University of Chicago Press, 1970.

Lappe, Marc. 1972. "Moral Obligations and the Fallacies of 'Genetic Control.'" *Theological Studies* 33 (September):411–427.

———. 1979. *Genetic Politics: The Limits of Biological Control.* New York: Simon and Schuster.

———. 1988. "Ethical Issues in Genetic Screening for Susceptibility to Chronic Lung Disease." *Journal of Occupational Medicine*, 30, no. 6:493–501.

Latour, Bruno, and Steve Woolgar. 1979. *Laboratory Life: The Social Construction of Scientific Facts.* Beverly Hills, Calif.: Sage Publications.

Laughlin, H. H., *The Scope of the Committee's Work,* Bulletin No. 10A, Cold Springs Harbor, New York: Eugenics Records Office, 1914:12–13.

Layde, P. M., et al. 1979. "Maternal Serum Alpha-Fetoprotein Screening: A Cost-Benefit Analysis," *American Journal of Public Health* 69, no. 6:566–572.

Lea, Henry C. 1906. *A History of the Inquisition of Spain.* New York: Macmillan.

Lebacqz, K. A. 1973. "Prenatal Diagnosis and Selective Abortion." *Linacre Quarterly* 40: 109–127.

Lederberg, J. 1972. "Biological Innovation and Genetic Intervention." In J. A. Behnke, ed., *Challenging Biological Problems.* N.Y.: Oxford University Press.

Lee, Sandra Soo-Jin, Joanna Mountain, and Barbara A. Koenig, "The Meanings of 'Race' in the New Genomics: Implications for Health Disparities Research, *Yale Journal of Health Policy, Law, and Ethics*, May 3, 2001, 12:15, 33–75.

Lench, Nicholas, Philip Stainer, and Robert Williamson. 1988. "Simple Non-Invasive Method to Obtain DNA for Gene Analysis." *Lancet* (June):1356–1358.

Lewis, C. S. 1965. *The Abolition of Man*. N.Y.: Collier-Macmillan.

Lewontin, R. C., Steven Rose, and Leon J. Kamin, eds. 1984. *Not in Our Genes: Biology, Ideology, and Human Nature*. New York: Pantheon.

Lieberson, Stanley. 1981. *A Piece of the Pie*. Berkeley, Calif.: University of California Press.

Lippman-Hand, Abby, and F. Clarke Fraser. 1979. "Genetic Counseling: Parents' Responses to Uncertainty." In Charles J. Epstein et al., eds., *Risk, Communication, and Decision-Making in Genetic Counseling*. New York: Liss, 325–339.

———. 1979. "Genetic Counseling: The Post Counseling Period." *American Journ. Medical Genetics* 4:51–71.

Loranger, A. W., J. M. Oldham, and E. H. Tulis. 1982. "Familial Transmission of DSM-III Borderline Personality Disorder." *Archives of General Psychiatry* 39:795–799.

Lowe, Alex L., Andrew Urquhart, Lindsey A. Foreman, Ian Evett, "Inferring Ethnic Origin by Means of an STR Profile," *Forensic Science International*, 2001, 119:17–22.

Ludmerer, Kenneth M. 1972. *Genetics and American Society*. Baltimore and London: Johns Hopkins University Press.

Luker, Kristin. 1984. *Abortion and the Politics of Motherhood*. Berkeley, Calif.: University of California Press.

Lumsden, Charles J., and E. O. Wilson. 1981. *Genes, Mind, and Culture: The Coevolutionary Process*. Cambridge, Mass.: Harvard University Press.

Lunsford, Terry F. 1982. "Informed Consent in Genetic Screening and Testing: New Opportunities, Hard Choices, and Legal Change" Working Paper Series, Social Issues in the New Genetics, Berkeley, Ca.: Institute for the Study of Social Change (January).

MacIntyre, Alasdair. 1980. "Epistemological Crises, Dramatic Narrative, and the Philosophy of Science." In Gary Gutting, ed., *Paradigms and Revolutions*. Notre Dame, Ind.: Notre Dame University Press, 54–74.

Malinowski, Bronislaw. 1948. *Magic, Science and Religion*. Boston: Beacon Press.

Mannheim, Karl. 1936. *Ideology and Utopia*. London: Routledge & Kegan Paul.

Margolin, C. R. 1978. "Attitudes Toward Control and Elimination of Genetic Defects," *Social Biology* 25, no. 1:33–37.

Marion, Janet P., et al. 1980. "Acceptance of Amniocentesis by Low-Income Patients in an Urban Hospital." *Amer. Journal of Obstet. Gynecol.* 138:11–15.

Marsh, Frank H., and Janet Katz, eds. 1985. *Biology, Crime, and Ethics: A Study of Biological Explanations for Criminal Behavior*. Cincinnati: Anderson.

McCollum, Audrey T., and Ruth L. Silverberg. 1979. "Psychosocial Advocacy." In Y. E. Hsia et al., eds., *Counseling in Genetics*. New York: Liss.

McCurdy, P. R. 1970. "Consistent Nomenclature for Sickle-Cell Trait." *New England Journal of Medicine* 282:1,158.

McGuffin, Pater, and Elizabeth Sturt. 1986. "Genetic Markers in Schizophrenia." *Human Heredity* 36:65–88.

McKusick, Victor A. 1988. *Mendelian Inheritance in Man: Catalogs of Autosomal Dominant, Autosomal Recessive, and X-Linked Phenotypes*. 8th ed. Baltimore: The Johns Hopkins University Press.

———. 1989. "Mapping and Sequencing the Human Genome," *New England Journal of Medicine*, 320, no. 14:910–915.

Mechanic, David. 1976. *The Growth of Bureaucratic Medicine*. New York: John Wiley.

Mednick, Sarnoff A. 1985. "Biosocial Factors and Primary Prevention of Antisocial Behavior." In Frank H. Marsh and Janet Katz, eds., *Biology, Crime, and Ethics*. Cincinnati: Anderson.

———, Patricia Brennan, and Elizabeth Kandel. 1988. "Predisposition to Violence." *Aggressive Behavior* 14, no. 1:25–33.

———, W. F. Gabrelli, Jr., and B. Hutchins. 1984. "Genetic Influences in Criminal Convictions: Evidence from an Adoption Cohort." *Science* 224:891–893.

Mehan, Hugh, Alma Hertweck, and J. Lee Meihls. 1986. *Handicapping the Handicapped: Decision Making in Students' Educational Careers*. Stanford, Calif.: Stanford University Press.

Meierhoefer, Barbara S., "The General Effect of Mandatory Minimum Prison Terms: A Longitudinal Study of Federal Sentences Imposed," *Federal Judicial Center*, Washington, D.C., 1992.

Meisel, Alan, and Lisa D. Kabnick. 1980. "Informed Consent to Medical Treatment: An Analysis of Recent Legislation." *University of Pittsburg Law Review* 41:407–564.

Mercer, Jane R. 1973. *Labeling the Mentally Retarded*. Berkeley, Calif.: University of California Press.

Merton, Robert K. 1973. *The Sociology of Science: Theoretical and Empirical Investigations*. N. Storer, ed. Chicago: University of Chicago Press.

Miller, Jerome G., *Hobbling A Generation: Young African American Males in the Criminal Justice System of America's Cities: Baltimore, Maryland*, National Center on Institutions and Alternatives, Alexandria, Virginia, 1992.

———. *Search and destroy: African-American males in the criminal justice system*, New York: Cambridge University Press, 1996.

Miller, W. A., D. Peck and R. M. Lowman. 1969. "Perenial Hematoma in Association with Renal Infarction in Sickle-Cell Trait." *Radiology* 92:351–352.

Milunsky, Aubrey. 1973. *The Prenatal Diagnosis of Genetic Disorders*. Springfield, Ill.: Charles C. Thomas.

———, ed. 1975. *The Prevention of Genetic Disease and Mental Retardation*. Philadelphia: W. B. Saunders.

———, and George J. Annas. 1976. *Genetics and the Law*. New York: Plenum Press.

———, and Philip Reilly. 1975. "The 'New' Genetics: Emerging Medicolegal Issues in the Prenatal Diagnosis of Hereditary Disorders." *American Journal of Law and Medicine* 71, no. 1.

Mintz, Morton. 1985. *At Any Cost: Corporate Greed, Women, and the Dalkon Shield*. New York: Pantheon.

Mokhiber, Russell. 1988. *Corporate Crime and Violence*. San Francisco: Sierra Club Books.

Moret, A., and G. Davy, From Tribe to Empire: Social Organization among Primitives and in the Ancient East, New York: Alfred A. Knopf, 1926.

Mosher, M. B. 1970. "Sickle-Cell Trait." *New England Journal of Medicine* 282:1,157.

Mulinare, Joseph. 1988. "Periconceptional Use of Multivitamins and the Occurrence of Neural Tube Defects." *Journal of the American Medical Association* December 2, 1988. 260, no. 21:3141–3145.

Murphy, E. A., G. Chase, and A. Rodriguez. 1978. "Genetic Intervention: Some Social, Psychological, and Philosophical Aspects." In B. H. Cohen, et al., eds., *Genetic Issues in Public Health and Medicine*. Springfield, Ill.: Charles C. Thomas.

Murphy, J. R. 1973. "Sickle-Cell Hemoglobin (Hemoglobin AS) in Black Football Players. *Journal of the American Medical Association* 225:981.

Murray, Robert F., et al. 1980. "Special Considerations for Minority Participation in Prenatal Diagnosis." *Journal of the American Medical Association* 243, no. 12:1,254–1,256.

Nader, Laura. 1972. "Up the Anthropologist: Perspectives Gained from Studying Up." In Dell Hymes, ed., *Re-Inventing Anthropology*. New York: Pantheon.

National Academy of Sciences. 1975. *Genetic Screening: Programs, Principles, and Research*. Washington, D.C.

National Academy of Sciences-National Research Council. 1973. *The S-Hemoglobinopathies: An Evaluation of Their Status in the Armed Forces*.

Neal-Cooper, Florence, and Robert B. Scott. 1988. "Genetic Counseling in Sickle-Cell Anemia: Experiences with Couples at Risk." *Public Health Reports* 103, no. 2 (March–April): 174–178.

"A Needling Controversy." 1982. *India Today*, August 15.

Nelkin, Dorothy. 1987. *Selling Science: How the Press Covers Science and Technology*. New York: W. H. Freeman.

———, and Judith P. Swazey. 1985. "Science and Social Control: Controversies over Research on Violence." In Frank H. Marsh and Janet Katz, eds., *Biology, Crime, and Ethics*. Cincinnati: Anderson.

Nelson, W. B., J. M. Swint, and C. T. Caskey. 1978. "An Economic Evaluation of a Genetic Screening Program for Tay-Sachs Disease." *American Journal of Human Genetics* 30:160–166.

Nichols, Eve K. 1988. *Human Gene Therapy*. Cambridge, Mass.: Harvard University Press.

Nichols, S. D. 1968. "Splenic and Pulmonary Infarction in a Negro Athlete." *Rocky Mountain Medical Journal* 65:49–50.

Nitowsky, H. M. 1973. "Prescriptive Screening for Inborn Errors of Metabolism: A Critique." *American Journal of Mental Deficiency* 77, no. 5:538–550.

Note. 1978. "Father and Mother Know Best: Defining Liability of Physicians for Inadequate Genetic Counseling." *Yale Law Journal* 87.

Oakley, G. P., et al. 1979. "A Community Approach to Prenatal Diagnosis." In E. B. Hook and I. H. Porter, eds., *Service and Education in Medical Genetics*. New York: Academic Press.

O'Rourke, D. H., et al. 1982. "Refutation of the General Single-Locus Model for the Etiology of Schizophrenia." *American Journal of Human Genetics* 34:630–649.

Osofsky, Gilbert. 1967. *The Burden of Race.* New York: Harper and Row.

Palca, Joseph. 1988. "National Research Council Endorses Genome Project." *Nature* 331, no. 6,156:467.

Pan, Philip P., "Prince George's Chief has used Serial Testing Before" *Washington Post,* January 31, 1998, B1.

Pauling, Linus, et al. 1949. "Sickle Cell Anemia: A Molecular Disease." *Science* 110:543–548.

———. 1968. "Reflections on the New Biology." *UCLA Law Review* 15, no. 3:269.

Pearn, J. H. 1973. "Patients' Subjective Interpretation of Risks Offered in Genetic Counseling." *Journal of Medical Genetics* 10:129–134.

Petersen, G. M., et al. 1983. "The Tay-Sachs Disease Gene in North American Jewish Populations: Geographic Variations and Origins." *American Journal of Human Genetics* 35:1258–1269.

Pickens, Donald K. 1968. *Eugenics and the Progressives.* Nashville, Tenn.: Vanderbilt University Press.

Polk, Kenneth, When Men Kill: *Scenarios of Masculine Violence,* New York: Cambridge University Press, 1994.

Pope, H. G., Jr., et al. 1982. "Failure to Find Evidence of Schizophrenia in First-Degree Relatives of Schizophrenic Probands." *American Journal of Psychiatry* 139:826–828.

Popper, Karl, *Conjectures and Refutations: The Growth of Scientific Knowledge,* New York: Basic Books, 1962.

Powledge, Tabitha M. 1974. "Genetic Screenings as a Political and Social Development." In D. Bergsman, ed., *Ethical, Social and Legal Dimensions of Screening for Human Genetic Disease.* New York: Stratton, 25–55.

———. 1983. "Toward a Moral Policy for Sex Choice." In Neil G. Bennett, ed., *Sex Selection of Children.* New York: Academic Press, 201–212.

President's Commission for the Study of Ethical Problems in Medicine and Biochemical and Behavioral Research. 1982. *Splicing Life: The Social and Ethical Issues of Genetic Engineering with Human Beings.* Washington, D.C.: U.S. Government Printing Office.

President's Commission on Law Enforcement and Administration of Justice. 1967. *The Challenge of Crime in a Free Society.* Washington, D.C.: U.S. Government Printing Office.

Proctor, Robert N., "Genomics and Eugenics: How Fair is the Comparison?" in George J. Annas and Sherman Elias, eds., *Gene Mapping: Using Law and Ethics as Guides,* New York: Oxford University Press, 1991: 57–93.

———, "Eugenics Among the Social Sciences: Hereditarian Thought in Germany and the United States," in JoAnne Brown and David K. van Keuren, eds., *The Estate of Social Knowledge,* Baltimore: Johns Hopkins University Press, 1991: 175–205.

Quinney, Richard. 1979. *Criminology: Analysis and Critique.* (2d ed.). Boston: Little Brown.

Rao, Radhakrishna. 1988. "Move to Ban Sex-Determination." *Nature* 33, no. 6,156:467.

———. 1986. "Move to Stop Sex-Test Abortion." *Nature* 324, no. 6,094:202.

Rapp, Rayna. 1988. "Chromosomes and Communication: The Discourse of Genetic Counseling." *Medical Anthropology Quarterly* 2, no. 2:143–157.

Reilly, Philip. 1977. *Genetics, Law, and the Social Policy.* Cambridge, Mass.: Harvard University Press.

———. 1975. "Genetic Screening Legislation." In H. Harris and K. Hirschhorn, eds., *Advances in Human Genetics*, 5:319–376. New York: Plenum.

Reilly, Philip, *The Surgical Solution: A History of Involuntary Sterilization in the United States*, Baltimore: Johns Hopkins University Press, 1991.

Reiman, Jeffrey H. 1984. *The Rich Get Richer and the Poor Get Prison.* New York: Wiley.

Reinarman, Craig and Harry G. Levine, *Crack in America: Demon Drugs and Social Justice*, Berkeley: University of California Press, 1997.

Risch, Neil, Esteban Burchard, Elad Ziv and Hua Tang, "Categorizations of humans in bio-medical research: genes, race and disease," *Genome Biology*, 2002, 3 (7) 2007.1–2007.12 2007.12 (also available at *http:// genomebiology.com/2002/3/7/com-ment/2007.1*).

Ritvo, E. R., et al. 1985. "Concordance for the Syndrome of Autism in 40 Pairs of Afflicted Twins." *American Journal of Psychiatry* 142, no. 1:74–77.

Robin, Stanley S., and Gerald E. Markle. 1987. "Let No One Split Asunder: Controversy in Human Genetic Engineering." *Politics and the Life Sciences* 6, no. 1:3–15.

Robinson, W. S. 1950. "Ecological Correlations and the Behavior of Individuals." *American Sociological Review* 15:351–357.

Rollnick, Beverly. 1984. "The National Society of Genetic Counselors: An Historical Perspective." *Birth Defects* 20:3–7.

Rose, G. and M. G. Marmot. 1981. "Social Class and Coronary Heart Disease." *British Heart Journal* 45:13–19.

Rosen, Charles. 1983. *The Structure of American Medical Practice, 1875–1941.* Philadelphia: University of Pennsylvania Press.

Rosenberg, NA, Pritchard, JK, Weber, JL, Cann, HM, Kidd, KK, Zhivotovsky, LA, Feldman, MW, "Genetic Structure of Human Populations," *Science*, 2002 Dec 20;298:2381–2385.

Rotter, R., et al. 1956. "Splenic Infarction in Sicklemia during Airplane Flight: Pathogenesis, Hemoglobin Analysis and Clinical Features in Six Cases." *Annals of Internal Medicine* 44:257–270.

Rowe, David C. 1986. "Genetic and Environmental Components of Antisocial Behavior: A Study of 265 Twin Pairs." *Criminology* 24, no. 3:513–532.

———, and D. Wayne Osgood. 1984. "Heredity and Sociological Theories of Delinquency: A Reconsideration." *American Sociological Review* 49:526–540.

Salk, Jonas. 1979. "Introduction" to Bruno Latour and Steve Woolgar, *Laboratory Life.* Beverly Hills, Calif.: Sage Publications.

Satcher, David, and Mary Ashby. 1974. "Beyond Screening: An Approach to Genetic Education and Counseling." *Journal of Black Health Perspectives*, 41–47.

Scheler, Max. 1926. *Die Wissensformen und die Gesellschaft.* Bern: Francke.

Scheper-Hughes, Nancy. 1979. *Saints, Scholars, and Schizophrenics: Mental Illness in Rural Ireland.* Berkeley, Calif.: University of California Press.

Schiff, Michael, and R. Lewontin. 1986. *Education and Class: The Irrelevance of IQ Genetic Studies.* New York: Oxford University Press.

———, et al. 1982. "How Much *Could* We Boost Achievement and IQ Scores? Direct Evidence from a French Adoption Study." *Cognition* 12:165–196.

Schuman, Howard, Charlotte Steeh, and Lawrence Bobo. 1985. *Racial Attitudes in America: Trends and Interpretations.* Cambridge, Mass.: Harvard University Press.

Schwartz, Barry. 1986. *The Battle for Human Nature: Science, Morality and Modern Life.* New York: W. W. Norton.

Scott, Roland B. 1971. "A Commentary on Sickle-Cell Disease." *Journal of the American Medical Association* (January).

Scriver, Charles R. 1979. "Genetic Screening: The Heterozygote Experience." In T. L. Sadick and S. M. Pueschel, eds., *Genetic Diseases and Developmental Disabilities: Aspects of Detection and Prevention.* Boulder, Colo.: Westview Press, 13–29.

Shawcross, William. 1979. *Sideshow: Kissinger, Nixon and the Destruction of Cambodia.* New York: Simon and Schuster.

Sherwood, J. J., and M. Nataupsky. 1968. "Predicting the Conclusions of Negro-White Intelligence Research from Biological Characteristics of the Investigator." *Journal of Personal and Social Psychology* 8:53–58.

Shibutani, Tomatsu, and Kian M. Kwan. 1965. *Ethnic Stratification: The Comparative Approach.* New York: Macmillan.

Shriver, Mark D., Michael W. Smith, Li Jin, Amy Marcini, Joshua M. Akey, Ranjan Deka, and Robert E. Ferrell, "Ethnic-Affiliation Estimation by Use of Population-Specific DNA Markers, *American Journal of Human Genetics,* 1997, 60:957–964.

Sibley, Elbridge. 1953. "Some Demographic Clues to Stratification." In S. M. Lipset and R. Bendix, *Class Status and Power.* Glencoe, Ill.: Free Press.

Simon, David R., and D. Stanley Eitzen. 1982. *Elite Deviance.* Boston: Allyn and Bacon.

Simonds, A. P. 1978. *Karl Mannheim's Sociology of Knowledge.* Oxford: Clarendon Press.

Simpson, Sally S., 1987. "Cycles of Illegality: Antitrust Violations in Corporate America." *Social Forces.* 64:943–63.

Singer, Peter, and Deane Wells. 1985. *Making Babies: The New Science and Ethnics of Conception.* New York: Scribner.

Sinsheimer, R. L. 1973. "Prospects for Future Scientific Development: Ambush or Opportunity." In B. Hilton, et al., eds., *Ethical Issues in Human Genetics.* N.Y.: Plenum Press.

Sissine, Fred J., et al. 1981. "Statistical Analysis of Genetic Counseling Impacts: A Multi-Method Approach to Retrospective Data." *Evaluation Review* 5, no. 6 (December): 745–757.

Skolnick, Jerome. 1966. *Justice without Trial: Law Enforcement in a Democratic Society.* New York: Wiley.

Smalley SL, Kustanovich V, Minassian SL, Stone JL, Ogdie MN, McGough JJ, McCracken JT, MacPhie IL, Francks C, Fisher SE, Cantor RM, Monaco AP, Nelson SF., "Genetic linkage of attention-deficit/hyperactivity disorder on chromosome 16p13, in a region implicated in autism," *Am J Hum Genet* 2002 Oct, 71 (4):959–63.

Smeraldi, E., et al. 1986. "Genetic Modeling in Schizophrenia According to HLA Typing." *Clinical Genetics* 30:157–166.

Smidt-Jensen, Steen, and Niels Hahnemann. 1988. "Transabdominal Chorionic Villus Sampling for Fetal Genetic Diagnosis: Technical and Obstetric Evaluation of 100 Cases." *Prenatal Diagnosis* 8:7–17.

Sofaer, Jeffrey A., and Alan H. Emery. 1981. "Genes for Super-Intelligence?" *Journal of Medical Genetics* 18:410–413.

Sogurno, G. 1987. "Urban Poor and Primary Health Care: An Analysis of Infant Mortality of an Inner City Community." *Journal of Tropical Pediatrics* 33:173–176.

Soloff, P.H., and J.W. Millward. 1983. "Psychiatric Disorders in the Families of Borderline Patients." *Archives of General Psychiatry* 40:37–44.

Solomon, Philip, et al. 1961. *Sensory Deprivation*. Cambridge, Mass.: Harvard University Press.

Sorenson, James. R. 1974. "Some Social and Psychologic Issues in Genetic Screening." In D. Bergsma, ed., *Ethical, Social and Legal Dimensions of Screening for Human Genetic Diseases*. N.Y.: Stratton.

———, J. P. Swazey, and N. A. Schotch. 1980. "Summary and Recommendations: A Two-year Study of Genetic Counseling at Clinics Receiving Support from the March of Dimes Birth Defects Foundation." Prepared for the Birth Defects Conference on Fetus and the Newborn, New York, June.

———. 1975. "From Social Movement to Clinical Medicine: The Role of Law and the Medical Profession in Regulating Applied Human Genetics." In *Genetics and the Law*, ed. G. J. Annas. New York: Plenum Press.

———, and Arthur J. Culbert. 1977. "The Genetic Counselors and Counseling Orientations: Unexamined Topics in Evaluation." In *Genetic Counseling*, ed. Felix de la Cruz. New York: Raven Press.

———, Carole M. Kavanagh, and Marc Mucatel. 1981. "Client Learning of Risk and Diagnosis in Genetic Counseling." *Birth Defects: Original Article Series* 17, no. 1:215–228 (March of Dimes Birth Defects Foundation).

———, Judith P. Swazey, and Norman A. Scotch. 1980. *Reproductive Pasts and Reproductive Futures: Genetic Counseling and Its Effectivess*. New York: Liss.

———, Judith P. Swazey, and Norman A. Scotch. 1980. "Summary and Recommendations: A Two-Year Study of Genetic Counseling at Clinics Receiving Support from the March of Dimes Birth Defects Foundation." *Prepared for Birth Defects Conference on Fetus and the Newborn*, New York (June).

Spencer, Herbert, *The Study of Sociology*, New York: D. Appleton and Co., 1896.

———, *Principles of Sociology*, New York: D. Appleton and Co., 1899, vol. 2.

Squires, G. D. 1982. "Runaway Plants: Capital Mobility and Black Economic Rights." In J. C. Raines et al., eds., *Community and Capital in Conflict: Plant Closings and Job Loss*. Philadelphia: Temple University Press.

SRTCST Report, House of Representatives. 1976. DNA Recombinant Molecule Research, *Supplemental Report II. Subcommittee on Science, Research and Technology*, Committee on Science and Technology, House of Representatives (December).

Stack, Carol B. 1974. *All Our Kin: Strategies for Survival in a Black Community*. New York: Harper and Row.

Stamatoyannopoulos, G. 1974. "Problems of Screening and Counseling in the Hemoglobinopathies." In A. G. Motulsky and F. J. B. Ebling, eds., *Birth Defects: Proceedings of the*

Fourth International Conference (Vienna, 1973). Amsterdam: Excerpta Medica, 268–276.

Stark, Werner. 1958. *The Sociology of Knowledge: An Essay in Aid of Deeper Understanding of the History of Ideas*. London: Routledge & Kegan Paul.

Starr, Paul. 1982. *The Social Transformation of American Medicine*. New York: Basic Books.

Stein, J., C. Berg, J. A. Jones, and J. C. Detter. 1984. "A Screening Protocol or a Prenatal Population at Risk for Inherited Hemoglobin Disorders: Results of Its Application to a Group of Southeast Asians and Blacks." *American Journal of Obstetrics and Gynecology* 150, no. 4 (October 15):333–341.

Stern, Curt. 1977. "Genes and People." In Adela S. Baer, ed., *Heredity and Society: Readings in Social Genetics*. 2d ed. New York: Macmillan, 409–415.

Stine, Gerald James. 1977. *Biosocial Genetics: Human Heredity and Social Issues*. New York: Macmillan.

Stone, W. J. 1970. "Sickle-Cell Trait." *New England Journal of Medicine*, 282:1,157.

Studer, Kenneth E., and D. E. Chubin. 1980. *The Cancer Mission: Social Contexts of Biomedical Research*. London and Beverly Hills: Sage Publications.

Suzuki, David T., and Anthony J. F. Griffiths. 1976. *An Introduction to Genetic Analysis*. San Francisco: W. H. Freeman and Sons.

———, and Peter Knudtson. 1989. *Genethics: The Clash between the New Genetics and Human Values*. Cambridge, Mass.: Harvard University Press.

Swinbanks, David. 1976. *Sons or Daughters: A Cross Cultural Survey of Parental Preferences*. Beverly Hills, Calif.: Sage Publications.

———. 1986. "Japanese Gynaecology: Gender Selection Sparks Row." *Nature* 321, no. 6,092:720.

Swinford, Ann E., and Mohamed H. El-Fouly. 1987. "Islamic Religion and Culture: Principles and Implications for Genetic Counseling." In B. Biesecker, P. A. Magyari, and N. W. Paul, eds., *Strategies in Genetic Counseling II: Religious, Cultural and Ethnic Influences on the Counseling Process*. White Plains, N.Y.: March of Dimes Birth Defects Foundation (November), 253–257.

Synnott, Marcia G. 1979. *The Half-Opened Door*. Westport, Conn.: Greenwood Press.

Szasz, Thomas. 1974. *The Myth of Mental Illness*. New York: Harper and Row.

Taviss, Irene. 1971. "Problems in the Social Control of Biomedical Science and Technology." In E. Mendelsohn, J. Swazey and I. Taviss, eds., *Human Aspects of Biomedical Innovation*. Cambridge, Mass.: Harvard University Press, 3–45.

Terman, Lewis M., and Melita H. Oden. 1947. *The Gifted Child Grows Up: Twenty-Five-Year Follow-Up of a Superior Group*. Stanford, Calif.: Stanford University Press.

Tesh, Sylvia Noble. 1988. *Hidden Arguments: Political Ideology and Disease Prevention Policy*. New Brunswick, New Jersey: Rutgers University Press.

Tong, Benjamin R. 1979. "The Ghetto of the Mind: Notes on the Historical Psychology of Chinese America." *Amerasia Journal* 1 (November):1–31.

Townes, Philip L. 1986. "Newborn Screening: A Potpourri of Policies." *American Journal of Public Health* 76, no. 10:1,191–1,192.

Tsuang, M. T., G. Winokur, and R. R. Crowe. 1980. "Morbidity Risks of Schizophrenia and

Affective Disorders among First Degree Relatives of Patients with Schizophrenia, Mania, Depression, and Surgical Conditions." *British Journal of Psychiatry* 137:497–504.

Tversky, A., and D. Kahneman. 1978. "Causal Schemas in Judgments under Uncertainty." In *Progress in Social Psychology*, ed. M. Fishbein, Hillsdale, N.J.: Lawrence Erlbaum Associates.

————, and D. Kahneman. 1981. "The Framing of Decisions and the Psychology of Choice." *Science* 211:453–458.

Tyler, Gus, *Organized Crime in America*, Ann Arbor: University of Michigan Press, 1962.

Tylor, Edward Burnett, Primitive Culture, London: John Murray, 1871, two volumes.

U.S. Senate, 94th Congress. 1975. Hearings, Subcommittee on Health, Committee on Labor and Public Welfare. First Session on S1619, S1620, S1714, S1715 (July 15).

Vichinsky, Elliott, et al. 1988. "Newborn Screening for Sickle Cell Disease: Effect on Mortality." *Pediatrics* 81, no. 6:749–755 (June).

Vincent, Paul. 1966. "The Measured Intelligence of Glasgow Jewish Schoolchildren." *Jewish Journal of Sociology*. 8:92–108.

Wagatsuma, Hiroshi. 1967. "A History of the Outcaste." In George DeVos and Hiroshi Wagatsuma, *Japan's Invisible Race*. Berkeley: University of California Press.

Wallerstein, Immanuel and Paul Starr, eds. 1971. *The University Crisis Reader*. New York: Random House. 2 vols.

Waltz, Jon R., and Carol R. Thigpen. 1973. "Genetic Screening and Counseling: The Legal and Ethical Issues." *Northwestern University Law Review* 68.

Warner, Richard. 1987. *Recovery from Schizophrenia: Psychiatry and Political Economy*. New York: Routledge & Kegan Paul.

Watson, James, D. 1969. *The Double Helix*. New York: Mentor.

Weaver, David D. 1988. "A Survey of Prenatally Diagnosed Disorders." In Roger A. Williamson, ed., *Clinical Obstetrics and Gynecology* 31, no. 3:253–269.

Wechsler, Harold S. 1977. *The Qualified Student: A History of Selective College Admission in America*. New York: Wiley.

Wegrocki, Henry J. 1962. "A Critique of Cultural and Statistical Concepts of Abnormality." in C. Kluckhohn, et al., *Personality in Nature, Society, and Culture*. New York: Knopf. 691–701.

Weitkamp, Lowell R., H. C. Stanger, E. Persad, C. Flood, and S. Guttormsen. 1981. "Depressive Disorders and HLA: A Gene on Chromosome 6 that Can Affect Behavior." *New England Journal of Medicine* 305, no. 22 (November): 1,301–1,306.

Wertz, Dorothy C., and John H. Fletcher. 1988. "Ethics and Medical Genetics in the United States: A National Survey." *American Journal of Medical Genetics* 29:815–827.

Wikler, Daniel and Norma J. Wikler, 1990. "Turkey-Baster Babies: The De-Medicalization of Artificial Insemination," (forthcoming) Millbank Quarterly, Spring.

Williamson, Nancy E. 1983. "Parental Sex Preferences and Sex Selection." In Neil G. Bennett, ed., *Sex Selection of Children*. New York: Academic Press, 129–145.

Wilson, E. O. 1971. *Insect Societies*. Cambridge, Mass.: Harvard University Press.

————. 1978. *On Human Nature*. Cambridge, Mass.: Harvard University Press.

Wilson, J. M. G., and G. Jungner. 1968. *Principles and Practice of Screening for Disease* (Public Health Papers no. 34). Geneva: World Health Organization.

Wilson, James F. et al. "Population genetic structure of variable drug response." *Nature Genetics*, 2001, 29 (November): 265–269.

Wilson, James Q., "Point of View," *The Chronicle of Higher Education*, June 10, 1992:A40.

——, "To Prevent Riots, Reduce Black Crime," *San Francisco Examiner*, May 13, 1992a, Reprinted from *The Wall Street Journal*.

——, and Richard J. Herrnstein, *Crime and Human Nature*, New York: Simon and Schuster, 1985.

Winslow, Ron "FDA is Prepared to Approve Heart Drug Intended for Treating African Americans," *Wall Street Journal*, March 21, 2001.

Wofsy, Leon. 1986. "Biotechnology and the University." *Journal of Higher Education* 57, no. 5:477–492.

Wolfgang, Marvin, *Patterns of Criminal Homicide*, Philadelphia: University of Pennsylvania Press, 1958.

Woo, Deborah A. 1989. "Psychiatry and Social Control in China," in Ron J. Troyer, John P. Clark, and Dean G. Rojek (eds.), *Crime and Social Control in the People's Republic of China*. New York, Westport Connecticut, and London: Praeger, 97–111.

——. 1983. "Social Support and the Imputation of Mental Illness: Chinese Americans and European Americans." Ph.D. diss., University of California, Berkeley.

Wright, S., "Physiological Genetics, Ecology of Populations and Natural Selection," *Perspectives in Biology and Medicine*, 3:107–151, 1959.

Xie, Hong-Guang, Richard B. Kim, Alastair JJ Wood, and C. Michael Stein, "Molecular Basis of Ethnic Differences in Drug Disposition and Response," *American Review of Pharmacology and Toxicology*, 2001:41:815–50.

Yap, Pow-meng. 1951. "Mental Diseases Peculiar to Certain Cultures: A Survey of Comparative Psychiatry." *Journal of Mental Science* 97:313–327.

Young, Matilda and Caroline Lieber. 1987. "Vitiligo in an Arab Family." In B. Biesecker, P. A. Magyari, and N. W. Paul, eds., *Strategies in Genetic Counseling II: Religious, Cultural and Ethnic Influences on the Counseling Process*. White Plains, N.Y.: March of Dimes Birth Defects Foundation, (November), 249–252.

Yoxen, Edward. 1983. *The Gene Business: Who Should Control Biotechnology?* London: Pan.

Zola, Irving Kenneth. 1966. "Culture and Symptoms: An Analysis of Patient's Presenting Complaints." *American Sociological Review* 31, no. 5:615–630.

Zuckerman, Harriett. 1977. *Scientific Elite: Nobel Laureates in the United States*. New York: Free Press.

Index

('n' indicates a note)